THE
CRAFT
BIBLE

THE CRAFT BIBLE

MORE THAN 100 PROJECTS – CROCHET, KNITTING & HOMEMADE GIFTS

LONDON, NEW YORK,
MELBOURNE, MUNICH, DELHI

Project Designers Alison Shackleton,
Katherine Raj
Project Editor Elizabeth Yeates
Indexer Hilary Bird
Senior Jacket Creative Mark Penfound
Pre-Production Producer Andy Hilliard
Senior Producer Toby Marshall
Sales Manager Nicholas Hayne
Special Sales Creative Project Manager
Alison Donovan

First published in Great Britain in 2014
by Dorling Kindersley Limited,
80 Strand, London, WC2R 0RL

Material in this publication was previously published in:
Big Book of Knitting (2013), Handmade Gifts (2013),
A Little Course In Crochet (2014), Easy World Craft
Baby Knits (2014), Easy World Craft Classic Knits (2014),
and Easy World Craft Crochet (2014)

A Penguin Random House Company

A CIP catalogue record for this book
is available from the British Library

ISBN 978-0-2411-8027-3

Printed and bound in China by
Hung Hing Printing Co. Ltd

Discover more at
www.dk.com/crafts

Contents

Conversion chart

This chart gives the closest equivalents between the three needle-sizing systems. The sizes don't match exactly in many cases, but are the nearest equivalents.

EU	Old UK	US Metric
1.5mm	N/A	000 00
2mm	14	0
2.25mm 2.5mm	13	1
2.75mm	12	2
3mm	11	N/A
3.25mm	10	3
3.5mm	N/A	4
3.75mm	9	5
4mm	8	6
4.5mm	7	7
5mm	6	8
5.5mm	5	9
6mm	4	10
6.5mm	3	10½
7mm	2	N/A
7.5mm	1	N/A
8mm	0	11
9mm	00	13
10mm	000	15
12mm	N/A	17
15mm	N/A	19
20mm	N/A	35
25mm	N/A	50

Knitting

This chapter is suitable for all knitters, whether you have never held a pair of needles before or are an experienced knitter. All key areas are covered – with over 15 patterns, plus tools and materials, and techniques. A vast array of techniques are featured, from simply understanding a pattern to more complicated cables, lace knitting, and colourwork. You'll find everything you need to knit with accuracy, confidence, and flair.

The patterns included are for a range of skill levels and a variety of techniques. Here you can bring your skills to fruition, knitting garments for all the family, plus a choice of accessories. The children's clothes are given in three sizes, specified by age, while the Men's sleeveless pullover includes four sizes – small, medium, large, and extra large.

Each project shows the yarn and stitch tension used, but if you substitute a yarn refer to p.12 for equivalent standard yarn weights from which to choose. Select one that has the same stitch and row count on the ballband as that in the pattern, and always work a tension swatch (see p.17). Adjust your needle size if necessary to achieve the correct stitch tension so that your project comes out at the correct size. Check that the tension swatch in the new yarn looks and feels suitable for the project. Calculate the amount of yarn by yardage/meterage, as the amount needed may vary.

Yarns

A yarn is the long, stranded, spun fibre that we knit with. There are many types of yarns, allowing knitters to enjoy a variety of sensory experiences as they express themselves through the medium. Yarns may be made of different fibres and have a range of textures. Their possibilities are exciting: you can, in theory, knit with anything – from a skein of supple silk sock yarn to the plastic bag that you brought it home in. Choose from a colour palette that sweeps from subtle, muted tones to eye-popping brights.

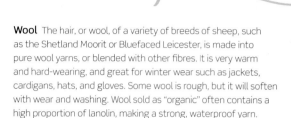

Wool

Merino wool

Alpaca

Wool The hair, or wool, of a variety of breeds of sheep, such as the Shetland Moorit or Bluefaced Leicester, is made into pure wool yarns, or blended with other fibres. It is very warm and hard-wearing, and great for winter wear such as jackets, cardigans, hats, and gloves. Some wool is rough, but it will soften with wear and washing. Wool sold as "organic" often contains a high proportion of lanolin, making a strong, waterproof yarn.

Merino wool This is wool from the merino sheep, which is said to have one of the softest wools of any sheep breed. The bouncy, smooth-surfaced fibre is just as warm as a more wiry, coarse wool. Merino is a fantastic choice for wearing against the skin, and is often treated to make it suitable for machine-washing. Good for soft scarves, arm warmers, and children's garments.

Alpaca This fibre has a luxurious feel and is one of the warmest natural fibres you can knit with. Even a fine, 4-ply garment provides sufficient insulation in bitterly cold weather. The alpaca is related to the llama. Alpaca yarn is perfect for ski hats, and thick, cosy jumpers and socks. You will also find baby alpaca yarn available, which is softer still.

Mohair This fibre is the hair of the angora goat, and it produces a unique natural "halo" when knitted up. Working with it is quite challenging, as its frizzy appearance makes it difficult to see the structure of the knitting and any mistakes made. Mohair makes particularly interesting oversized jumpers or accessories. It is not advisable to use it for babywear as it may shed hair when newly made, which could be dangerous if inhaled.

Mohair

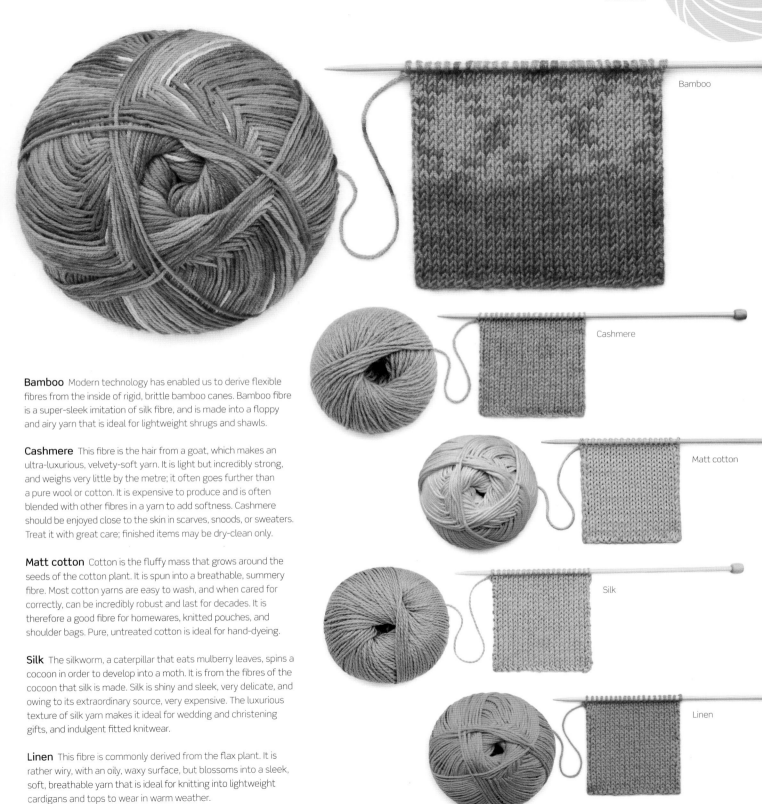

Bamboo

Cashmere

Matt cotton

Silk

Linen

Bamboo Modern technology has enabled us to derive flexible fibres from the inside of rigid, brittle bamboo canes. Bamboo fibre is a super-sleek imitation of silk fibre, and is made into a floppy and airy yarn that is ideal for lightweight shrugs and shawls.

Cashmere This fibre is the hair from a goat, which makes an ultra-luxurious, velvety-soft yarn. It is light but incredibly strong, and weighs very little by the metre; it often goes further than a pure wool or cotton. It is expensive to produce and is often blended with other fibres in a yarn to add softness. Cashmere should be enjoyed close to the skin in scarves, snoods, or sweaters. Treat it with great care; finished items may be dry-clean only.

Matt cotton Cotton is the fluffy mass that grows around the seeds of the cotton plant. It is spun into a breathable, summery fibre. Most cotton yarns are easy to wash, and when cared for correctly, can be incredibly robust and last for decades. It is therefore a good fibre for homewares, knitted pouches, and shoulder bags. Pure, untreated cotton is ideal for hand-dyeing.

Silk The silkworm, a caterpillar that eats mulberry leaves, spins a cocoon in order to develop into a moth. It is from the fibres of the cocoon that silk is made. Silk is shiny and sleek, very delicate, and owing to its extraordinary source, very expensive. The luxurious texture of silk yarn makes it ideal for wedding and christening gifts, and indulgent fitted knitwear.

Linen This fibre is commonly derived from the flax plant. It is rather wiry, with an oily, waxy surface, but blossoms into a sleek, soft, breathable yarn that is ideal for knitting into lightweight cardigans and tops to wear in warm weather.

Yarn weights

The yarn "weight" refers to the thickness of a yarn. Some yarns are spun by manufacturers to fall into what are considered as "standard" yarn weights, such as UK double-knitting and aran, and US sport or worsted. These standard weights have long histories and will probably be around for some time to come. However, even within these standard weights there is slight variation in thickness, and textured novelty yarns are not easy to categorize by thickness alone.

Visual yarn thickness is only one indicator of a yarn-weight category. A yarn can look thicker than another yarn purely because of its loft, the air between the fibres, and the springiness of the strands. By pulling a strand between your hands you can see how much loft it has by how much the thickness diminishes when the yarn is stretched. The ply of a yarn is also not an indication of yarn

thickness. Plies are the strands spun together around each other to form the yarn. A yarn with four plies can be very thick or very thin depending on the thickness of each individual ply.

In order to help knitters attempting to match like for like when looking for a substitute yarn for their knitting pattern, yarn manufacturers have created a table of yarn weights. This table (opposite) demonstrates how to find the nearest yarn substitute if you are unable to purchase the yarn specified in a knitting pattern. The very best indication of a yarn weight is the manufacturer's recommended tension and needle size for the yarn. (These will produce a knitted fabric that is loose enough to be soft and flexible but not so loose that it loses its shape.) Two yarns with the same fibre content and the same recommended tension and needle size will be ideal substitutes for each other.

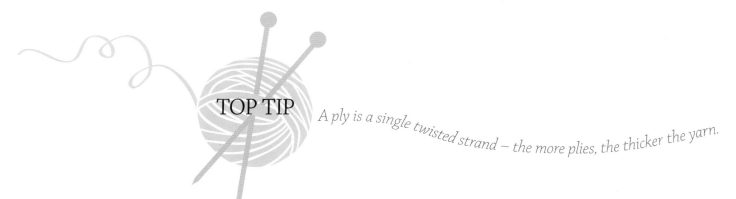

TOP TIP   *A ply is a single twisted strand – the more plies, the thicker the yarn.*

Yarn labels

Yarn is usually packaged with a label that provides all the information you need to knit successfully. Before you buy, always read the label carefully to establish the type of yarn, suggested needle size, care instructions, and ball length.

Decide whether you require an easy-care yarn and check the care instructions. Fibre content will indicate whether the yarn is synthetic, natural, or a mix of fibres. The ball length will enable you to calculate how many balls are required especially when substituting yarn. Check the dye lot number if you are purchasing several balls, as variations in colour can occur across different dye lots.

Lace/2-ply Extremely light and often sold in a plentiful quantity. If worked on needles of the recommended size, the yarn produces a very fine-knit, delicate result. It can be more pleasurable to use the yarn with slightly larger needles for a more open fabric and a quicker knit.

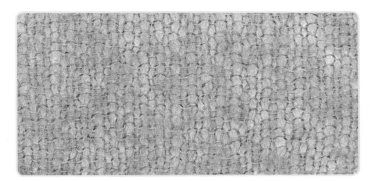

Superfine/3-ply An ideal choice for lightweight lace work. It goes a long way per ball, and requires very slim needles. A gossamer yarn such as this one (above) highlights stitch definition and fine detail, which is why intricate lace work looks stunning in superfine yarn.

Fine/4-ply Many knitters prefer fine to superfine yarn as it uses a more comfortable needle size yet still produces a lightweight knit. It is ideal for socks and baby clothes. The small stitches and neat appearance also suit delicate texture and colourwork items.

Double knit (DK)/Light worsted/ 5–6-ply DK yarn is used for anything from blankets and toys to jumpers and cardigans. It is commonly associated with 4mm (UK8/US6) needles, and knits up quickly. Many projects in this book are knitted in DK yarn.

Aran/Worsted/12-ply A thick, warm yarn that requires 5mm (UK6/US8) needles. It is good for men's garments with thick cabled detail, and functional items. Many yarns in this thickness employ a variety of fibres to make them machine-washable.

Bulky/chunky/14-ply Although bulky, the yarn consists mainly of lightweight fibres to prevent garments from misshaping. Commonly worked on 7mm (UK2/USn/a) needles, it makes a chunky knitted fabric perfect for outerwear, hats, and leg warmers.

Super bulky/Super chunky/16-ply+ The yarn thickness varies, but it is mostly used with large needles from 10mm (UK000/US15) upwards. A great choice for beginners as stitches are so large that mistakes are easily visible. Good for rugged scarves.

Yarns

In its simplest form, yarn is made from combed fibres spun together for strength and durability. There are, however, numerous fibre mixes, textures, and effect yarns now available offering exciting creative possibilities to the hand knitter.

Yarn weights

In its simplest form, yarn is made from combed fibres spun together for strength and durability. There are, however, numerous fibre mixes, textures, and effect yarns now available offering exciting creative possibilities to the hand knitter.

Yarn weight chart

What do you want to knit?	Yarn weight	Yarn symbol	Recommended needle sizes		
			EU Metric	Old UK	US
Lace	Lace, 2-ply, fingering	**0** Lace	2mm 2.5mm	14 13	0 1
Fine-knit socks, shawls, babywear	Superfine, 3-ply, fingering, baby	**1** Superfine	2.75mm 3mm 3.25mm	12 11 10	2 N/A 3
Light jumpers, babywear, socks, accessories	Fine, 4-ply, sport, baby	**2** Fine	3.5mm 3.75mm 4mm	N/A 9 8	4 5 6
Jumpers, light-weight scarves, blankets, toys	Double-knit (DK), light worsted, 5–6-ply	**3** Light	4.5mm	7	7
Jumpers, cabled menswear, blankets, hats, scarves, mittens	Aran, medium, worsted, Afghan, 12-ply	**4** Medium	5mm 5.5mm	6 5	8 9
Rugs, jackets, blankets, hats, legwarmers, winter accessories	Bulky, chunky, craft, rug, 14-ply	**5** Bulky	6mm 6.5mm 7mm 8mm	4 3 2 0	10 10½ N/A 11
Heavy blankets, rugs, thick scarves	Super bulky, super chunky, bulky, roving, 16-ply and upwards	**6** Super Bulky	9mm 10mm	00 000	13 15

Yarn labels

Everything you need to know about a yarn is on its label, represented by a symbol. Always keep the labels as they are vital for identifying the yarn if you run short and need more. New yarn needs to have the same dye lot number as the original purchase in order to avoid a slight difference in colour in the finished item.

 ## Symbols

Yarn manufacturers may use a system of symbols to give details of a yarn. These include descriptions of suitable needles and the required tension.

Yarn weight and thickness

4.5mm (UK 7/US 7)

Recommended needle size

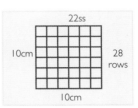

Tension over a 10cm (4in) sample square

50g

Nett at standard condition in accordance with BS984
Approx. length 115m (126yds)

Weight and length of yarn in ball

Shade/Colour

520

Shade/colour number

Dye lot number

313

Dye lot number

100%
wool

Fibre content

Machine-wash cold

Machine-wash cold, gentle cycle

Do not bleach

Dry-cleanable in any solvent

Dry-cleanable in certain solvents

Hand-wash cold

Hand-wash warm

Do not dry-clean

Do not tumble-dry

Do not iron

Iron on a low heat

Iron on a medium heat

Straight needles

If you are new to knitting, start with straight needles because they give a great deal of support to the hand when knitting. Short needles are recommended for small projects; longer needles are more suitable for wider knits such as a pullover or a baby's blanket, and for knitters who like to work by holding the needles underneath their arms or elbows.

Needles are sold in different sizes

Plastic needles

Metal needles

Bamboo needles

Ebony/rosewood needles

Square needles

Double-pointed needles

Size Knitting needles vary in diameter, from just 1.5mm (1/16in) thick to over 25mm (1in). There are three common needle-sizing systems: European metric, old British sizes, and American sizes. If you have older needles, use a knitting needle gauge to find their equivalent modern size. Needles are also available in various lengths to suit different projects and different ways of holding needles.

Plastic needles For needles with a surface that is halfway between that of metal and that of bamboo, choose plastic. It remains at a steady temperature during use, which may suit people who have arthritis. Avoid plastic needles of 4mm (UK8/US6) or smaller, as heavy projects may bend or break them.

Metal needles When working with hairy fibres such as mohair or wool, which may stick, slippery metal needles are great. If you find that you tend to knit too tightly, the slippery surface can help as it will cause a knitter's tension to loosen. Needles of more than 8mm (UK0/US11) in diameter can be clunky to work with, so are rarely available.

Bamboo needles Bamboo is a lightweight, flexible material, and makes excellent knitting needles. It helps to keep stitches regularly spaced, creating an even knitted fabric with a good tension. Great for slippery fibres such as silk and bamboo yarn. Recommended for arthritis sufferers. Thin needles will gradually warp slightly with use, to fit the curvature of your hand.

Ebony/rosewood needles These wooden needles feel luxurious to work with, and can be quite expensive. They often have a waxy surface, which becomes smooth with wear, creating a soft and tactile surface. Like bamboo needles, they help to create an even tension; they hold their shape and remain straight when used, giving them a solid feel.

Square needles Most needles are cylindrical with a pointed tip; these unusual new needles have a faceted surface and a pointed tip. Made from metal, they lie over each other better, which is particularly useful when working with double-pointed needles, and cause less strain on the hands, making them especially suitable for arthritis sufferers.

Double-pointed needles The recommended option for socks, gloves, and narrow tubes. These needles are short and do not accommodate a large number of stitches. At first, some knitters may find that ladders form on each corner between the needles; however, this problem will disappear as you practise.

Other equipment

Hundreds of different gadgets are available to knitters. Some are merely for convenience, whereas others are absolutely vital and perform specific tasks. Here are the basics, to which you can add more advanced items as you progress. These basic items should always be at hand when you are working on a project. Most knitters have a portable knitting bag or case to keep them in, so that it is easy to take everything to wherever they want to sit and knit. The tools below are relatively inexpensive, and can be purchased from haberdashery stores and knitting suppliers.

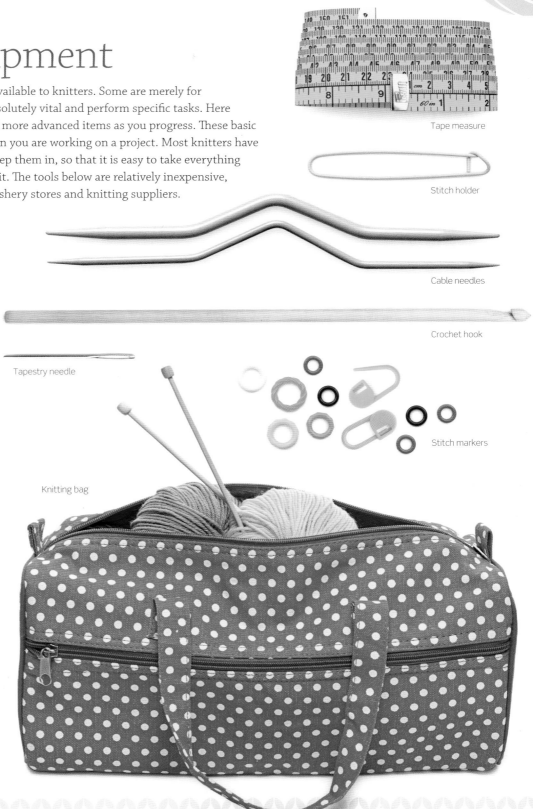

Tape measure

Stitch holder

Cable needles

Crochet hook

Tapestry needle

Stitch markers

Knitting bag

Tape measure Use this to accurately gauge sizing, to check tension, and to measure your knitting. Stick to using either metric or imperial measures.

Stitch holder Use it to hold stitches that you will return to later. Make your own stitch holder from a length of lightweight cotton yarn, or a safety pin.

Cable needle A kinked or v-shaped cable needle is used when working cables; this shape prevents cable stitches from sliding away. Choose a size that is closest to that of the needles used for the main body of the knitting.

Crochet hook A crochet hook makes it much easier to pick up previously dropped stitches. You can also use a crochet hook for inserting tassels.

Tapestry needle This has a blunt tip that will not damage yarn. Make sure that the eye is an appropriate size for the type of yarn you are using.

Stitch markers Use these to mark the beginning and end of a panel of stitches, and to identify the end of each row when working in the round. As you arrive at a marker, transfer it with the stitches and continue working the row as normal.

Knitting bag Bags for knitters often have many compartments, perfect for storing equipment and materials for your current project.

Following a pattern

Knitting patterns can look daunting to a beginner knitter, but if approached step by step they are easy to understand. This section provides an explanation of how to follow simple knitting patterns and gives tips for finishing details and seams. The best advice for a beginner wanting to knit a first project from a knitting pattern is to start with a simple accessory. Cushion covers are especially good practice as the instructions are straightforward and usually the only finishing details are seams. This is an example of a pattern for a simple, striped, stocking stitch cushion cover.

Summer cushion cover

Check the size of the finished item. If it is a simple square like this cushion, you can adjust the size easily by adding or subtracting stitches and rows.

Size of finished cushion
40.5 x 40.5cm (16 x 16in)

Always purchase the same total amount in metres/yards of a substitute yarn; not the same amount in weight.

Materials
3 x 50g (1¾oz)/125m (137yd) balls in each of branded Pure Wool DK in Lavender 039 (A) and Avocado 019 (B). Pair of 4mm (US size 6) knitting needles. Cushion pad to fit finished cover.

Use the yarn specified, but if you are unable to obtain this yarn, choose a substitute yarn of the same weight.

If desired, select different colours to suit your décor; the colours specified are just suggestions.

Extra items needed for your project will usually be listed under Notions or Additional materials.

Tension
22sts and 30 rows to 10cm (4in) over stocking stitch on 4mm (UK8/US6) needles or size necessary to achieve correct tension. To save time, take time to check tension.

Make a tension swatch before starting to knit and change the needle size if necessary (see opposite page).

Front
Using 4mm (UK8/US6) needles and A, cast on 88sts. Beg with a K row, work in st st until work measures 14cm (5½in) from cast on edge, ending with RS facing for next row.
Cut off A and change to B.
Cont in st st until work measures 26.5cm (10½in) from cast on edge, ending with RS facing for next row.
Cut off B and change to A.
Cont in st st until work measures 40.5cm (16in) from cast on edge, ending with RS facing for next row.
Cast off.

Consult the abbreviations list with your pattern for the meanings of abbreviations (see also p.19).

Instructions for working a piece of knitted fabric always start with how many stitches to cast on and what yarn or needle size to use. If there is only one needle size and one yarn, these may be absent here.

Work in the specified stitch pattern, for the specified number of rows or cm/in.

Colours are usually changed on a right-side row, so end with the right side facing for the changeover row.

The back of a cushion cover is sometimes exactly the same as the front or it has a fabric back. In this case, the stripes are reversed on the back for a more versatile cover.

If no stitch is specified for the cast off, always cast off knitwise (see p.26).

Back
Work as for Front, but use B for A, and A for B.

After all the knitted pieces are complete, follow the Making up (or Finishing) section of the pattern.

Making up
Darn in loose ends.
Block and press lightly on wrong side, following instructions on yarn label. With wrong sides facing, sew three sides of back and front together. Turn right-side out, insert cushion pad, and sew remaining seam.

See p.40 for how to darn in loose ends.

Make sure you look at the yarn label instructions before attempting to press any piece of knitting. The label may say that the yarn cannot be pressed or to press it only with a cool iron. (See p.40 for blocking tips.)

See pp.40-41 for seaming options. Take time with seams on knitting. Practise on odd pieces of knitting before starting your main project.

Garment patterns

Choosing the right size and knitting a tension swatch are the two most important things to get right if you want to create a successful garment. It is also possible to make simple alterations to patterns worked in plain garter or stocking stitch.

Choosing a garment size

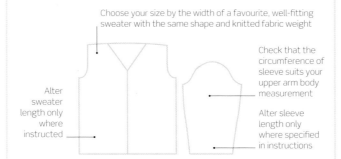

Choose your size by the width of a favourite, well-fitting sweater with the same shape and knitted fabric weight

Check that the circumference of sleeve suits your upper arm body measurement

Alter sweater length only where instructed

Alter sleeve length only where specified in instructions

Rather than looking at specific "sizes" when choosing which size to knit, select the one nearest to how you want the garment to fit. The best way to do this is to find a similar garment that fits you. Lay it flat and measure its width – choose the width on the pattern that is the closest match to your body shape.

Photocopy your pattern and highlight the figures for your size throughout. Start with the number of balls of yarn, then the number of stitches to cast on, the length to knit to the armhole, and so on. The smallest size is given first and larger sizes follow in parentheses. Where only one figure is given, this applies to all sizes.

Altering patterns

Alter the length of garment patterns worked in plain garter or stocking stitch, but avoid altering armholes, necklines, or sleeve heads. As sleeves and some bodies have shaping, this must also be adjusted. In this example, length is added to a sleeve:

1 Photocopy or draw out the pattern diagram. Write the new required length on the diagram (eg 48cm (19in)).
2 Find the number of rows to 10cm (4in) in the tension note. Divide number by 10 to calculate how many rows there are in 1cm. For example, 30 rows per 10cm (4in). 30 ÷ 10 = 3 rows per 1cm ($\frac{1}{2}$in).
3 Multiply the required new length by the number of rows in 1cm ($\frac{1}{2}$in). The resulting figure is the total number in the new length. For example, 48 × 3 = 144 rows.
4 Any increasing will also have to be re-calculated. From the pattern, note the number of stitches to cast on at the cuff and how many there will be on the needle just before the start of the underarm shaping (this figure should be shown at the end of the written instruction for the increases).
5 Subtract the smallest from the largest amount of stitches. The answer is the total number of stitches to be increased. Divide the answer by two (because a sleeve has two sides), to give the number of stitches to increase on each side. For example. 114 - 60 = 54 sts. 54 ÷ 2 = 27 sts.
6 To calculate the number of rows between each increase, divide the new number of rows found in Step 3 by the number of increases calculated in Step 5. If you have a fraction in this answer, round the number down. For example, 144 ÷ 27 = 4.22. Increase one stitch each side every 4 rows. Knit the remaining rows straight before underarm cast offs.

Measuring tension

Always knit a swatch before starting your project to make sure that you achieve the recommended stitch size (tension). Only if you achieve the correct tension will your knitting have the correct measurements.

1 Using the specified needle size, knit a 13cm (5in) square. Mark 10cm (4in) across the centre with pins and count the number of stitches between the pins.

2 Count the number of rows to 10cm (4in) in the same way. If you have fewer stitches and rows than you should, try again with a smaller needle size; if you have more, change to a larger needle. Use the needle size for your knitting that best matches the correct tension. (Matching stitch width is more important than matching row height.)

Understanding written instructions

Anyone who can cast on, knit and purl, and cast off will be able to work from simple knit-and-purl-combination stitch pattern instructions with little difficulty. It is just a question of following the instructions one step at a time and getting used to the abbreviations. A list of common knitting abbreviations is given opposite, but for simple knit and purl textures all you need to grasp is that "k1" means "knit one stitch", "k2" means "knit two stitches", and so on. And the same applies for the purl stitches – "p1" means "purl one stitch", "p2" means "purl two stitches", and so on.

To begin a stitch pattern, cast on the number of stitches that it tells you to, using your chosen yarn and the yarn manufacturer's recommended needle size. Work the stitch row by row, then repeat the rows as instructed and the stitch pattern will grow beneath the needles. When your knitting is the desired size, cast off in pattern (see pp.26–28).

The best tips for first-timers are to follow the rows slowly; mark the right side of the fabric by knotting a coloured thread onto it; use a row counter to keep track of where you are; and pull out your stitches and start again if you get in a muddle. If you love the stitch pattern you are trying out, you can make a scarf, blanket, or cushion cover with it – no need to buy a knitting pattern.

The principles for following stitch patterns are the same for lace and cables. Some stitch patterns will call for "slipping" stitches and knitting "through the back of the loop". To learn more about knitting terminlogy, consult the table (opposite) for the most common knitting abbreviations.

Slipping stitches purlwise

1 Always slip stitches purlwise, for example when slipping stitches onto a stitch holder, unless instructed otherwise. Insert the tip of the right needle from right to left through the front of the loop on the left needle.

2 Slide the stitch onto the tip of the right needle and off the left needle without working it. The slipped stitch now sits on the right needle with the right side of the loop at the front just like the worked stitches next to it.

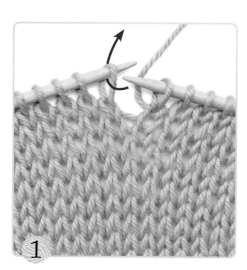

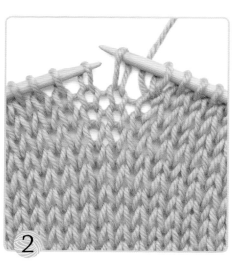

Slipping stitches knitwise

1 Slip stitches knitwise only if instructed to do so, or if working decreases (see pp.38-39), as it twists the stitch. First insert the tip of the right needle from left to right through the front of the loop on the left needle.

2 Slide the stitch onto the right needle and off the left needle without working it. The slipped stitch now sits on the right needle with the left side of the loop at the front of the needle unlike the worked stitches next to it.

Symbols, charts, and abbreviations

Knitting instructions for stitch patterns can also be given in chart form. Some knitters prefer working with stitch-symbol charts because they are easy to read, and they build up a visual image of the stitch repeat that is quick to memorize.

Even with charted instructions, there are usually written directions for how many stitches to cast on. If not, you can calculate the cast on from the chart, where the number of stitches in the pattern "repeat" are clearly marked. Cast on a multiple of this number, plus any edge stitches, three stitches are shown on the example chart, below, outside the six-stitch repeat.

Each square represents one knitted stitch and each horizontal line of squares represents a row on your knitted fabric. After casting on, work from the bottom of the chart upwards to start creating the knitted fabric. Read odd-numbered rows (usually RS rows) from right to left and even-numbered rows (usually WS rows) from left to right. Work the edge stitches, then work the stitches inside the repeat as many times as required. Some symbols may mean one thing on a RS row and another on a WS row (see below).

Once you have worked all the charted rows, start again at the bottom of the chart to begin the "row repeat" once more.

Charts

④ After completing row 16, start again at row 1

Rep = 16 rows

② Read row 1 and all other RS rows from right to left

③ Read row 2 and all other WS rows from left to right

① Cast on a multiple of 6 stitches, plus 3 extra stitches at each end

3 edge sts   Rep = 6sts   Start at the bottom

Stitch symbols

These are some of the commonly used knitting symbols in this book. Any unusual symbols will be explained in the pattern. Symbols can vary, so follow the explanations in your pattern.

☐	K on RS rows, p on WS rows
⬤	P on RS rows, k on WS rows
O	Yarnover
╱	K2tog
╲	Ssk
╱│╲	S1 k2tog psso (sk2p)
╱╲╲	Sk2 k1 p2sso (s2kpo)

Knitting abbreviations

These are the most frequently used knitting abbreviations found both in this book and in popular knitting patterns throughout the world. Any special abbreviations in knitting instructions are always explained within the pattern.

alt alternate

beg begin(ning)

cm centimetre(s)

cont continu(e)(ing)

dec decreas(e)(ing)

foll follow(s)(ing)

g gram(s)

g st garter stitch

in inch(es)

inc increas(e)(ing)

k knit

k1 tbl knit st through back of loop

k2tog (or dec 1) knit next 2sts together (see p.38)

kfb (or inc 1) knit into front and back of next st

LH left hand

m metre(s)

M1 (or M1k) make one stitch (see pp.34–35)

mm millimetre(s)

oz ounce(s)

p purl

p2tog (or dec 1) purl next 2sts together (see p.38)

patt pattern, or work in pattern

Pfb (or inc 1) purl into front and back of next st (see p.33)

psso pass slipped stitch over

rem remain(s)(ing)

rep repeat(ing)

rev st st reverse stocking stitch

RH right hand

RS right side (of work)

s1 k1 psso (skpo) slip one, knit one, pass slipped st over (see p.39)

s1 k2tog psso (or sk2p) slip one st, knit 2sts together, pass slipped sts over

ssk slip, slip, knit (see p.39)

s slip stitch(es)

s2 k1 p2sso (or s2kpo) slip 2, knit one, pass slipped stitches over

st(s) stitch(es)

st st stocking stitch

tbl through back of loop(s)

tog together

WS wrong side (of work)

yd yard(s)

yfwd yarn forward (US yo; see p.36)

yfrn yarn forward round needle (US yo; see p.37)

yon yarn over needle (US yo; see p.37)

yrn yarn round needle (US yo; see p.36)

[ ] * Repeat the instructions between the brackets, or after or between the asterisks, as many times as instructed in the pattern

Holding yarn and needles

Learning to knit is a very quick process. There are only a few initial techniques to pick up before you are ready to make simple shapes, such as scarves, blankets, and cushion covers. Basics include casting stitches onto the needles, knit and purl stitches, and casting stitches off the needles. Before starting to knit, familiarize yourself with how to hold the yarn and needles. See below for two common methods.

Knitting English style

1 Wrap yarn around fingers on your right hand. The aim is to control the yarn firmly but with a relaxed hand. Release the yarn to flow through fingers as the stitches are formed.

2 You need to be able to tension the yarn just enough with your fingers to create even stitches that are neither too loose nor too tight.

3 Hold the needles with the stitches about to be worked in the left hand and the working needle in the right hand. Use the right forefinger to wrap the yarn around the needle.

Knitting Continental style

1 Wrap the yarn around the fingers of your left hand in any way that feels comfortable. Try this technique to see if you can both release and tension the yarn easily to create uniform loops.

2 This alternative tensioning technique may suit you better. Here the yarn is wrapped twice around the forefinger.

3 Hold the needle with the unworked stitches in the left hand and the working needle in the right. Position the yarn with the left forefinger and pull it through the loops with the right needle.

Making a slip knot

After reading about the two knitting styles on the previous page you are now ready to place the first loop of yarn on your needle and start creating a piece of knitting. This initial loop is called the slip knot and it is the first stitch formed when casting on stitches.

1 Begin by crossing the yarn coming from the ball over the yarn end (called the yarn tail) to form a large circle, or loop, of yarn.

2 Insert the tip of a knitting needle through the circle of yarn, then wrap the needle tip around the ball end of the yarn and pull the yarn through the circle.

3 This forms a loop on the needle and a loose, open knot below the loop.

4 Pull both ends of the yarn firmly to tighten the knot and the loop on the needle.

5 Make sure the completed slip knot is tight enough on the needle that it will not fall off but not so tight that you can barely slide it along the needle.

6 The yarn tail on the slip knot should be at least 10-15cm (4-6in) long so it can be threaded onto a blunt-ended yarn needle and darned in later. Your knitting pattern, however, may instruct you to leave an extra-long yarn tail (called a long loose end) to use for seams or other purposes.

Yarn coming from ball

Yarn tail

1

2

3

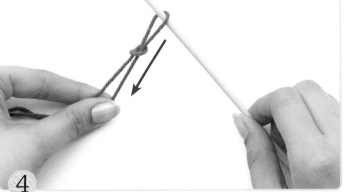

4

Make sure the loop is secure but slides easily

Ball end of yarn

5

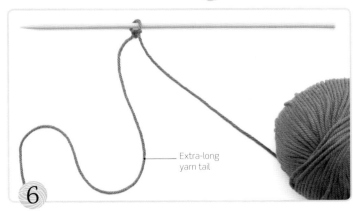

Extra-long yarn tail

6

Single strand cast ons

Casting on gives a closed edge to your knitting that won't unravel. There are several methods of casting on, but the basic techniques shown here are the quickest and simplest ways to get started.

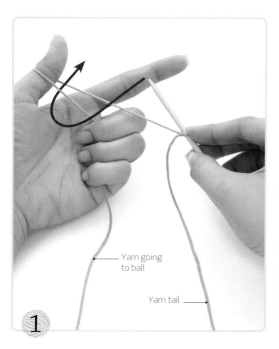

Yarn going
to ball

Yarn tail

1

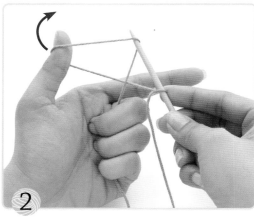

2

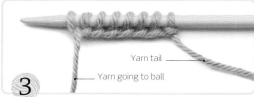

Yarn tail

Yarn going to ball

3

Single cast on
(also called thumb cast on)

1 This is the easiest cast on technique. Hold the needle with the slip knot in your right hand. Then wrap the yarn around your left thumb as shown and hold the yarn in place in the palm of your left hand. Insert the needle tip under and up through the loop on your thumb following the arrow.

2 Release the loop from your thumb and pull the yarn to tighten the new cast on loop on the needle, sliding it up close to the slip knot.

3 Loop the yarn around your thumb again and continue making loops in the same way until the required number of stitches is on the needle.

Knit on cast on
(also called knit stitch cast on)

1 Place the needle with the slip knot in your left hand. Insert tip of right needle from left to right through centre of loop on left needle. With yarn behind needles, wrap it under and around tip of right needle. (While casting on, use your left forefinger to hold loops on left needle in position.) Using tip of right needle, carefully draw yarn through loop on left needle.

2 Transfer the loop on the right needle to the left needle by inserting the left needle from right to left through the front of the loop. Pull both yarn ends to tighten the new cast on loop on the needle, sliding it up close to the slip knot.

3 Continue casting on stitches in the same way for the required number of stitches. For a looser cast on, hold two needles together in your left hand while casting on.

Yarn going to ball

Long yarn tail

1

2

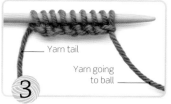

Yarn tail

Yarn going
to ball

3

Yarn going to ball

Long yarn tail

1

2

3

Cable cast on

1 Begin by working Steps 1–2 of the knit on cast on (opposite). Then insert the tip of the right needle between the two loops on the left needle and wrap the yarn under and around the tip of the right needle.

2 With the tip of the right needle, draw the yarn through to form a loop on the right needle.

3 Transfer the loop on the right needle to the left needle (see Step 2 Knit on cast on). Continue, inserting the needle between the first two loops on the left needle when beginning each new cast on stitch.

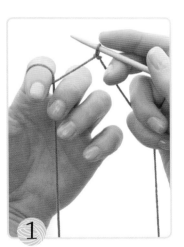

1

2

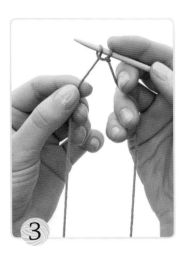

3

Finger loop cast on

1 This gives a soft cast on. Hold the needle with the slip knot in your right hand. Lift the yarn from underneath with your left index finger pointing away from you. Bend and turn your finger to point towards you.

2 Insert the needle into the loop that lies on top of your finger from behind.

3 Release your index finger and tighten the stitch on the needle.

TOP TIP *If your casting on is always too tight, use a needle one size larger.*

Two strand cast ons

These cast on techniques all use two strands of yarn, but generally only one needle, and are strong, elastic, and versatile. They are usually followed by a wrong side row, unless the reverse is the right side. As with double cast on, start all these with a slip knot made after a long tail at least three times as long as the planned knitting width.

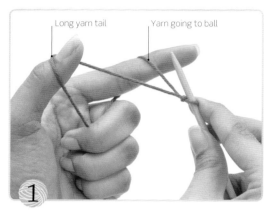

Long yarn tail   Yarn going to ball

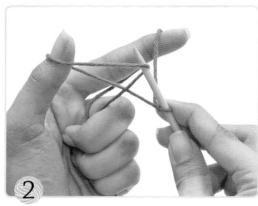

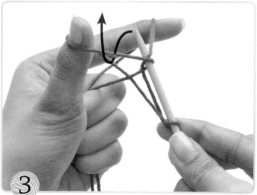

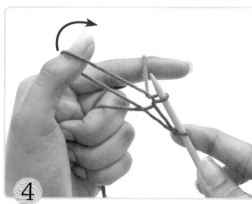

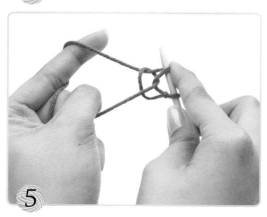

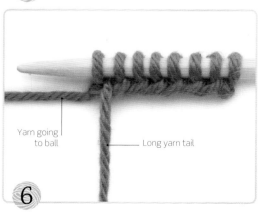

Yarn going
to ball   Long yarn tail

Double cast on
(also called long-tail cast on)

1 Make a slip knot on the needle, leaving a long yarn tail – allow about 3.5cm (1⅜in) for each stitch being cast on. Hold the needle in your right hand. Loop the yarn tail over your left thumb and the ball yarn end over your left forefinger as shown. Hold both strands in the palm of your left hand.

2 Insert the tip of the needle under and up through the loop that is around your left thumb.

3 Wrap the tip of the needle around the loop on your forefinger from right to left and use it to pull the yarn through the loop on your thumb as shown by the arrow.

4 Gently release the loop by bending down the thumb and sliding the yarn off.

5 Pull both yarn ends to tighten the new cast on loop on the needle, sliding it up close to the slip knot.

6 Loop the yarn around the thumb again and cast on another stitch in the same way. Make as many stitches as you need.

Twisted double cast on

This cast on is very stretchy, so is useful before a rib. It can be made even stretchier by working it over two needles held together.

1 Hold the yarn and needle as for double cast on. Bring the needle towards you and then back under both thumb loops.

2 Bring the needle towards you over the top of the furthest thumb loop and down between both thumb strands. The thumb loop is now a figure of eight.

3 Take the needle over the first loop on your index finger.

4 Bring the needle towards you. Drop the end of your thumb away from you and let the loop slide down towards the end to open the thumb loop. Bring the needle down through the open thumb loop.

5 Release the thumb loop keeping the yarn around your index finger ready to start the next cast on loop. Pull the short strand to tighten the stitch. Loop the yarn around the thumb again and repeat to this point to cast on another stitch in the same way. The stitches will create a stretchy double twist effect.

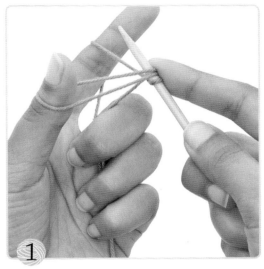

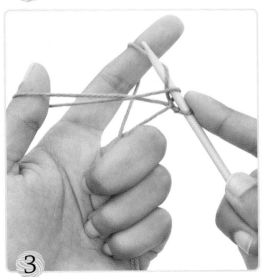

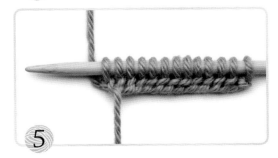

 **TOP TIP** *It is important to use the correct method of casting on.*

Simple cast offs

When your piece of knitted fabric is complete you need to close off the loops so that they cannot unravel. This is called casting off the stitches. Although casting off is shown here worked across knit stitches, the principle is the same for purl stitches. If instructed to retain stitches for future use, slip your stitches onto a spare needle or a stitch holder.

Casting off knitwise

1 Begin by knitting the first two stitches. Then insert the tip of the left needle from left to right through the first stitch and lift this stitch up and over the second stitch and off the right needle.

2 To cast off the next stitch, knit one more stitch and repeat Step 1. Continue until only one stitch remains on the right needle. If your pattern says "cast off in pattern", work the stitches in the specified pattern as you cast off.

3 To stop the last stitch from unravelling, cut the yarn, leaving a yarn tail 20cm (8in) long, which is long enough to darn into the knitting later. (Alternatively, leave a much longer yarn end to use for a future seam.) Pass the yarn end through the remaining loop and pull tight to close the loop. This is called fastening off.

Slipping stitches off needle

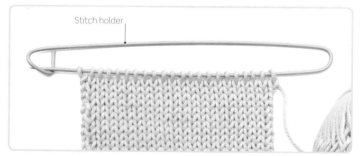

Stitch holder

Using a stitch holder: If you are setting stitches aside to work on later, your instructions will tell you whether to cut the yarn or keep it attached to the ball. Carefully slip your stitches onto a stitch holder large enough to hold all the stitches. If you are only slipping a few stitches, use a safety pin.

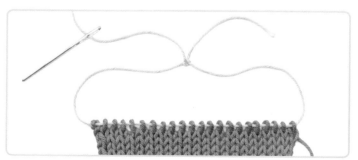

Using a length of yarn: If you do not have a stitch holder or do not have one large enough, use a length of cotton yarn instead. Using a blunt-ended yarn needle, pass the yarn through the stitches as you slip them off the knitting needle. Knot the ends of the cotton yarn together.

Alternative cast offs

Try using one of these casting off techniques to complement your project. Consider using a contrast colour, either in the basic cast off or combined with a decorative style. Cast offs are included that give more stretch to ribs or loosen an edge, and an adaptation of the three needle cast off can be used to join pockets and hems.

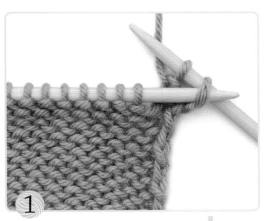

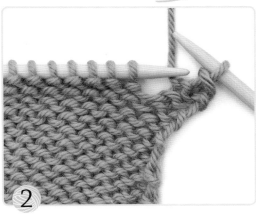

Purl cast off

1 Purl two stitches, then take the yarn to the back. Insert the tip of the left needle into the first stitch and pass it over the second stitch and off the right needle.

2 Bring the yarn to the front, repeat Steps 1 and 2 across row, but purl only one stitch in Step 1. Pull the end stitch through itself as for casting off knitwise (see opposite).

Casting off in rib effect

Use after a single rib fabric to maintain the rib corrugations. This method adds a little more stretch than casting off in either all knit or all purl.

1 Work one knit and one purl. Move the yarn to the back. Insert the left needle into the first stitch. Pass over the second and off the right needle.

2 Knit the next stitch then pass the first stitch over the second and off the right needle as before.

3 Yarn to front and purl next stitch. Repeat Steps 2 and 3 across the row. Pull the final stitch through itself to fasten off.

Tubular cast off

1 In preparation, and over an even number of stitches, work two rows as follows: knit the first stitch, bring yarn to front and slip the purl stitch that follows without twisting it (purlwise), take yarn to back. Repeat across row.

2 Stretch your ribbing out and cut the yarn end to about four times the length of the required cast off edge. Thread onto a blunt-ended yarn needle. Hold the knitting with the tip to the right. Insert the yarn needle into the first stitch knitwise. Pull the yarn through and drop the stitch.

3 Bring the yarn across the front and insert the needle purlwise into the third (knit) stitch. Pull the yarn through but not too tightly. Take it to the right and insert purlwise into the second (purl) stitch, taking the yarn through to the back.

4 Take the yarn behind the third (knit) stitch, bring it to the front between the third and fourth stitch and insert it as shown into the fourth (purl) stitch. Then insert the needle through the centre of the preceding knit stitch, and out to the front around the left leg.

5 Repeat Steps 3–4. Tension the stitches evenly as you work.

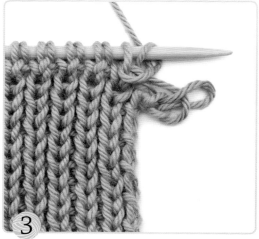

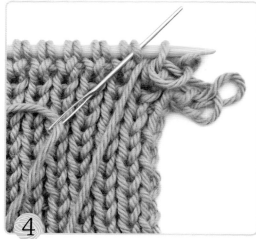

TOP TIP *Thread the yarn gently for a straight edge.*

Knit and purl stitches

All knitting is made up of only two basic stitches – knit and purl. These examples are shown on stocking stitch. The purl stitch is a little more difficult, but becomes effortless with practise. Once you are a seasoned knitter, your hands will know how to work these basic stitches in your sleep. Work your first purl row after you have cast on and knitted a few rows of garter stitch (see p.30).

Knit stitch (abbreviation: k)

1 Hold needle with unworked stitches in your left hand and other needle in your right hand. With yarn at back of knitting, insert right needle from left to right under front loop and through centre of next stitch to be worked on left needle.

2 Wrap yarn under and around right needle, keeping an even tension as the yarn slips through your fingers.

3 With right needle, draw yarn through stitch on left needle. Hold yarn reasonably firmly. Let old loop drop off left needle to complete knit stitch on right needle. Work all stitches on left needle onto right needle in same way. To start new row, turn work and transfer right needle to left hand.

Yarn at back of knitting

Purl stitch (abbreviation: p)

1 With yarn at front of knitting, insert right needle from right to left through centre of next stitch to be worked on left needle. Wrap yarn over and around right needle. Keep an even tension on yarn as you release it.

2 With needle, draw yarn through stitch on left needle. Keep your hands relaxed and allow yarn to slip through fingers in a controlled manner.

3 Let old loop drop off left needle to complete purl stitch. Work all stitches on left needle onto right needle in the same way. To start next row, turn work and transfer the knitting to your left hand.

Yarn at front of knitting

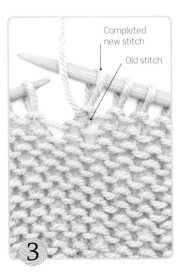

Completed new stitch

Old stitch

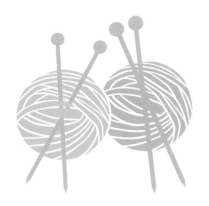

Basic pattern stitches

Once you know how to work knit and purl stitch with ease, you will be able to work the most frequently used stitch patterns – garter stitch and stocking stitch. Stocking stitch and reverse stocking stitch are commonly used for plain knitted garments and many more complicated patterns are based on these stitches.

Garter stitch (abbreviation: g st)

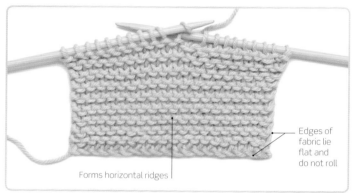

Forms horizontal ridges

Edges of fabric lie flat and do not roll

Knit right side (RS) rows: Garter stitch is the easiest of all knitted fabrics because whichever side is facing you, all rows are worked in knit stitch.
When the right side of the fabric is facing you, knit all the stitches in the row. Both sides look the same. The resulting fabric is soft, textured, and slightly stretchy. More rows are needed than in stocking stitch to make the same length of fabric.

Single ribbing (abbreviation: k1, p1 rib)

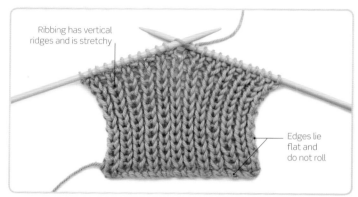

Ribbing has vertical ridges and is stretchy

Edges lie flat and do not roll

Right side (RS) rows: Single ribbing is formed by working alternating knit and purl stitches over an even number of stitches. Bring the yarn forwards before working the second (purl) stitch, and take it backwards before the third (knit) stitch, and so on. Both sides look the same and are worked in the same way. Ribbed fabric is stretchy and, therefore, ideal for cuffs and collars on knitted sweaters.

Stocking stitch (abbreviation: st st)

Side edges roll slightly to back

Right side is smooth

Bottom edge naturally rolls up at front

Knit right side (RS) rows: Stocking stitch is formed by working alternate rows of knit and purl stitches. When the right side is facing you, knit all the stitches in the row.

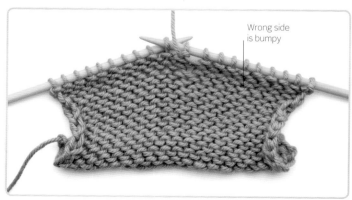

Wrong side is bumpy

Purl wrong side (WS) rows: When the wrong side is facing you, purl all the stitches in the row. The wrong side is often referred to as the "purl side".

Joining yarn

To calculate if there is sufficient yarn to complete two rows, fold the remaining yarn in half and make a slip knot at the fold. Knit the first row. If the knot comes before the end of the row you do not have enough yarn and need to join on a fresh ball.

End of old ball

New ball

1

Knot close to knitting

New ball joined on

2

Joining on a new ball

1 Always join on a new ball at the beginning of a row. Knot the new end of yarn onto the old yarn.

2 Slide the knot up very close to the edge of the knitting. The knot can be hidden in the seam later. If you are knitting a scarf or blanket, tie the knot loosely so you can undo it later and darn in the ends.

Weaver's knot

Use this knot when joining yarns of different thickness.

1 Make a loop of the thick yarn and pinch the neck together. Thread a longish end of the thin yarn through the loop from above, and wrap it over the neck of the loop from back to front, pinch this to the loop with your fingers.

2 Take the thin yarn end that is wrapped around the loop under the front thread of the thick yarn loop. Pass it over itself as you take it towards the back and then pass it under the rear thread of the thick yarn loop.

3 Holding both thick yarns in one hand and both thin in the other, gently pull the short ends apart with your fingers to close the knot.

1

2

3

Square knot

This is made like a granny knot, but take left over right, then right over left. This is best made at the point where it is needed in the knitting so you can make sure it goes to the back.

Correcting mistakes

The best thing to do if you make a mistake in your knitting is to unravel it back to the mistake by unpicking the stitches one by one. If you drop a stitch, be sure to pick it up quickly before it comes undone right back to the cast on edge.

Unpicking a knit row

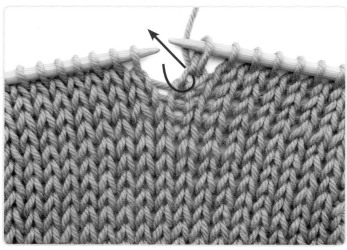

Unravelling on RS: Hold the needle with the stitches in your right hand. To unpick each stitch individually, insert the tip of the left needle from front to back through the stitch below the first knit stitch on the right needle, then drop the old knit stitch off the needle and pull out the loop.

Unpicking a purl row

Unravelling on WS: Hold the needle with the stitches in your right hand. Unpick each purl stitch individually with the tip of the left needle in the same way as for the knit stitch. When unpicking stitches, do not split the yarn or you will add two stitches to your needle. Count the stitches before you start knitting again.

Picking up a dropped stitch

Reclaim a dropped stitch on st st: You can easily reclaim a dropped stitch with a crochet hook. With the right side of the knitting facing you, insert the hook through the dropped loop. Grab the strand between the stitches and pull a loop through the loop on the hook. Continue up the rows in this way until you reach the top. Then slip the stitch back onto your needle.

Simple increases

Increasing the number of stitches on the needle is one way knitting is shaped, changing the edges from straight vertical sides to curves and slants. The following techniques are simple increases used for shaping knitting.

Knit into front and back of stitch

(abbreviation: kfb or inc 1)

This popular invisible increase for a knit row is also called a bar increase because it creates a little bar between the stitches.

1 Knit the next stitch, leaving the stitch being worked on the left needle. Insert the right needle through the back of the loop from right to left.

2 Wrap the yarn around the tip of the right needle, draw the yarn through the loop to form the second stitch and drop the old stitch off the left needle.

3 Knitting into both the front and the back of the stitch creates two new stitches out of one, and increases one stitch overall in the row.

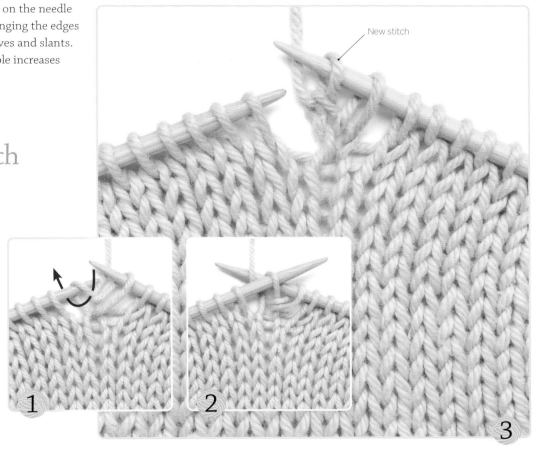

New stitch

Purl into front and back of stitch (abbreviation: pfb or inc 1)

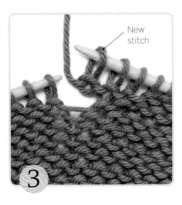

New stitch

1 Purl the next stitch, leaving the stitch being worked on the left needle. Insert the right needle through the back of the loop from left to right.

2 Wrap the yarn around the tip of the right needle, draw the yarn through the loop to form the second stitch and drop the old stitch off the left needle.

3 Purling into the front and the back of the stitch like this creates two stitches out of one and increases one stitch in the row.

Lifted increase on knit row (abbreviation: inc 1)

1 Insert the tip of the right needle from front to back through the stitch below the next stitch on the left needle. Knit this lifted loop.

2 Knit the next stitch (the stitch above the lifted stitch on the left needle) in the usual way.

3 This creates two stitches out of one and increases one stitch in the row. (The purl version of this stitch is worked using the same principle.)

"Make one" left cross increase on a knit row (abbreviation: M1 or M1k)

1 Insert the tip of the left needle from front to back under the horizontal strand between the stitch just knit and the next stitch. Then insert the right needle through the strand on the left needle from right to left behind the left needle.

2 Wrap the yarn around the tip of the right needle and draw the yarn through the lifted loop. (This is called knitting through the back of the loop.)

3 This creates an extra stitch in the row. (Knitting through the back of the loop twists the base of the new stitch to produce a crossed stitch that closes up the hole it would have created.)

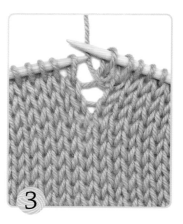

"Make one" right cross increase on a knit row (abbreviation: M1 or M1k)

Knitting patterns do not always differentiate between left and right "make one" increases. Choose the most suitable increase for your project.

1 Insert the tip of the left needle from back to front under the horizontal strand between the knitted stitch and the next one. Insert the right needle from left to right into the front of this new loop, twisting the stitch.

2 Wrap the yarn around the tip of the needle and draw the yarn through the lifted loop, knitting into the front of the stitch.

3 This action crosses the lifted stitch, and closes the hole made by picking up the loop. The resulting increase slants to the right and is normally worked at the end of a knit row.

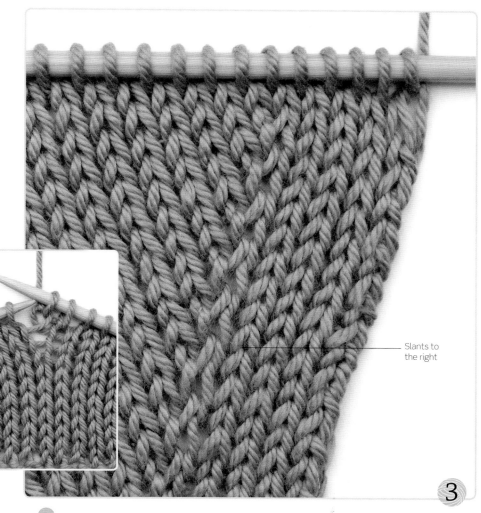

Slants to the right

TOP TIP   *M1 means to make a new, separate stitch between two stitches.*

Yarnover increases

Also known as "visible increases", yarnover increases add stitches to a row and create holes at the same time. They are used to produce decorative lace patterns. A yarnover is made by looping the yarn around the right needle to form an extra stitch. It is important to wrap the loop around the needle in the correct way or it will become crossed when it is worked in the next row, which closes the hole.

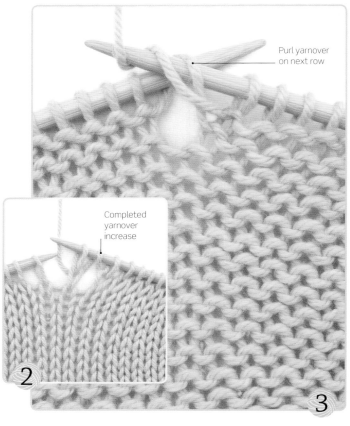

Purl yarnover on next row

Yarnover between knit stitches

(abbreviation: UK yfwd; US yo)

1 Bring the yarn forwards (yfwd) to the front of the knitting between the needles. Take the yarn over the top of the right needle to the back and work the next knit stitch in the usual way.

2 When the knit stitch is complete, the yarnover is correctly formed on the right needle with the right leg of the loop at the front.

3 On the following row, when you reach the yarnover, purl it through the front of the loop. This will create an open hole under the purl stitch.

1

Completed yarnover increase

2

3

Yarnover between purl stitches (abbreviation: UK yrn; US yo)

1

Completed yarnover increase

2

Knit yarnover on next row

3

1 Bring the yarn to the back of the work over the top of the right needle, then to the front between the needles. Work the next purl stitch in the usual way.

2 When the purl stitch is complete, the yarnover is correctly formed on the right needle with the right leg of the loop at the front of the needle.

3 On the following row, when you reach the yarnover, knit it through the front of the loop in the usual way. This creates an open hole under the knit stitch.

Yarnover between knit and purl stitches (abbreviation: UK yfrn and yon; US yo)

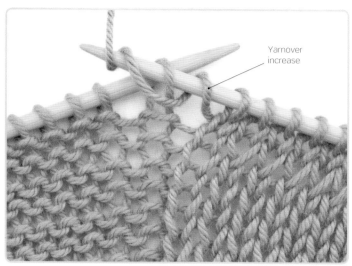

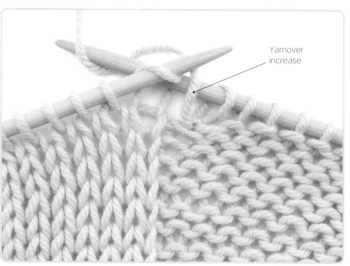

After a knit stitch and before a purl stitch (yfrn): Bring the yarn to the front between the needles, then over the top of the right needle and to the front again. Purl the next stitch. On the following row, work the yarnover through the front of the loop in the usual way to create an open hole.

After a purl stitch and before a knit stitch (yon): Take the yarn over the top of the right needle and to the back of the work, then knit the next stitch. On the following row, work the yarnover through the front of the loop in the usual way to create an open hole.

Yarnover at the beginning of a row (abbreviation: UK yfwd and yrn; US yo)

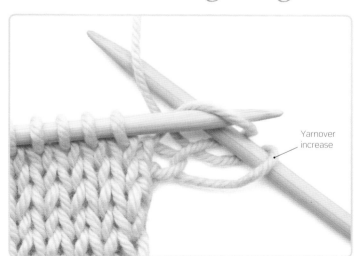

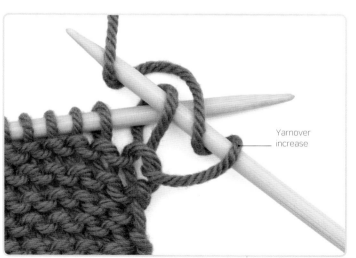

At the beginning of a row before a knit stitch (yfwd): Insert the right needle behind the yarn and into the first stitch knitwise. Take the yarn over the top of the right needle to the back and complete the knit stitch. On the following row, work yarnover through front of loop to create an open scallop at the edge.

At the beginning of a row before a purl stitch (yrn): Wrap the yarn from front to back over the top of the right needle and to the front again between the needles. Then purl the first stitch. On the following row, work the yarnover through the front of the loop in the usual way to create an open scallop at the edge.

Simple decreases

To shape knitting, and for creating textured stitches, when paired with increases, decreases are essential. Complicated decreases are always explained in knitting instructions. Most of the decreases that follow are single decreases that subtract only one stitch from the knitting, but the most common double decreases are included.

Completed decrease slants right

Knit two together
(abbreviation: k2tog or dec 1)

1 Insert the tip of the right needle from left to right through the second stitch then the first stitch on the left needle.

2 Wrap the yarn around the tip of the right needle, draw the yarn through both loops and drop the old stitches off the left needle.

3 This makes two stitches into one and decreases one stitch in the row. The completed stitch slants to the right.

Purl two together (abbreviation: p2tog or dec 1)

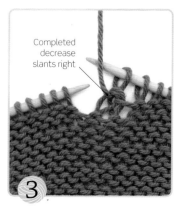

Completed decrease slants right

1 Use the p2tog decrease where a pattern specifies "decrease 1" on a purl row. Insert the tip of the right needle from right to left through the first, then the second stitch on the left needle.

2 Wrap the yarn around the tip of the right needle, draw the yarn through both loops and drop the old stitches off the left needle.

3 This makes two stitches into one and decreases one stitch in the row.

Slip one, knit one, pass slipped stitch over (abbeviation: s1 k1 psso or skpo)

1 Slip the first stitch on the left needle knitwise onto the right needle without working it. Then knit the next stitch.

2 Pick up the slipped stitch with the tip of the left needle and pass it over the knit stitch and off the right needle.

3 This makes two stitches into one and decreases one stitch in the row.

Slipped knitwise onto right needle

Completed decrease slants left

Slip, slip, knit (abbreviation: ssk)

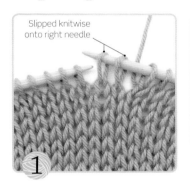
Slipped knitwise onto right needle

Completed decrease slants left

1 Slip the next two stitches on the left needle knitwise, one at a time, onto the tip of the right needle without working them.

2 Insert the tip of the left needle from left to right through the fronts of the two slipped stitches (the right needle is now behind the left). Knit these two stitches together.

3 This makes two stitches into one and decreases one stitch in the row.

Slip, slip, purl (abbreviation: ssp)

1 Keeping yarn at the front, slip two stitches, one at a time, knitwise onto the right needle without working them as for ssk decrease. Holding needles tip to tip, insert left needle into both stitches and transfer back to left needle without twisting.

2 Holding the right needle at the back, bring the tip upwards from left to right through the back of the two stitches. Bring the right needle in front of left as it comes through the stitches.

3 Lay the yarn between the needles as for purl. Take the right needle down and back through both loops, then slide them off the left needle together. This makes one stitch out of the two, and decreases one stitch.

Seams and blocking

After you have finished knitting, and before you sew it together, your project will need blocking. This means to pin out and set the knitted shape using steam, or by wet-pressing. Always refer to the yarn label, or pattern instructions beforehand. Textured stitches may lose their shape when steam blocked.

Wet blocking

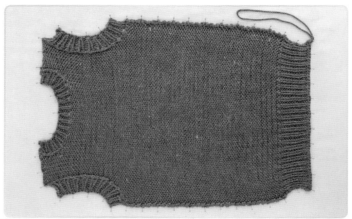

Wet the knitting: Wet blocking is the best way to even out your knitting on certain yarns (see ballband). Using lukewarm water, either wash the piece or simply wet it. Squeeze and lay it flat on a towel, then roll the towel to squeeze out more moisture. Pin the piece into shape on layers of dry towels covered with a sheet. Leave to dry.

Steam blocking

Steam the knitting: Only steam block if your yarn allows. Pin the piece to the correct shape, then place a clean damp cloth on top. Use a warm iron to create steam, barely touching the cloth. Do not rest the iron on the knitting, and avoid any garter stitch or ribbed areas. Before removing the pins, let the piece dry completely.

Darning in an end

A professional finish: Completed knitting will have at least two yarn ends – one at the cast on and one at the cast off edges. For every extra ball used, there will be two more ends. Thread each end separately onto a large-eyed needle and weave it vertically or horizontally through stitches on the wrong side of your work.

Edge-to-edge seam

Suitable for most stitch patterns: Align the pieces of knitting with the wrong sides facing upwards. Using a large-eyed needle and matching yarn, sew the seam together through the little pips formed along the edges of knitting, as shown. Do not pull the seam too tight.

Backstitch seam

Right sides of knitting together

Suitable for almost any seam on knitting: Align the pieces of knitting with the right sides together. Make one stitch forwards, and one stitch back into the starting point of the previous stitch as shown. Work the stitches as close to the edge of the knitting as possible. A backstitch seam is not suitable for super-bulky yarns.

Overcast seam

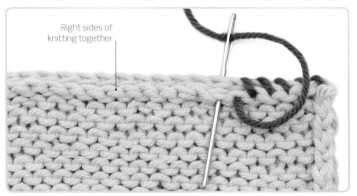

Right sides of knitting together

Oversewn seam (or whipped stitch seam): With the right sides facing each other, insert the needle from back to front through both layers of knitted fabric, working through the centres of the edge stitches and not through the pips at the edge of the fabric. Create each stitch in the same way as you sew the seam together.

Grafted seam

This seam is worked along two pieces of knitting that have not been cast off or along two cast off edges as shown here; the principle for both is the same.

1 With the right sides facing you, follow the path of a row of knitting along the seam as shown. Do not pull the stitches too tight.

2 When worked in a matching yarn as here, the seam blends in completely and makes it look like a continuous piece of knitting.

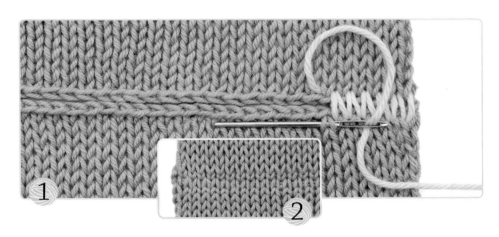

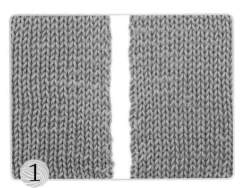

Mattress stitch

1 The best seam technique for ribbing and stocking stitch, mattress stitch is practically invisible. Start by aligning the edges of the pieces to be seamed with both right sides facing.

2 Insert the needle from front through centre of the first knit stitch on one piece of knitting and up through centre of stitch two rows above. Repeat on other piece, working up seam and pulling edges together every few stitches.

This tiny bonnet sits against the baby's head, holding its shape with soft ribbing that is just snug enough to retain warmth.

Newborn hat

This quick and easy hat is designed to match the Newborn booties on pages 44-45 and Newborn cardigan on pages 46-49. It is sized to fit a newborn baby, but can be made bigger by using a thicker yarn with the appropriate needles. For example, try a different DK yarn with 4mm (UK8/US6) needles to make a hat for a baby aged three to six months.

you will need

size
To fit a newborn baby

materials
Rowan cashsoft DK 50g in
Sky pink (540) × 1
1 pair of 3.25mm (UK10/US3)
needles
Large-eyed needle

tension
25sts and 34 rows to 10cm (4in)
over st st on 3.25mm (UK10/US3)
needles

special abbreviations
rib: Work in rib, knitting all
presented k sts and purling all
presented p sts
rib2tog: Working in rib, k2tog

how to make

Pattern
Cast on 83sts using the cable cast on
method.
Row 1 (RS): *K1, p1, rep from * to last st,
k1.
Row 2: *P1, k1, rep from * to last st, p1.
Rep last 2 rows once more.
Row 5: [Rib 13, rib2tog] × 5, rib to end.
(78sts)
Next row: P.
Next row: K.
These 2 rows form st st.
Work in st st for a further 17 rows.

Shape crown
Row 1 (RS): [K6, k2tog] × 9, k to end.
(69sts)
Row 2 and every foll alt row: P.
Row 3: K.
Row 5: [K5, k2tog] × 9, k to end. (60sts)
Row 7: [K4, k2tog] × 9, k to end. (51sts)
Row 9: [K3, k2tog] × 10, k to end. (41sts)
Row 11: [K2, k2tog] × 10, k to end. (31sts)
Row 13: [K1, k2tog] × 10, k to end. (21sts)
Row 15: [K2tog] × 10, k1. (11sts)

Break off yarn, leaving a long yarn tail and
draw this through rem sts twice. Use this
end to join the back seam with mattress
stitch (see p.41). Steam block lightly.

By tightly pulling the yarn through the
stitches twice at the top of the hat, you will
prevent gaps from forming in the future.

top tip

The seams along the base of the booties sit flat for comfort.

The fold-down cuff is knitted as one long piece, then folded and stitched to create a casing for the ribbon. The cast off adds a wavy edge.

Newborn booties

These tiny booties curve gently to follow the shape of a baby's foot, providing plenty of room for growth. Increases and decreases curve the booties as you knit. We've chosen a soft DK yarn and used smaller than usually recommended needles to achieve a firm fabric suitable for keeping tiny toes warm and protected.

you will need

size
To fit a newborn baby

materials
Rowan Cashsoft Baby DK 50g in Sky pink (540) × 1
1 pair of 3mm (UK11/USn/a) needles
1 pair of 2.75mm (UK12/US2) needles
70cm (27½in) co-ordinating ribbon, 3–7mm (⅛–⅜in) wide
Large-eyed needle

tension
25sts and 46 rows to 10cm (4in) over g st on 3mm (UK11/USn/a) needles

how to make

Booties (Make 2)
Using 3mm (UK11/USn/a) needles, cast on 37sts.
Row 1 (WS): K.
Row 2: Inc in next st, k15, inc in next st, k3, inc in next st, k15, inc in last st. (41sts)
Rows 3, 5, and 7: K.
Row 4: Inc in next st, k17, inc in next st, k3, inc in next st, k17, inc in last st. (45sts)
Row 6: Inc in next st, k19, inc in next st, k3, inc in next st, k19, inc in last st. (49sts)
K 16 rows, ending with a WS row.

Shape for toe
Row 1 (RS): K17, skpo, k11, k2tog, k17. (47sts)
Row 2: K17, skpo, k9, k2tog, k17. (45sts)
Row 3: K17, skpo, k7, k2tog, k17. (43sts)
Row 4: K17, skpo, k5, k2tog, k17. (41sts)
Row 5: K17, skpo, k3, k2tog, k17. (39sts)
Row 6: K17, skpo, k1, k2tog, k17. (37sts)
Row 7: K17, sk2p, k17. (35sts)

Shape for ankle
Change to 2.75mm (UK12/US2) needles and work as follows:

Next row (RS): K1, *p1, k1, rep from * to end.
Next row: P1, *k1, p1, rep from * to end.
Rep last 2 rows × 2.
Eyelet row: K1, *yon, k2tog, rep from * to end.
Next row: P1, *k1, p1, rep from * to end.

Work edging
Next row: (Casting off) *k2, pass first st over second so that 1st rem on RH needle as if casting off, place this 1st back on LH needle, rep from * until 1st remains.

Making up
Fasten off, leaving a long yarn tail. Join row ends with mattress stitch (see p.41) using the yarn tail from cast off edge. Fold over ribbed edging and catch to main bootie with a long running stitch. Thread ribbon through eyelets and tie in a bow. Sew a few stitches through the yarn and ribbon to prevent the ribbon coming undone.

top tip
The garter stitch edging keeps the stocking stitch from curling.
(See p.30)

🌿 you will need

size
To fit a newborn baby

materials
Rowan Cashsoft DK 50g in Sky pink (540) x 3
1 pair of 3.25mm (UK10/US3) needles
Stitch holder
Large-eyed needle
1 button

tension
27sts and 37 rows to 10cm (4in) over st st on 3.25mm (UK10/US3) needles

Newborn cardigan

This soft, luxurious cardigan is perfect for a newborn baby. You only need to know stocking stitch for the body and garter stitch for the yoke, edges, and sleeves. Boys' and girls' buttonholes are worked on different sides, so follow the relevant instructions below. Choose a button to complement your yarn colour choice.

 ## how to make

Back
Using cable cast on method, working between stitches, cast on 62sts.
Row 1 (WS): K.
Rows 2 and 3: As row 1.
Row 4 (RS): K.
Row 5: P.
Last 2 rows set st st. Cont working in st st until work measures 17cm (6¾in) from cast on edge, ending with a WS row.

Shape arms
Next 2 rows: Cast on 36sts, k to end. (134sts)
Cont in g st as set for a further 32 rows.

Shape right front
Next row: K57 and turn, leaving rem 77sts on a stitch holder.

Shape neck
Row 1 (WS): K1, skpo, k to end. (56sts)
Row 2 (RS): K to last 3sts, k2tog, k1. (55sts)
Row 3: As row 1. (54sts)
K 11 rows ending with a RS row.
Inc row (WS): K1, M1, k to end. (55sts)
K 3 rows without shaping.
Cont increasing at neck edge as set by inc row on next and foll 3 alt rows, then at

neck edge of foll 2 rows. (61sts)
Next row: Cast on and k7, k to end. (68sts)
For a girl only:
Place buttonhole: K to last 5sts, cast off 3sts, k1.
Next row: K2, cast on 3sts, k to end.
For a boy only:
K 2 rows.
For boy and girl:
Shape underarm (RS): Cast off 36sts, k to end.
Row 1 (WS): K5, p to end.
Row 2 (RS): K to end.
Last 2 rows set st st with g st border.
Rep last 2 rows until work measures 16cm (6¼in) from underarm, ending with a RS row.
K 3 rows.
Cast off.

Shape left front
With RS facing, rejoin yarn to rem sts.
Cast off next 20sts, k to end. (57sts)
Row 1 (WS): K to last 3sts, k2tog, k1. (56sts)
Row 2 (RS): K1, skpo, k to end. (55sts)
Row 3 (WS): As row 1. (54sts)
K 12 rows without shaping, ending with a WS row.

Inc row (RS): K1, M1, k to end. (55sts)
K 2 rows without shaping.
Cont increasing at neck edge as set by inc row on next and foll 3 alt rows, then at neck edge of foll 2 rows. (61sts)
Next row (WS): K.
Next row (RS): Cast on and k7, k to end. (68sts)
For a girl only:
K 2 rows.
For a boy only:
Place buttonhole: K to last 5sts, cast off 3sts, k1.
Next row: K2, cast on 3sts, k to end.
For boy and girl:
Shape underarm (WS): Cast off 36sts, k to end.
Row 1 (RS): K to end.
Row 2 (WS): P to last 5sts, k5.
Rep last 2 rows until work measures 16cm (6¼in) from underarm, ending with a RS row.
K 3 rows.
Cast off.

Making up
Join side and underarm seams using mattress stitch (see p.41). Steam gently and attach the button.

Flower headband

This flower headband will keep hair out of your little one's eyes, or just act as a pretty accessory. It's so simple to knit you can have it completed in just a few hours. The flower-centre button can be left off the finished headband if you want a completely soft headband suitable for young babies.

❧ how to make

Headband
Cast on 9sts in yarn A.
Row 1: K2, [yfwd, k2tog] x 3, k1.
Next row: P2, k5, p2.
K 2 rows.
Rep last 4 rows x 27 (29:31).
Cast off.

Outer flower petals
Cast on 10sts in yarn B.
Row 1: [Inc 1st] x 2.
Turn and work on 4sts just knitted.
Work 9 rows in st st beg with a p row.
Next row: K2tog, ssk. Lift first st on needle over second st. (1st)
*Next row: K1 into next cast on st, inc 1st.
Turn and work on 4sts on needle only.
Work 9 rows in st st beg with a p row.
Next row: K2tog, ssk. Lift first st on needle over second st.** (1st)
Rep from * to ** x 3.
K into first cast on st to complete final petal. (2sts)
Cast off 1st. Break yarn and pull it through rem st.

Inner flower petals
Cast on 10sts in yarn B.
Row 1: [Inc 1st] x 2.

Turn and work on 4sts just knitted.
Work 5 rows in st st beg with a p row.
Next row: K2tog, ssk. Lift first st on needle over second st. (1st)
*Next row: K1 into next cast on st, inc 1st.
Turn and work on 4sts on needle.
Work 5 rows in st st beg with a p row.
Next row: K2tog, ssk. Lift first st on needle over second st.** (1st)
Rep from * to ** x 3.
K into first cast on st to complete final petal. (2sts)
Cast off 1st. Break yarn and pull it through rem st.

Making up
Seam the two short ends of the headband together using mattress stitch (see p.41).

Join both the outer and inner petals into a circle. Place the inner petals onto the outer petals so that each inner petal lies between two outer petals. Secure the flower in place on the headband and stitch the button to the flower centre with cream sewing thread.

Practise your increase and decrease skills (see pp.33-39) to knit the undulating flower petals in this pretty two-tiered bloom.

🌿 you will need

size
To fit a child, aged 0–6 (9–12: 12–36) months

materials
Sublime Baby Cashmerino Silk
DK 50g in
A: Gooseberry (004) × 1
B: Cheeky (048) × 1
1 pair of 3.75mm (UK9/US5)
needles

Large-eyed needle
Sewing needle
Cream sewing thread
1 × 16mm (¾in) mother-of-pearl
button

tension
23sts and 40 rows to 10cm (4in)
over lace st on 3.75mm (UK9/
US5) needles

Cuddly baby toys

Suitable for newborns to older babies, these stylized tiny cot toys are quick to knit. The patterns include stocking stitch and garter stitch with embroidered detailing.

Essential information

SIZE 14.5 x 6.5cm (6 x 2½in) approx.

YARN

Sublime Baby Cashmere Merino Silk DK 50g

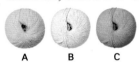

A   B   C

A: 278 Muffin x 1 B: 03 Vanilla x 1

C: 124 Splash x 1

Scrap of yarn for embroidery (we've used 051 Button)

NEEDLES

A: 1 pair of 3.25mm (UK10/US3) needles

B: 1 pair of 4mm (UK8/US6) needles

A
B

TENSION

22sts and 28 rows to 10cm (4in) over st st on 4mm (UK8/US6) needles

NOTIONS

Large-eyed needle

Polyester toy filling

Water-soluble pen

Spray bottle (optional)

Knitted lamb toy

The body and head are knitted together from the base to the top of the head.

Body and head (make 2)

Using needles A and yarn A, cast on 18sts.

K 34 rows.

Break yarn and join yarn B.

Work 10 rows in st st.

NEXT ROW: K2, k2tog, k to last 4sts, ssk, k2. (16sts)

NEXT ROW: P2tog, p to last 2sts, p2tog. (14sts)

Rep last 2 rows once more. (10sts)

Cast off.

Ears (make 2)

Using needles A and yarn B, cast on 10sts.

ROW 1: P.

ROW 2: K1, k2tog, k4, ssk, k1. (8sts)

ROW 3: P2tog, p4, p2tog. (6sts)

ROW 4: K1, k2tog, ssk, k1. (4sts)

ROW 5: [P2tog] x 2. (2sts)

ROW 6: K2tog. (1st)

Break yarn and pull through rem st.

Forelock

Using needles B and yarn A, cast on 5sts.

ROW 1: Inc 1st, k2, inc 1st, k1. (7sts)

K 2 rows.

NEXT ROW: K2tog, k3, ssk. (5sts)

Cast off.

Making up

Join the side seams and top seam of the lamb using mattress stitch (see p.41) and matching yarns. Make sure all yarn tails are secure and on the inside of your toy. Stuff fairly lightly with toy filling. Sew the lower edge using mattress stitch. Fold the ears in half lengthways with RS on the outside. Oversew the seam close to the edge. Oversew the ears in place so that the seams are at the front. Secure the forelock in place by working a circle of running stitch around the edge. Using the photograph as a guide, draw on the lamb's features using the water-soluble pen. Work French knots for the eyes using an oddment of yarn and a large-eyed needle. Embroider three straight stitches in a "Y" shape for the nose and mouth. Spray the toy lightly with water to remove the pen marks and leave to dry.

TOP TIP   *Give the toys different expressions by varying your embroidery.*

Knitted kitten toy

The body and head are knitted together from the base to the top of the head.

Body and head (make 2)

Cast on 18sts in yarn C.

K 34 rows.

Break yarn and join yarn A.

Work 12 rows in st st.

ROW 47: K8, cast off 2sts, k to end.

ROW 48: P8, turn and work on these 8sts only, leaving rem sts on needle.

ROW 49: K1, k2tog, k to end. (7sts)

ROW 50: P.

Rep last 2 rows x 2. (5sts)

ROW 55: K1, k2tog, k2. (4sts)

ROW 56: [P2tog] x 2. (2sts)

ROW 57: K2tog. (1st)

Break yarn and pull through rem st.

Rejoin yarn to rem sts on WS of work.

ROW 58: P.

ROW 59: K to last 3sts, ssk, k1. (7sts)

ROW 60: P.

Rep last 2 rows x 2. (5sts)

ROW 65: K2, ssk, k1. (4sts)

ROW 66: [P2tog] x 2. (2sts)

ROW 67: Ssk. (1st)

Break yarn and pull through rem st.

Making up

Join the side seams using mattress stitch (see p.41) and matching yarns. Turn the kitten inside out and oversew round the ears. Turn the kitten RS out again. Make sure all yarn tails are secure and on the inside of your toy. Stuff with polyester toy filling. Sew the lower edge closed. Using the photograph as a guide, draw on the kitten's features using the water-soluble pen. Embroider the features in backstitch (see p.41), using an oddment of yarn and a large-eyed needle. Spray the toy lightly with water to remove the pen marks and leave to dry.

Rattle ball

You don't need to know how to knit in the round to make this simple striped ball; it is knitted on straight needles and then joined together with mattress stitch. The contrasting colour stripes and rattle, sewn inside, make it of both visual and auditory interest to curious babies. Choose black and white yarns for even more contrast if you wish.

❧ how to make

Pattern

Cast on 6sts in yarn A.
1st row: (Inc 1st) × 6. (12sts)
K 2 rows.
Next row: [K1, M1] to last st, k1. (23sts)
Next row: K.
Next row (RS): K4, [M1, k3] × 5, M1, k4. (29sts)
Next row: K.
Leave yarn A at side and join yarn B.
K 2 rows.
Next row: K4, [M1, k3] × 7, M1, k4. (37sts)
K 3 rows.
Leave yarn B at side and use yarn A.
K 2 rows.
Next row: [K3, M1] × 11, k4. (48sts)
K 3 rows.
Leave yarn A at side and use yarn B.
K 2 rows.
Next row: [K3, M1] × 15, k3. (63sts)
K 3 rows.
Leave yarn B at side and use yarn A.
K 2 rows.
Next row: K1, [k2tog, k3] × 12, k2tog. (50sts)
K 3 rows.
Leave yarn A at side and use yarn B.
K 2 rows.
Next row: [K3, k2tog] to end. (40sts)

K 3 rows.
Break yarn B and use yarn A for remainder of toy.
K 2 rows.
Next row: [K2, k2tog] to end. (30sts)
Next row: K.
Next row: [K2tog] to end. (15sts)
Next row: K.
Next row: [K2tog] × 3, sk2p, [k2tog] × 3. (7sts)
Break yarn, thread it through rem sts and secure.

Making up

Prepare the rattle by wrapping it in a layer of toy filling about 2cm (¾in) thick, and winding a length of yarn round the "parcel" to secure the rattle in the centre. This is necessary to stop the rattle working its way to the edge of the filling when it is inside the ball.

Join the side seam of the ball using mattress stitch (see p.41), leaving a gap of a few centimetres (1in) for filling. Stuff the ball firmly and insert the wrapped rattle in the centre. Close the opening using mattress stitch. Weave in any yarn ends and cut.

Wrap the rattle in a layer of filling and secure it with scrap yarn. This will prevent it from moving around.

Be sure to line up your stripes in straight rows as you stitch up the seam using mattress stitch (see p.41).

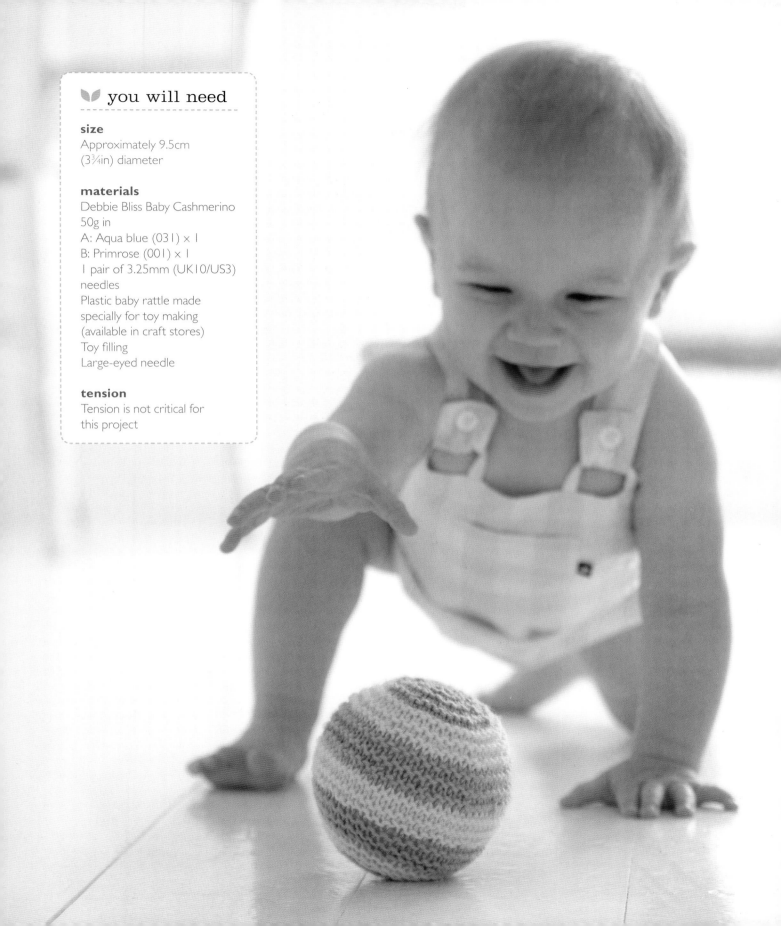

you will need

size
Approximately 9.5cm
(3¾in) diameter

materials
Debbie Bliss Baby Cashmerino
50g in
A: Aqua blue (031) × 1
B: Primrose (001) × 1
1 pair of 3.25mm (UK10/US3)
needles
Plastic baby rattle made
specially for toy making
(available in craft stores)
Toy filling
Large-eyed needle

tension
Tension is not critical for
this project

🌱 you will need

size
62 × 87cm (24½ × 34¼in)

materials
Rowan Cashsoft DK
50g in
Lime (509) × 7
1 pair of 4mm (UK8/US6)
needles
Large-eyed needle

tension
22sts and 30 rows to 10cm
(4in) over patt on 4mm
(UK8/US6) needles

Diamond blanket

This is an ideal project for improving your knitting and purling skills. You don't have to follow any complex charts to create the attractive diamond pattern, you just need to be able to create basic knit and purl stitches. A double-sided moss stitch is used to border the blanket and prevent the edges from curling.

 ## how to make

Bottom border
Cast on 137sts.
Moss st row: [K1, p1] to last st, k1.
This row forms moss st.
Rep the row × 5.

Commence pattern
Row 1 (RS): [K1, p1] × 2, k4, *p1, k7, rep from * to last 9sts, p1, k4, [p1, k1] × 2.
Rows 2 and 8: [K1, p1] × 2, p3, *k1, p1, k1, p5, rep from * to last 10sts, k1, p1, k1, p3, [p1, k1] × 2.
Rows 3 and 7: [K1, p1] × 2, k2, *p1, k3, rep from * to last 7sts, p1, k2, [p1, k1] × 2.
Rows 4 and 6: [K1, p1] × 2, p1, *k1, p5, k1, p1, rep from * to last 4sts, [p1, k1] × 2.
Row 5: [K1, p1] × 2, *p1, k7, rep from * to last 5sts, p1, [p1, k1] × 2.
Rep rows 1–8 until work measures 84cm (33in) from cast on edge, ending with row 8.

Top border
Moss stitch row: [K1, p1] to last st, k1.
This row forms moss st.
Rep this row × 5.
Cast off in patt.
Darn in ends on WS and block according to ballband instructions.

This subtle knit and purl texture adds interest. Very dark colours may disguise a great deal of carefully created detail, so try to choose a yarn colour that will show off your hard work.

The benefit of using a knit and purl stitch pattern is that the reverse side of the work will feature a negative relief image of the right side. This makes it double-sided – perfect for blankets.

A moss stitch edging is used to help the blanket to lie flat and also adds a soft frame to the finished piece. This edging is easy to create and looks very attractive.

Tiny tank top

This project, knitted in stocking stitch, can be worn on its own, or as an extra layer when it's chilly outside. Worked in a soft cashmere merino silk 4-ply yarn, it will make a great garment for a boy or a girl depending on the colours you choose..

❧ how to make

Back

Using 3.75mm (UK9/US5) needles and yarn B, cast on 62 (66:70) sts.
Rib row 1 (RS): K2, [p2, k2] to end.
Change to yarn A.
Rib row 2: P2, [k2, p2] to end.
These 2 rows form the rib.
Work a further 4 rows, inc 2sts evenly across last row. (64 (68:72) sts)
Change to 4mm (UK8/US6) needles.
Work in stripe patt of [2 rows in yarn B, 4 rows in yarn C, 2 rows in yarn B, 4 rows in yarn A] throughout.
Beg with a k row, cont in st st until back measures 15 (17:19)cm (6 (6¾:7½)in) from cast on edge, ending with a p row.

Shape armholes

Cast off 6sts at beg of next 2 rows. (52 (56:60) sts)
Next row: K2, skpo, k to last 4sts, k2tog, k2.
Next row: P to end.
Rep the last 2 rows x 3 (4:5). (44 (46:48) sts)**
Cont in st st until back measures 26 (29:32)cm (10 (11½:12½)in) from cast on edge, ending with a WS row.

Shape back neck

Next row: K12 (12:13), turn and leave rem sts on a spare needle.
Next row: P to end.
Next row: K to last 3sts, k2tog, k1.
Next row: P to end 11 (11:12) sts.
Shape shoulder.

Cast off.
With RS facing, place centre 20 (22:22) sts on a stitch holder, rejoin yarn to rem sts, k to end.
Next row: P to end.
Next row: K1, skpo, k to end.
Next row: P to end 11 (11:12) sts.
Shape shoulder.
Cast off.

Front

Work as given for Back to **.
Cont in st st until front measures 20 (23:26)cm (8 (9¼:10)in) from cast on edge, ending with a WS row.

Shape front neck

Next row: K16 (17:18), turn and leave rem sts on a spare needle.
Next row: P to end.
Next row: K to last 3sts, k2tog, k1.
Next row: P to end.
Rep the last 2 rows x 4 (5:5). (11 (11:12) sts)
Work straight until front measures same as back to shoulder, ending at armhole edge.
Shape shoulder.
Cast off.
With RS facing, place centre 12sts on a holder, rejoin yarn to rem sts, k to end.
Next row: P to end.
Next row: K1, skpo, k to end.
Rep the last 2 rows x 4 (5:5). (11 (11:12) sts)
Work straight until front measures same as back to shoulder, ending at armhole edge.

Shape shoulder.
Cast off.

Neckband

Join right shoulder seam.
With 3.75mm (UK9/US5) needles and yarn A, RS facing, pick up and k24 down LS of front neck, k12 from front neck holder, pick up and k24 up RS of front neck, 6sts down RS of back neck, k20 (22:22) sts from back neck holder, inc 2 (4:4) sts evenly across the back neck sts.
Pick up and k6 up RS of back neck. (94 (98:98) sts)
Next row: P2, [k2, p2] to end.
This row sets the rib.
Work a further 2 rows.
Change to yarn B.
Work 1 row.
Cast off in rib.

Armbands

Join left shoulder and neckband seam.
With 3.75mm (UK9/US5) needles and yarn A, RS facing, pick up and k70 (74:78) sts.
Next row: P2, [k2, p2] to end.
This row sets the rib.
Work a further 2 rows.
Change to yarn B.
Work 1 row.
Cast off in rib.

Making up

Join side and armband seams.

you will need

size

To fit a child, aged 1 (2:3)
years

materials

Sublime Baby Cashmere
Merino Silk 4-ply 50g in
A: Vanilla (003) × 1 (1:2)
B: Sleepy (123) × 1 (1:2)
C: Paddle (100) × 1 (1:1)
1 pair of 3.75mm (UK9/US5)
needles
1 pair of 4mm (UK8/US6)
needles
2 stitch holders and spare
needles
Large-eyed needle

tension

22sts and 28 rows to 10cm
(4in) over st st on 4mm
(UK8/US6) needles

you will need

size
40cm (16in) square

materials
Sublime Egyptian Cotton DK 50g
321 Frothy × 5
1 pair of 4mm (UK8/US6) needles
1 pair of 3.25mm (UK10/US3)
needles

tension
22sts and 28 rows to 10cm (4in)
over st st on 4mm (UK8/US6)
needles

notions
1 × 1.5cm (4¾in) mother-of-pearl
button for centre of flower
3 × 2cm (¾in) mother-of-pearl
buttons for back
Large-eyed needle
40cm (16in) square cushion pa

Daisy cushion

A delicate project knitted in 100 per cent cotton yarn, this cushion is formed of knitted daisies and embellished with a flower and scallop shell lace edging.

how to make

Front

With needles A, cast on 89sts.
Work 4 rows st st starting with a k row.
Rows 1 and 3: K to end.
Rows 2 and 4: P to end.
Row 5: K2, [*k1, count 2sts ahead on the LH needle and 4 rows down, then put the point of the RH needle into the centre of this stitch from front to back and draw a loop through to the front and put it on the RH needle, k2, draw a 2nd loop through the same st, k2, make a 3rd loop into same st*, k5] × 8, rep from * to * once more, k2.
Row 6: P2 [*p loop and next st tog, p1, p loop and next st tog, p1, p loop and next st tog*, p5] × 8, rep from * to * once more, p2.
Rows 7 and 9: K to end.
Rows 8 and 10: P to end.
Row 11: K2, [k5, count 2sts ahead on the LH needle and 4 rows down, then put the point of the RH needle into the centre of this stitch from front to back and draw a loop through to the front and put it on the RH needle, k2, draw a 2nd loop through the same st, k2, make a 3rd loop into same stitch] × 8, k7.
Row 12: P2 [p5, p loop and next st tog, p1, p loop and next st tog, p1, p loop and next st tog*] × 8, p7.
Rep rows 1–12 × 8 then rows 1–6 once more.
Work 4 rows st st starting with a k row.
Cast off.

Back (make 2)

With needles A, cast on 89sts.
Work 54 rows st st, starting with a k row.
Change to needles B.
Row 1 and 3: [K1, p1] to last st, k1.
Row 2: [P1, k1] to last st, p1.
Row 4: [P1, k1] × 10, p1, yon, p2tog. [k1, p1] × 10, k1, yon, k2tog, [p1, k1] × 10, p1, yon, p2tog, [k1, p1] × 10.
Rows 5 and 7: As row 1.
Row 6: As row 2.
Cast off in stitch.
Work two pieces, replacing row 4 on the second piece with a repeat of row 2.

Scallop shell lace (make 2)

With needles A, cast on 107sts using finger loop method (see p.25).
Row 1: K1, yon, *k5, 1 at a time lift 2nd, 3rd, 4th, and 5th sts just worked over the 1st st and off needle, yon* rep from * to * to last st, k1.
Row 2: P1, *[p1, yon, k1 tbl] into next st, p1*, rep from * to * to end.
Row 3: K2, k1 tbl, *k3, k1 tbl*, rep from * to * to last 2sts, k2.
Work 3 rows g st.
Cast off.

Flower

With needles A, cast on 57sts.
Row 1: P to end.
Row 2: K2, *k1, slip this st back to LH needle, lift next 8sts on LH needle over this st and off needle, yon twice, knit first st again, k2*. Rep from * to * to end. (27sts)
row 3: P1, *p2tog, drop 1 yon loop, [kfb] × 2 in rem yon of previous row, p1*. Rep from * to * to last st, p1. (32sts)
Row 4: K1, [k3tog] × 10, k1. (12sts)
Row 5: (P2tog) to end. (6sts)
Slip 2nd, 3rd, 4th, 5th, and 6th st over first st. Fasten off.

Making up

Steam and block the front and back pieces. Lay out the cover front, RS up. Pin the lace strips, RS facing, to the edges of the front pieces, with the cast off edge of the lace lined up with the outer edge of the front. Lay the back piece with buttonholes on top, RS down and with the cast on edge over the cast off edge of the front piece. Lay the second back piece on top, RS down, with the cast on edge over the cast on edge of the front piece, overlapping the two back pieces in the centre. Pin, then backstitch the pieces together around all four edges. Turn the cover RS out and sew the flower to the cushion cover with the button in centre. Sew three buttons along the cast off edge on the back, aligning each one with the buttonholes. Insert a cushion pad and button up to close.

Floral ear warmer

This classic ribbed band is tapered at the back and embellished with a stylized flower worked as one piece in garter stitch. Knit this pattern in a cotton yarn for a lightweight headband that can be worn in warm weather.

Essential information

SIZE To fit an adult female

YARN

King Cole Baby Alpaca DK/Classic Elite Inca Alpaca 50g

A   **B**

A: 513 Lilac x 1/1179 Santo grape x 1
B: 501 Fawn x 1/1116 Natural x 1

NEEDLES

A: 1 pair of 3.25mm (UK10/US3) needles
B: 1 pair of 3mm (UK11/USn/a) needles

———————————————————— A
———————————————————— B

NOTIONS

1 x 2.5cm (1½in) button
Large-eyed needle

TENSION

35sts and 30 rows to 10cm (4in) over rib patt on 3.25mm (UK10/US3) needles

SPECIAL ABBREVIATIONS

M1K or **M1P** Make a stitch by picking up bar between sts and knitting or purling into back of it (see p.33)

Headband

With needles A and yarn A, cast on 19sts.
ROW 1 (RS): K1, [p1, k1] to end.
ROW 2: P1, [k1, p1] to end.
These 2 rows form the rib.
Rib 2 rows more.

Shape sides

ROW 1: K1, M1k, rib to last st, M1k, k1.
ROW 2: P2, rib to last 2sts, p2.
ROW 3: K2, rib to last 2sts, k2.
ROW 4: As row 2.
ROW 5: K1, M1p, rib to last st, M1p, k1.
ROWS 6–8: Rib 3 rows straight.
Rep last 8 rows x 2, then work rows 1–5. (35sts)
Cont straight until work measures 40cm (16in) from beg, ending after WS row.

Shape sides

ROW 1: Skpo, rib to last 2sts, k2tog.
ROW 2: P2, rib to last 2sts, p2.
ROW 3: K2, rib to last 2sts, k2.
ROW 4: As row 2.
ROW 5: As row 1.
ROWS 6–8: Rib 3 rows straight.
Rep these 8 rows x 3. (19sts)
Cast off in rib.

Flower

Beg at centre. Using needles B and yarn B, cast on 5sts. K 1 row.
INC ROW: [Kfb] to end.
NEXT ROW: K.
Rep last 2 rows once more. (20sts)
NEXT ROW: [Kfb, k1] to end. (30sts)
K 1 row.

Divide for petals.
***NEXT ROW:** K6, turn.
K 4 rows on these 6sts.
NEXT 2 ROWS: K2, k2tog, k2; turn and k5.
NEXT 2 ROWS: K1, k2tog, k2; turn and k4.
NEXT ROW: [K2tog] x 2, then pass second st over first st and fasten off.**
Return to sts on LH needle.*
Rep from * to * x 3, then work from * to **.

Making up

Join first to last petal and neaten edges of flower. Join headband into a ring and sew cast on and cast off edges together. Sew flower in place, then sew button to centre of flower.

Tapered headband Shape the back of this easy-to-knit headband using the M1 increase, and the k2tog and skpo decrease techniques. Cast off in rib effect and sew a flat edge-to-edge seam to form the band.

Rosette snood

This ladies' winter knit is worked in a medium-weight yarn spun from the fleece of Peruvian alpacas and sheep, making it both luxurious and thick, but any aran yarn will work just as well. The simple pattern is embellished with knitted rosettes.

Essential information

SIZE 36cm x 1.4m (14¼ x 55in)

YARN

Artesano Alpaca Aran/Berroco Ultra Alpaca 100g

A   **B**

A: 2200 Laxford x 2/6258 Cyclamen x 2
B: 5083 Lomond x 1/6233 Rose spice x 1

NEEDLES

A: 1 pair of 10mm (UK000/US15) needles
B: 1 pair of 7.5mm (UK1/USn/a) needles

A
B

TENSION

10sts and 12 rows to 10cm (4in) over patt on 10mm (UK000/US15) needles

NOTIONS

Large-eyed needle
3 x 2cm (¾in) mother-of-pearl buttons

Using needles A and yarn A, cast on 40sts.
ROW 1: K.
ROW 2: K.
ROW 3: *K1, p1, rep from * to end of row.
ROW 4: *K1, p1, rep from * to end of row.
Rep rows 1–4 until work measures 1.4m (55in).
Cast off loosely.
Sew cast on edge to cast off edge.
Block (see p.40).

Rosettes

Using needles B and yarn B, cast on 15sts.
ROW 1: K.
ROW 2: Kfb into every st.
ROW 3: K.
ROW 4: K.
ROW 5: Kfb into every st.
ROW 6: K.
ROW 7: K.
Cast off loosely.
Roll strip into flower shape, stitching as you go.
Attach button to centre of flower and sew flowers to snood.

Knitted rosettes An easy mini project, these pink roses "grow" when you knit into the front and back of each stitch to increase the fabric. They are attached to the snood with mother-of-pearl buttons.

TOP TIP *Add mother-of-pearl buttons for a delicate, shimmering finish.*

Striped snake scarf

This child's scarf, worked in moss stitch, is a simple project for a beginner. The cotton yarn is a joy to work with and the pattern is quick to complete. Finish your creation with a pom-pom tail.

Essential information

SIZE 15cm x 1.5m (6 x 59in)

YARN

Debbie Bliss DK Cotton 50g

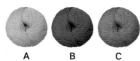

A   **B**   **C**

A: 20 Green x 2   **B:** 62 Blue x 2   **C:** 47 Red x 1

NEEDLES

1 pair of 4mm (UK8/US6) needles

TENSION

20sts by 30 rows to 10cm (4in) over st st on 4mm (UK8/US6) needles

NOTIONS

Large-eyed needle

SPECIAL ABBREVIATIONS

MB Make a bobble

Striped pattern

Using yarn A, k 10 rows.
Using yarn B, k 6 rows.
Rep throughout, until row 188, then cont in yarn B only.

Body

In yarn A cast on 2sts.
ROW 1: *K1, p1.
ROW 2: P1, k1.
Rep from *.
Cont in moss st as above and inc (kfb or pfb) into the first and last st every 4th row. Cont stripe as stated until you are left with 36sts and have 68 rows.
Cont knitting straight in moss st and foll the stripe layout until 177 rows have been knitted.
ROWS 178–188: Cont in moss st, dec 1st (k2tog or p2tog) at beg and end of row 178, row 182, and row 188. (30sts)
ROWS 189–200: Cont in moss st for 12 rows inc into first and last stitch every 2 rows. (42sts)
ROWS 201–225: Cont in moss st straight.
ROW 226: Cont in moss st. Dec 1st at beg and end of each row. At sts 17 and 23 MB, (using yarn A, k into front, back, front, back of st, turn, p4, turn, k4, turn, p4, k2, k2tog, then pass third and fourth sts over first st).
ROWS 227–242: Cont in moss st. Dec 1st at beginning and end of each row.
ROW 243: Change to yarn C. (8sts)
Cont knitting in moss st for 15 rows.

Forked tongue

ROW 259: *K1, p1, k1, p1, turn.
ROW 260: P1, k1, p1, k1, turn.
ROW 261: K1, p1, k1, p1, turn.
ROW 262: P1, k1, p1, k1, turn.
ROW 263: K1, p1, k1, p1, turn.
Break yarn and cast off these 4sts.
Reattach yarn to rem 4sts and rep from *.
Cast off.

Pom-pom

Cut two circles of card (6cm (2½in) diameter); cut a smaller circle out of the centre. Place two circles on top of each other. Wrap yarn C around the circle until there is no hole left in the centre (it is easier to wrap with small bundles of yarn). Using scissors, cut all the way around the edge of the circle, take a separate piece of yarn and wrap it around the middle of the pom-pom, making sure to go between the two pieces of circular card; secure tightly. Remove the card circles and puff up the pom-pom. Sew the pom-pom onto the bottom of the snake as a tail.

Essential information

SIZE To fit an adult female, shoe size UK 4-6

YARN

Debbie Bliss Baby Cashmerino 50g

A   B   C

A: 027 Denim x 3
B: 006 Candy pink x 2
C: 002 Apple x 2

NEEDLES

1 pair of 3.75mm (UK9/US5) needles

TENSION

25sts and 34 rows to 10cm (4in) over st st on
3.75mm (UK9/US5) needles

NOTIONS

1 stitch holder and spare needle
Stitch markers
Large-eyed needle

Striped knee-high socks

Adjust the length by knitting fewer or more rows after you shape the heel. Measure your legs first and work out the number of rows needed before you cast on.

Socks (make 2)

With yarn A, cast on 66sts.
ROW 1: K1, *k2, p2. Rep from * to last st, k1.
Rep until your work measures 3.5cm (1³⁄₈in).
ROWS 1–4: Join in yarn B and work 4 rows st st.
ROWS 5–8: Join in yarn C and work 4 rows st st.
ROWS 9–14: With yarn A, work 6 rows st st.
Cont to work 14 rows stripe sequence, until your work measures 45cm (17³⁄₄in) from cast on edge, finishing with a RS row.
NEXT ROW: P4, [p2tog, p5] x 8, p2tog, p4. (57sts)
Cont in stripe as set until work measures 61cm (23¹⁄₂in) from cast on edge.
Break off yarn.

Divide for heel

With RS facing, slip first 14sts onto RH needle, slip next 29sts onto a stitch holder for instep, slip rem 14sts onto a spare needle.
With WS facing, join yarn A to instep edge of 14sts on RH needle from previous row, p to end, turn spare needle around and p14 on spare needle. (28sts)
With yarn A, cont as follows:
NEXT ROW: K1, *k1, s1p, rep from * to last st, k1.
NEXT AND EVERY FOLL ALT ROW: P.
Rep these 2 rows x 9.

Turn heel

ROW 1: K15, skpo, k1, turn.
ROW 2: P4, p2tog, p1, turn.
ROW 3: K5, skpo, k1, turn.
ROW 4: P6, p2tog, p1, turn.
ROW 5: K7, skpo, k1, turn.
ROW 6: P8, p2tog, p1, turn.
ROW 7: K9, skpo, k1, turn.
ROW 8: P10, p2tog, p1, turn.
ROW 9: K11, skpo, k1, turn.

ROW 10: P12, p2tog, p1, turn.
ROW 11: K13, skpo, k1, turn.
ROW 12: P14, p2tog, p1. (16sts)
Break off yarn.
With RS facing, join yarn A to instep edge, pick up and k11 evenly along side edge of heel, k across 16sts of heel, then pick up and k11 along other side of heel. (38sts)
P 1 row.
ROW 1: K1, skpo, k to last 3sts, k2tog, k1. (36sts)
ROW 2 AND EVERY FOLL ALT ROW: P.
ROW 3: K.
ROW 4: As row 2.
Rep these 4 rows x 4. (28sts)
Cont in st st until work measures 18cm (7in) from back of heel, finishing with RS facing. (Length can be adjusted here, allowing 3.5cm (1³⁄₈in) for the toe shaping.)

**Shape toe

ROW 1: K1, skpo, k2, *p2, k2, rep from * to last 3sts, k2tog, k1. (26sts)
ROW 2: P2, *p2, k2, rep from * to last 4sts, p4.
ROW 3: K1, skpo, k1, *p2, k2, rep from * to last 6sts, p2, k1, k2tog, k1. (24sts)
ROW 4: P3, *k2, p2, rep from * to last 5sts, k2, p3.
Keeping continuity of rib as set, cont to dec 1st at each end of next and foll 4 alt rows. (14sts)
NEXT ROW: P2, *k2, p2, rep from * to end. **
Break off yarn and leave these 14sts on a spare needle.

Instep (RS facing)

Keeping continuity of stripes, k across 29sts on stitch holder, dec 1st at centre (28sts). (Place markers at each end of this row.)
Starting with a p row, work in st st and stripes

Each solid blue sole is seamed with a striped instep (see main picture, left) to form an enclosed foot.

as set until work measures the same as sole to toe shaping from markers.

Shape toe

With yarn A, work as for lower foot from ** to **.
Placing RS of upper foot facing, cast off as follows: P2tog 1st from upper and lower foot, across all sts, casting off as each st is worked.

Making up

Join the upper and lower foot seams and back seam (see pp.40–41).

Essential information

SIZE To fit an adult male S (97cm/38in):
M (104cm/41in): L (112cm/44in): XL (119cm/47in)

YARN

Sublime Cashmere Merino Silk DK 50g

223 Latte x 7 (8:8:9)

NEEDLES

A: 1 pair of 3.75mm (UK9/US5) needles
B: 1 pair of 4mm (UK8/US6) needles

A
B

TENSION

22sts and 28 rows to 10cm (4in) over st st using
4mm (UK8/US6) needles

NOTIONS

2 stitch holders
Large-eyed needle

Men's sleeveless pullover

A timeless v-necked tank top knitted in stocking stitch with a 2x2 ribbed border. The yarn used here is a cashmere, merino wool and silk blended quality.

Back

With needles A, cast on 106 (118:130:142) sts.
RIB ROW 1: K2, [p2, k2] to end.
RIB ROW 2: P2, [k2, p2] to end.
Rep the last 2 rows x 4 (5:6:7).
Change to needles B.
Beg with a k row cont in st st until back measures 44 (45:46:47)cm (17$\frac{1}{2}$ (17$\frac{3}{4}$:18:18$\frac{1}{2}$)in) from cast on edge, ending with a p row **.

Shape armholes

Cast off 10 (11:12:13) sts at beg of next 2 rows. (86 (96:106:116) sts)
NEXT ROW: K1, skpo, k to last 3sts, k2tog, k1.
NEXT ROW: P to end.
Rep the last 2 rows x 3 (4:5:6). (78 (86:94:102) sts)
Work straight until back measures 65 (67:69:71)cm (26 (26$\frac{1}{4}$:27:28)in) from cast on edge, ending with a WS row.

Shape shoulders

Cast off 8 (9:11:12) sts at beg of the next 2 rows and 9 (10:11:12) sts at beg of foll 2 rows.
Leave rem 44 (48:50:54) sts on a stitch holder.

Front

Work as given for Back to **. (106 (118:130:142) sts)

Shape armholes and neck

NEXT ROW: Cast off 10 (11:12:13) sts, k until there are 42 (47:52:57) sts on the needle, turn, and work on these sts for first side of neck shaping.
NEXT ROW: P to end.

NEXT ROW: K1, skpo, k to last 3sts, k2 tog, k1.
NEXT ROW: P to end.
Rep the last 2 rows x 3 (4:5:6). (34 (37:40:43) sts)
Keeping armhole edge straight cont to dec 1st at neck edge on every RS row until 17 (19:22:24) sts rem.
Cont straight until front measures the same as back to shoulder shaping, ending at armhole edge.

Shape shoulders

Cast off 8 (9:11:12) sts at beg of the next row.
Work 1 row.
Cast off rem 9 (10:11:12) sts.
With RS facing, slip next 2sts on a holder, rejoin yarn to rem sts, k to end.
NEXT ROW: Cast off 10 (11:12:13) sts, p to end. (42 (47:52:57) sts)
NEXT ROW: K1, skpo, k to last 3sts, k2 tog, k1.
NEXT ROW: P to end.
Rep the last 2 rows x 3 (4:5:6). (34 (37:40:43) sts)
Keeping armhole edge straight cont to dec 1st at neck edge on every RS row until 17 (19:22:24) sts rem.
Cont straight until front measures the same as back to shoulder shaping, ending at armhole edge.

Shape shoulders

Cast off 8 (9:11:12) sts at beg of the next row.
Work 1 row.
Cast off rem 9 (10:11:12) sts.

Neckband

Join right shoulder seam.
With RS facing and using needles A, pick up and k50 (52:56:58) sts evenly down left side of front neck, k2 from safety pin, pick up and k50

(52:54:56) sts evenly up RS of front neck, k44 (48:50:54) sts from back neck holder. (146 (154:162:170) sts)
1st and 4th sizes only
ROW 1: K2, [p2, k2] to end.
2nd and 3rd sizes only
ROW 1: P2, [k2, p2] to end.
All sizes
This row sets the rib patt.
ROW 2: Rib 49 (51:55:57), k2tog, skpo, rib to end.
ROW 3: Rib to end.
ROW 4: Rib 48 (50:54:56), k2tog, skpo, rib to end.
ROW 5: Rib to end.
ROW 6: Rib 47 (49:53:55), k2tog, skpo, rib to end.
ROW 7: Rib to end.
Cast off in rib, dec on this row as before.

Armbands

Join left shoulder seam and neckband.
With RS facing and using needles A, pick up and k118 (122:130:134) sts evenly around armhole edge.
ROW 1: K2, [p2, k2] to end.
ROW 2: P2, [k2, p2] to end.
These 2 rows set the rib patt.
Work a further 5 rows.
Cast off in rib.

Making up

Join side and armband seams (see pp.40–41 for more information).

Essential information

SIZE 32 x 38cm (12½ x 15in)

YARN

Rowan Colourscape Chunky 100g

447 Jungle x 2

NEEDLES

1 pair of 7mm (UK2/US n/a) needles

TENSION

(Before felting) 14sts and 28 rows to 10cm (4in)
over st st on 7mm (UK2/US n/a) needles

NOTIONS

20 (approx.) rhinestone studs

Felted tote bag

A roomy bag ideal for storing your yarn and needles, this project is worked in stocking stitch, then felted, and embellished with rhinestone studs. Refer to the felting instructions here, or follow the manufacturer's information on your ballband.

Cast on 50sts.

Starting with a k row, and working in st st, inc at both ends of 5th row. Work 9 rows without shaping. (52sts)

ROW 15 (RS): Inc in first st, k15, cast off 20sts, k15, inc in last st. (54sts)

ROW 16: P17, cast on 20sts, p to end.

Cont working in st st, inc at each end on 8th and every foll 10th row, until there are 66sts.

Work 19 rows without shaping.

Dec at each end of next and every foll 10th row until 54sts remain.

Work 8 rows without shaping.

NEXT ROW (WS): P17, cast off 20sts, p to end.

NEXT ROW: S1 k1 psso, k15, cast on 20sts, k to last 2sts, k2tog. (52sts)

Cont working in st st, dec on foll 10th row.

Work 5 more rows without shaping. Cast off.

Fold work with WS facing you so that cast on and cast off edges meet. Join row ends using a long backstitch (see p.41), and felt the bag in the washing machine at 60°C (140°F), (see right). Stuff the felted bag with clean plastic bags to hold it in its pear shape and leave to dry. Add rhinestone studs on the bag, using the photograph as a guide.

How to felt your knitting

First, hand test the yarn to see if it will felt. Roll a 90cm (36in) long strand into a ball. Add a drop of detergent and rub it together for 2 minutes under hot running water. If the yarn clumps and is difficult to pull apart, it is a good candidate for test-felting. Next, knit and block a 10cm (4in) swatch. Submerge it in soapy hand-hot water. Squeeze and knead it gently, adding more hot water as required for up to 30 minutes. Rinse and squeeze out the water (do not wring) and roll in a towel. Pat the felt, right-side up, into a rectangle and leave to dry overnight. If the yarn has felted successfully, test a bigger swatch in a washing machine.

Preparing for test-felting

By test-felting a swatch of your yarn you can determine how much it will shrink, although felting is not an exact science. Washing machine agitation, water temperature, detergent type, and yarn fibre content, spin, and colour all vary.

Knit a swatch of stocking stitch at least 20cm (8in) square (accurate shrinkage measurements cannot be obtained with smaller swatches). Block the swatch carefully. If unblocked, the side edges will felt too thickly due to the curling.

Machine felting

Put a swatch in the washing machine along with a large towel (this increases the agitation). Add half the amount of detergent used for a full load. Wash at 40°C (104°F) for yarn that contains mohair, and 60°C (140°F) for 100 per cent wool yarns, using the full washing and spin cycle. Tug the washed swatch gently in both directions, lay it right-side up and pat into a rectangle. Leave to dry completely. If necessary, do more tests with new swatches, altering the temperature or the length of the wash cycle. Keep detailed records of tension, needle size, sizes of pre-felted and felted swatches, wash settings, and type and amount of detergent used.

Tips for felting

If you are trying felting for the first time, make several test swatches in different weights of yarn and felt them together in the same load. This way you can get a feel for the different thicknesses of knitted felt. When using highly contrasting colours, put a colour catcher sheet in the machine to absorb loose dye and prevent colours from running. Wool will fade slightly when felted, due to the high temperatures and the detergent, but this adds an attractive quality to the felt. Clean your washing machine after a felting load by wiping it out with a damp cloth to remove any stray fibres.

Mobile phone sock

Protect your phone with a knitted cover in a choice of three different colourways.
Knitted in single rib, the sock includes a slim pocket to store a memory card or
earphones. An ideal project for a beginner.

Essential information

SIZE 7 x 15cm (2³/₄ x 6in)

YARN

Patons Diploma Gold/Berroco Vintage DK 50g

A   B   C   D

A: 6220 Blue x 1/51190 Cerulean x 1 or
B: 6245 Plum x 1/5180 Dried plum x 1 or
C: 6125 Apple green x 1/5162 Envy x 1
D: 6142 White x 1/5100 Snow day x 1

NEEDLES

1 pair of 3.25mm (UK10/US3) needles

TENSION

30sts and 30 rows to 10cm (4in) over 1x1 rib on
3.25mm (UK10/US3) needles

NOTIONS

Large-eyed needle

Front and back (make 2)

In the colour of your choice (A, B, or C) cast
on 21sts.
ROW 1: K1, [p1, k1] to end.
ROW 2: P1, [k1, p1] to end.
Rep these 2 rows to form 1x1 rib until your
work measures 12cm (5in).
Work 1x1 rib, as above, 1 row in yarn D and
1 row in yarn A, B, or C x 4.
To halve the number of yarn ends when
knitting single rows, cut off a piece of yarn
about eight times the width of the work and
knit the first row, starting from the middle of
the strand. Do this again for the next colour,
and then pick up the tail of the first yarn to knit
the 3rd row. Continue in this way with a new
strand of yarn introduced for every 2 rows of
a colour instead of every row.
Cast off in stitch using yarn D.

Pocket

In yarn A, B, or C cast on 21sts.
ROW 1: K1, [p1, k1] to end.
ROW 2: P1, [k1, p1] to end.
Rep these 2 rows until your work measures
5cm (2in).
Work 1 row of 1x1 rib in yarn D and 1 row
in yarn A, B, or C x 4.
Cast off in stitch using yarn D.

Making up

Lay the back piece RS up. Lay the pocket on top,
RS down, lining up the cast on edges. Lay front
piece on top with RS down, lining up the cast
on edges. Backstitch (see p.41) down sides and
across bottom. Turn through.

Protective cover This stitch is stretchy so the sock will
fit most phones. Refer to p.30 for information on how to
knit single ribbing.

Essential information

SIZE 12 x 12cm (5 x 5in)

YARN

Debbie Bliss Rialto DK 50g

A   B   C

A: 12 Scarlet x 1
B: 01 White x 1
C: 42 Pink x 1

NEEDLES

1 pair of 3.75mm (UK9/US5) needles

TENSION

26sts and 30 rows to 10cm (4in) over st st on
3.75mm (UK9/US5) needles

NOTIONS

Large-eyed needle
Polyester toy stuffing
90cm (35in) x 6mm (¼in)-wide red ribbon
Sewing needle and red sewing thread
3 x 1cm (½in) mother-of-pearl buttons

Heart sachets

A trio of hanging hearts that sport knitted and embroidered motifs.

Red heart (make 2)

With yarn A, cast on 3sts.
K 1 row and p 1 row.
Now shape sides as follows:
ROW 1: K1, yon, k1, yon, k1.
ROW 2: P1, yrn, p into back of yon on previous row, p1, p into back of yon on previous row, yrn, p1.
ROW 3: K1, yon, k into back of yrn on previous row, k3, k into back of yrn on previous row, yon, k1.
ROW 4: P1, yrn, p into back of yon on previous row, p5, p into back of yon on previous row, yrn, p1.
ROW 5: K1, yon, k into back of yrn on previous row, k to last 2sts, k into back of yrn on previous row, yon, k1.
ROW 6: P1, yrn, p into back of yon on previous row, p to last 2sts, p into back of yon on previous row, yrn, p1.
Rep the last 2 rows until there are 35sts, ending with a p row. *

Cont in st st, beg with a k row, work 20 rows straight.
**Shape top.
NEXT ROW: K17, turn and cont on these sts only for first side.
Now dec 1st at both ends of next 5 rows. (7sts)
Cast off.
With RS of work facing, rejoin yarn to rem sts. K2tog and then k to end.
Dec 1st at both ends of next 5 rows. (7sts)
Cast off.
Following Chart 1, below left, and using yarn B, cross-stitch a heart in the centre of both sides.

Pink heart (make 2)

Using yarn C, work as for Red Heart until there are 31sts, ending with a p row. Cont to shape sides as set until there are 35sts, at the same time now work in patt from Chart 2, below centre. Odd numbers are RS rows and read from right to left, even numbered rows are WS rows and read from left to right. Use a separate ball

of yarn for each area of colour, twisting yarns tog when joining colours to avoid a hole from forming. When chart is complete, work a further 6 rows st st using yarn C only.
Complete as given for Red Heart from ** to end.

White heart (make 2)

Using yarn B, work as for Red Heart to *.
Following Chart 3, below right, work 14 rows in Fair Isle patt.
When chart is complete, work a further 6 rows st st using yarn B only.
Complete as given for Red Heart from ** to end.

Making up

Place front and back together with RS facing and stitch around outer edges, leaving a small opening in one straight edge. Turn RS out. Stuff the hearts and stitch closed. Cut a length of ribbon 30cm (12in) long and sew it to the top of the front with matching thread. Sew on one button to cover the raw ends of the ribbon.

Chart 1

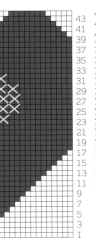

Chart 2

Chart 3

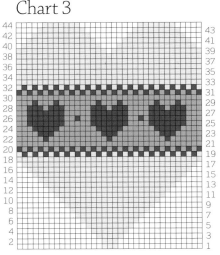

KEY

■	Scarlet
□	White
▨	Pink

Gifts to Give

Sometimes a box of chocolates or another pair of socks simply won't do. For a truly thoughtful present, making your own gifts is the way forward: you can create something beautiful, unique, and affordable, regardless of whether you have an hour or two to spend or an afternoon.

Every idea in this chapter is explained in step-by-step photographs so you can be sure that your gift will have a professional finish, and will be well worth the time you invest. If the project needs a template, we include one so you know it will work. There are lots of ideas for how you can add your own twist, so you can make the gift that is exactly right for the person you have in mind.

We have included a range of gift ideas, each requiring different levels of skill and time. We hope you have a wonderful time making your gifts... and that you find time to make something for yourself!

Beaded
necklace

There is such a wealth of beautiful beads to choose from, including ceramic, glass, enamel, and hand-painted. Design a unique piece of jewellery using this simple and versatile knot technique.

To make a beaded necklace you will need

Tools: scissors

Materials: reel of 1mm-wide, black, waxed cotton thread
• 5 large beads • 6 small beads

1
Choose beads with holes that are large enough to thread onto the waxed cotton thread. Plan out the order of your beads, and lay them in order on the work surface.

2
Cut two lengths of waxed cotton thread roughly twice the length you want the necklace to be. You could tie the thread around your neck first to judge the length.

3

Lay the two strands of waxed cotton thread together. Fold the strands in half and tie a knot at this mid-point. This doesn't need to be very accurate, as the threads will be trimmed later.

4

Take the middle bead from your design and thread it onto one of the strands from either side. Slide it down until it reaches the first knot.

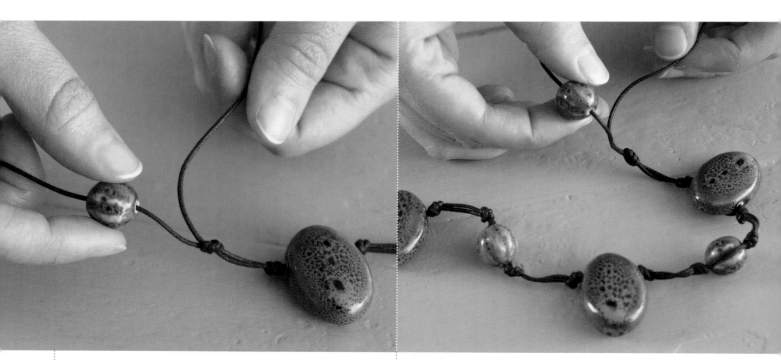

7

Take the next bead in your design and thread onto one strand. Again, pass the other strand behind the bead, then take both strands and tie a knot to secure the bead in position.

8

Take the next bead from your design and thread and knot as before, leaving a 2cm (¾in) gap each time. Repeat until you have finished one side of the necklace, then thread and knot the other side.

5

Pass the other strand behind the bead and tie both strands together in a knot on the other side of the bead to secure the bead in position.

6

Leave a gap of approximately 2cm (¾in), and tie another knot with both threads together.

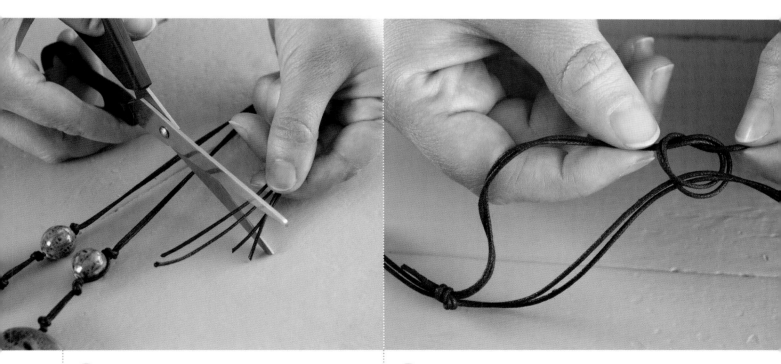

9

When you have threaded on your final bead, secure it with a knot. Place the ends of the necklace alongside each other and cut the strands of thread to the same length.

10

Knot one end of the necklace around the other end. Then knot the remaining loose end around the other end. You can now adjust the length of the necklace by sliding the knots.

Colour variation

Once you have mastered the technique on pp.79–81, you can experiment with different bead colours and sizes. Keeping colours within the same palette works well, and you can introduce different sizes without your necklace becoming fussy.

} *Tip: Opaque and tinted beads from the same colour palette work well together.*

Painted beads

Hand-painted beads are expensive but making your own jewellery is a cost-effective way to showcase just a few hand-picked beautiful beads. If using beads with a varied pattern, keep the size the same.

} *Tip: Use coloured waxed cotton thread to match or contrast with your beads and help colours stand out.*

Button-bead necklace

Flat button beads work well knotted together. This design knots the beads closely for a more formal look.

1. Tie a knot. Thread each strand through a bead as if sewing a button, passing through the bead from opposite sides.

2. Pull both strands tight, and tie a knot to secure. Repeat with the next bead, tying them close.

Tip: The knotting technique also works for flat or unusual-shaped beads.

Make all of these pretty brooches in exactly the same way as the bird brooch on pp.84–87. Templates for the other shapes are given on p.233.

Embellished
felt brooches

It's hard to believe that scraps of fabric and felt, buttons, ribbon, and beads are all that are needed to make these whimsical brooches. Turn a brooch into a key ring or bag charm by attaching a split ring to the top with a ribbon.

. . . .

To make a bird brooch you will need

Tools: pencil • dressmaker's scissors • iron • damp cloth *Materials:* double-sided bonding web • patterned fabric
• 3 squares of felt in contrasting colours • 1 skein of stranded cotton embroidery thread • extra-heavy-weight sew-in interfacing
• 35 seed beads • 1 black bead • 15cm (6in) narrow ribbon • 1 small button • cotton sewing thread • brooch pin

1

Trace the bird template on p.233 onto the paper side of the bonding web. Cut around the bird and iron it, textured side down, onto the reverse of the patterned fabric. Cut out the bird.

2

Peel off the backing paper. Place the bird face side up on the first felt square. Cover with a damp cloth and iron for a few seconds until the bird is bonded to the felt.

85

3

Using three strands of the cotton embroidery thread, stitch around the bird shape using an overstitch.

4

Cut the felt around the bird, leaving a felt border of approximately 3–5mm (⅛–¼in).

7

Using the wing template on p.233, cut a wing out of the first colour of felt. Stitch the wing onto the bird with the embroidery thread using a small running stitch.

8

Stitch on the black bead for the eye. Cut the ribbon in half and sew on two small ribbon loops for the tail. Using the embroidery thread, sew on the button to cover the ends of the ribbon.

5

Place the bird onto the contrasting shade of felt with the interfacing underneath. Using sewing cotton, sew on the seed beads, sewing through all three layers.

6

Carefully cut around the bird shape, again leaving a border of approximately 3–5mm (⅛–¼in). Make sure that you cut through both the contrasting felt and the interfacing.

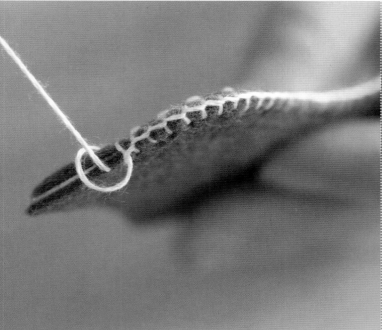

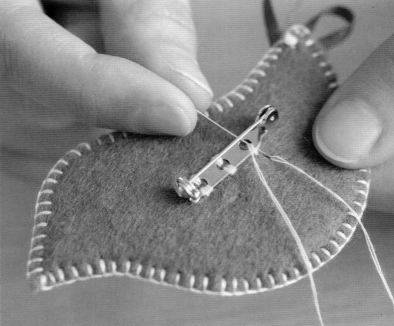

9

Using the brooch as a guide, cut an identical shape out of the last colour of felt to use as the backing. Using the embroidery thread, attach the backing with blanket stitch.

10

Using doubled sewing thread for strength, stitch the brooch pin on the reverse side of the brooch. Ensure you only stitch through the backing felt.

Silver clay jewellery

Make beautiful silver jewellery items easily with silver clay. Available from craft shops, silver clay is 99% silver. When fired with a kitchen torch, the clay burns off, leaving behind a fully silver item.

For a silver leaf pendant you will need

Tools: Teflon mat or greaseproof paper • small rolling pin or piece of pipe • playing cards • craft knife • small straw • wet and dry sandpaper (600 grit) or sanding pad (220 grit) • kitchen blowtorch • firing brick or ceramic tile • timer • tweezers • soft wire brush • 2 pairs of pliers *Materials:* oil (cooking spray is ideal) • 7g (¼oz) silver clay • real leaves or leaf skeletons • silver jump ring

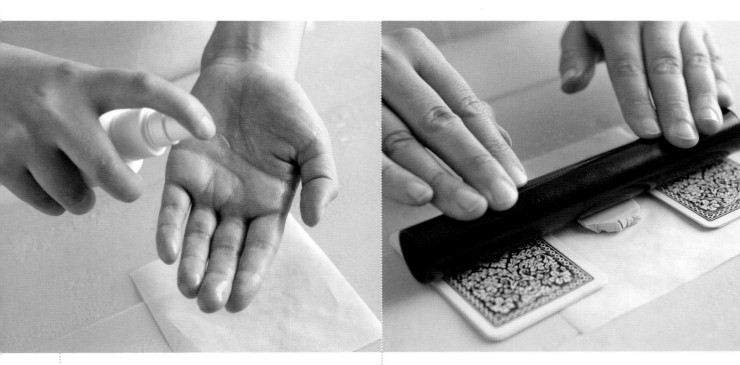

1

Cut out a square of greaseproof paper or use a Teflon mat. Prepare your work surface by rubbing a small amount of oil over the paper or mat, your hands, and the rolling pin.

2

Place two stacks of four playing cards each about 5cm (2in) away from each other to act as rolling guides. Soften the clay in your hands and roll it flat.

3

Lift up the rolled clay carefully and place a leaf underneath and on top of it as shown, ensuring you line up the stems and tips of the leaves. Roll over the clay again to imprint both sides.

4

Carefully remove the leaves, and lay the clay on a cutting mat or chopping board. Using the craft knife and the template from p.233, carefully cut a leaf shape from the clay.

7

Place the leaf on the firing brick or tile in a dimly lit, well-ventilated room. Hold the torch 5cm (2in) from the clay and move the flame evenly over it. The leaf will start to glow a peachy orange colour.

8

Once the leaf begins to glow, set the timer for two minutes. If the leaf turns bright red or shiny silver, it is too hot – move the flame away. Once fired, pick up the leaf with tweezers and quench it in water.

5

Using the straw, make a hole in the leaf about 5mm (¼in) from the top. This needs to be big enough for your jump ring, bearing in mind that the clay may shrink by up to 10% when fired.

6

Leave the clay to dry overnight, or to speed up the process use a hairdryer or put the clay in an oven at 150°C (300°F/Gas 2) for 10 minutes. Once dry, sand it very carefully to smooth the edges.

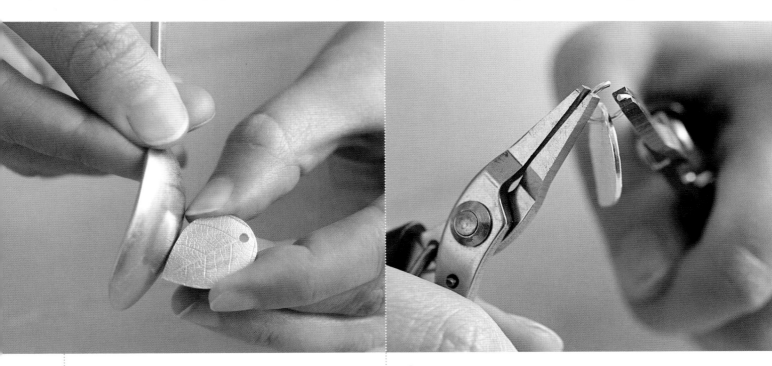

9

The leaf will now be a matt-white colour, even though it is pure silver. Gently brush it with a soft wire brush to reveal the silver colour. To achieve a high shine, rub with the back of a metal spoon.

10

Using two pairs of pliers, gently twist the ends of the jump ring away from each other. Thread it through the hole in your leaf, and then twist the jump ring closed.

Simple button cufflinks

A huge array of textured paper is available from most craft shops; a snakeskin pattern has been used to create these cufflinks made using the same technique as the silver leaf pendant on pp.89–91 and the cufflink templates on p.233. To make, roll out and texture approximately 20g (¾oz) of silver clay. Carefully cut out two discs measuring 2cm (¾in) in diameter, and another two of 1.5cm (⅝in) in diameter. Pierce each of these discs twice using a cocktail stick (the holes should be positioned to resemble the holes in a button). Dry out and fire the clay as for the silver leaf pendant. Burnish for a high shine, then using a needle and silver thread stitch the silver clay buttons onto a cufflink chain: 1.5–2cm (⅝–¾in) of chain with roughly 5mm (¼in) links is ideal. Tie off the thread, and use a tiny dot of superglue to ensure the end doesn't come loose.

Wallpaper earrings

Patterned wallpaper can be ideal for texturing metal clays, and the variety of designs available is huge. Make these earrings using the same technique as for the silver leaf pendant on pp.89–91, using 15g (½oz) of silver clay. Using the wallpaper, roll and texture your clay as before. Cut ovals from the clay approximately 3cm (1¼in) in length using the template on p.233, and pierce at the top with your straw. Dry out, and torch fire. Burnish for a high shine, and attach ear wires.

Leaf bracelet

This simple leaf bracelet requires approximately 25g (1oz) of silver clay. Roll and texture your clay as for the silver leaf pendant on pp.89–91. Then cut out seven pointed ellipses 2.5cm (1in) in length. Pierce each end of the ellipses with your straw. While the pieces of clay are still soft lay them over a rolling pin to give them a curved shape. Leave them to dry, and then torch fire as before. Link the elements together using jump rings, and finally attach a simple clasp.

Lace heart key ring

Fabrics, in particular lace, can be used to produce beautifully delicate patterns in metal clays. To make this heart key ring in the same way as the silver leaf pendant on pp.89–91, roll out approximately 10g (⅜oz) of silver clay. Texture it using lace, and then cut out a heart shape 3.5cm (1⅜in) in length using the template on p.233. Pierce the top of the heart with your straw. Dry out and fire the clay, then burnish to a high shine. Use a jump ring to attach the heart to a key ring and chain.

Crochet
necklace

This beautiful necklace is a great crochet project for beginners as it uses just one stitch – the chain stitch. For a quick lesson on how to make the stitch, turn to crochet basic stitches on pp.250–255 before starting work.

To make a crochet necklace you will need

Tools: 2mm (B/1) crochet hook • 1mm (10 steel) crochet hook (if needed) • darning needle

Materials: cotton yarn • approximately 15 beads in different sizes and shapes (ensure the holes are large enough for the beads to pass easily over at least a 1mm (10 steel) crochet hook)

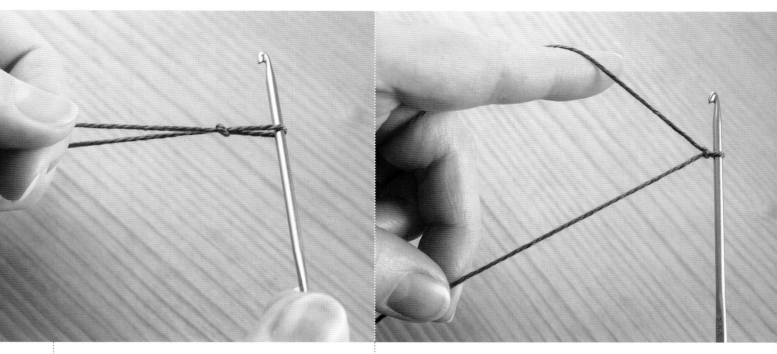

1
Make a slip knot by first crossing the yarn coming from the ball over itself to form a circle. Insert the 2mm (B/1) hook through the circle and pull the ball end through the circle. Tighten.

2
Pull both ends of the yarn firmly to tighten the slip knot around the shank of the hook, ensuring that the knot is tight but not so tight that you can't move it along the hook.

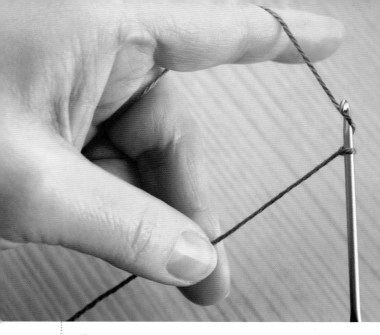

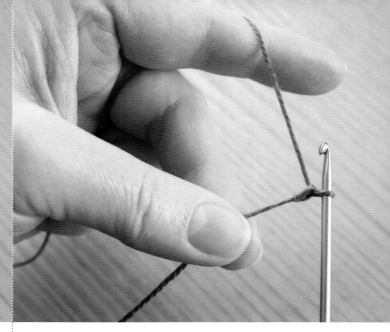

3

To begin the foundation chain, wrap the yarn from the ball around the hook. This action is called "yarn over hook" (abbreviated yo). Use the lip of the hook to grip the yarn as shown.

4

With the lip of the hook, pull the yarn through the loop on the shank of the hook, and tighten it. This makes the first chain of your foundation chain (see p.250).

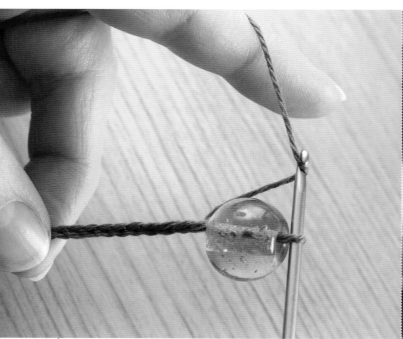

7

If you switched hooks in Step 6, switch back to the 2mm (B/1) hook. Yo. Grasp the yarn going to the ball with the lip of the hook (see Step 3).

8

Pull the yarn through the loop to secure the bead in place. Continue chaining and adding beads in this way, until the necklace is the length you require.

5

Yo and draw a loop through the loop on the shank of the hook for the next chain. Continue making chains in this way, making a total of 10 to start.

6

Thread a bead onto the hook and insert it back through the loop (see inset). Pass the bead onto the loop, pulling the loop through it. If necessary, use a 1mm (10 steel) hook for this step.

9

Make a slip stitch (ss) (see p.251) in the first chain to join the necklace ends. Cut the yarn, leaving a tail. Pass the tail through the last loop and tighten to finish off.

10

Using a darning needle, work both yarn tails through the chains on either side of the last ss to finish.

Découpage bangle

To make these stylish bangle bracelets, paper cut-outs are glued down and varnished to create a smooth, shiny surface. Almost any paper can be used for this technique, making these bangles the ultimate bespoke gift.

To make a découpage bangle you will need

Tools: ruler • scissors • paintbrushes

Materials: bangle (wooden or plastic) • solid, coloured or patterned backing paper • craft glue • decorative paper motifs • white tack • craft paint • glitter (optional) • clear varnish

1

Measure the distance around the side of the bangle. Cut paper strips, 1.5cm (⅝in) wide and long enough to wrap around the bangle. Cut enough strips to cover the bangle.

2

Spread glue all over the back of one paper strip, but don't soak it. Position the strip around the edge of the bangle so that the ends overlap on the inside. Remove any air.

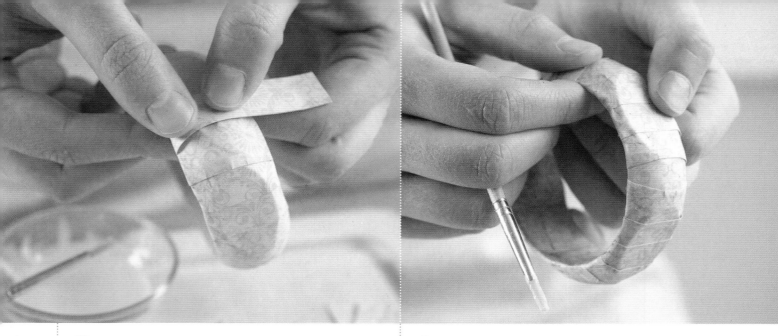

3

Continue adding strips, overlapping slightly with each previous strip, until you have covered the bangle completely with the backing paper.

4

When you have finished this stage, check that each strip of paper is firmly glued down. Smooth out any bumps or wrinkles, adding more glue as necessary.

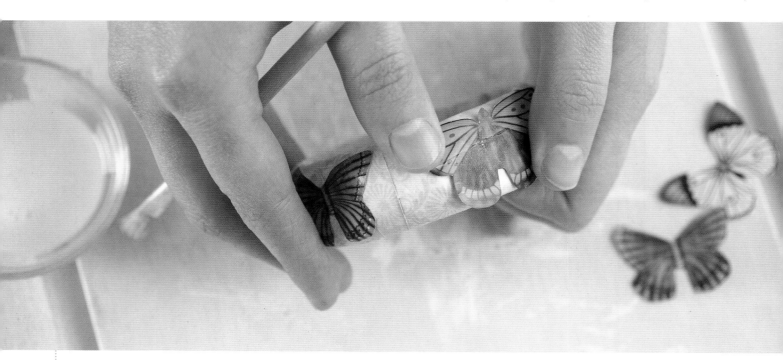

7

Glue the motifs onto the bangle. Take care when sticking down the motifs as they are likely to tear easily when wet with glue, and will be difficult to reposition.

5

Cut another strip of the backing paper for the inside of the bangle. This will need to cover the entire inside surface for a neat finish. Glue in place and leave to dry.

6

Carefully cut out the motifs. Position them around the bangle using white tack, moving them around until you have decided on a design that works for you.

8

Paint a thin border around the top edge of the bangle; leave to dry. Turn the bangle around and paint the other edge. Add glitter, if desired, and leave to dry.

9

Varnish the bangle and leave to dry for two to three days, turning occasionally. When hardened, repeat with a second coat. Leave to dry as before.

Crochet
flower brooches

These pretty crochet flowers would brighten up any jacket or bag. They are more difficult to make than the crochet necklace (pp.94–97), but once you get the hang of it they are quick to create. Make them in different colours, adding a statement button to the centre, for endless variations. You will need to know four different stitches to make these brooches: chain stitch (ch), slip stitch (ss), double crochet (dc), and half treble crochet (htr). For a guide to these stitches, turn to crochet basic stitches on pp.250–255.

To make a crochet flower brooch you will need

Tools: 4mm crochet hook • sewing needle
Materials: cotton yarn • button • cotton sewing thread • brooch pin

1

Make a slip knot and tighten it (see Steps 1–2 on p.95).

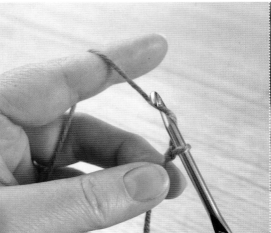

2

To make the first chain (ch) (see p.250) first bring the yarn over the hook (yo).

3

Pull the yarn through the loop to make the first ch.

4

Work 5 more ch.

5

Ss (see p.251) into the first chain you made.

6

Tighten the ss to form a circle. Work 1 ch.

10

Work 6 ch.

11

Skip 2 dc and ss into next stitch to create first petal.

14

Work 7 half trebles (htr) (see p.254) into first petal.

15

Work 1 dc into first petal to finish. Then ss into next ch to join.

16

Repeat Steps 13–15 for the other petals. Pull yarn through last loop to finish off.

7

Work 1 dc (see p.252) into the centre of the circle.

8

Continue working 14 more dc into the centre of the circle.

9

Ss into the first dc to join the circle.

12

Repeat Steps 10–11 to create four more petals. Then ss into the first ch to finish round.

13

Work 1 dc into the centre of the first petal.

17

Combine two flowers and add a button to the centre.

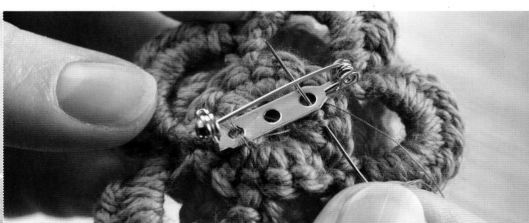

18

Using sewing cotton, sew a brooch pin to the back of the brooch to complete it.

Jewellery case

This slim case makes the perfect gift box for jewellery and other small items likely to slip out of a looser box. Wrap your gift in tissue paper and close the box with a ribbon tied in a bow to ensure that it stays safe until opened.

To make a jewellery case you will need

Tools: pencil • scalpel • cutting mat • ruler • blunt knife (or pair of scissors) • eraser
Materials: card • tracing paper • tissue paper • glue stick

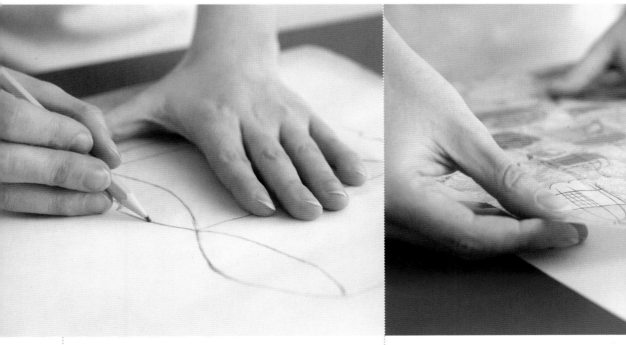

1

Use a photocopier to re-size the template on p.109 if necessary. Transfer it onto a sheet of card using tracing paper and a pencil.

2

Flip the card over. Glue a sheet of tissue paper or decorative paper to the card, ensuring that it is stuck down completely. You could also use patterned card.

3

Using a scalpel and a cutting mat, cut around the outside lines of the box. Take care not to cut into the folding lines.

4

Using a ruler and one side of a pair of scissors, or a blunt knife, score along all the internal folding lines. You can rub out the pencil lines at this point.

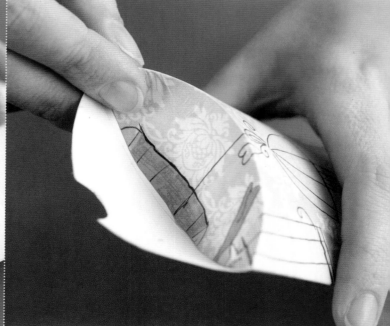

5

Fold the side flap up and spread glue on the patterned side. Fold the case in half and attach the flap to the inside of the opposite edge. Hold it in place until it sticks.

6

Choose one end to be the bottom of the case. Fold in the first flap along the curved line, and then the other. Fill the box and fold in the flaps at the other end to close.

Jewellery case template

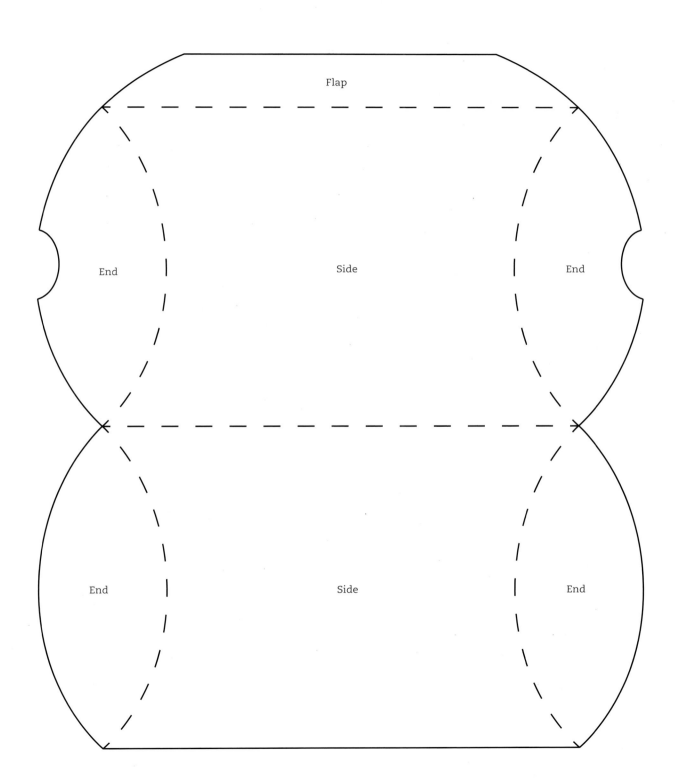

Flap

End

Side

End

End

Side

End

Each of these scented soaps has been made using the method on pp.111–113 and varying the ingredients. See pp.114–117 for variations of the soap recipe.

All natural
luxury soap

Handmade soaps make indulgent gifts, and with the melt-and-pour method require no specialist skill to make. Create naturally scented and coloured soaps using spices, dried fruit or flowers, essential oils, and natural mineral dyes.

To make lemon soap you will need

Tools: gloves • heatproof bowl • pan • spatula • spoon • square mould • knife

Materials: 1kg (2¼lb) white melt-and-pour soap base • ¼–¾ tsp yellow natural mineral colour • dried lemon peel granules • lemon essential oil • surgical spirit in a spray bottle • 9 dried lemon slices • clingfilm

Makes
9 bars

1
Wearing gloves, chop the melt-and-pour soap into pieces and heat in a heatproof bowl over a pan of boiling water, stirring occasionally, until all lumps have melted.

2
Add the desired amount of colouring to the melted soap base and stir until the powder has mixed in and the colour is evenly distributed.

3

Add the lemon peel granules a little at a time, stirring gently. Continue stirring until the granules are spread evenly throughout the soap mixture.

4

Just before you pour the soap mixture into the mould, slowly add the essential oil and stir gently until it is evenly distributed throughout.

7

Spray the almost-set layer again with surgical spirit. This will act as a glue and help it to bond to the next layer of soap.

8

Slowly pour the remaining mixture into the mould and add the dried lemon slices. You will need to act fast, as the top layer will begin to set as soon as it is poured in.

5

Pour approximately three-quarters of the mixture into the mould. Leave the remainder in the bowl over the hot water to keep it melted and warm.

6

Spray the mixture with surgical spirit to remove any bubbles. Leave this first layer for 20–25 minutes until it is almost set. It should be hard but warm.

9

Create a 3 x 3 pattern so that each slice of soap will contain a lemon slice. Spritz the surface with surgical spirit to remove any bubbles and leave until hard.

10

Remove the soap from the mould and cut it with a knife into nine even squares. Wrap each square in clingfilm to prevent it attracting moisture.

Soap recipe variations

Make a variety of soaps by choosing different scent and colour combinations. All these soaps are made in the same way as the lemon soap (see pp.111–113), using 1kg (2¼lb) of white melt-and-pour soap base and make nine square bars of soap.

A. *Bergamot soap*
¼–¾ tsp orange natural mineral colour
2½ tsp bergamot essential oil
9 whole dried orange slices

B. *Rose soap*
2½ tsp rose absolute diluted in 5% grapeseed oil
100g (3½oz) rose buds

C. *Cinnamon soap*
¼–¾ tsp caramel natural mineral colour
2½ tsp cinnamon leaf essential oil
9 cinnamon sticks

D. *Camomile soap*
¼–¾ tsp dark green natural mineral colour
2½ tsp camomile essential oil
35g (1¼oz) dried camomile flowers

E. *Lavender soap*
¼–¾ tsp purple natural mineral colour
2½ tsp English lavender essential oil
10g (¼oz) dried lavender

F. *Vanilla soap*
¼–¾ tsp cream natural mineral colour
2½ tsp vanilla essential oil
30g (1oz) vanilla pods (use the seeds in the mixture)

G. *Juniper soap*
¼–¾ tsp pink natural mineral colour
2½ tsp juniper essential oil
100g (3½oz) juniper berries

H. *Sandalwood soap*
¼–¾ tsp light brown natural mineral colour
2½ tsp sandalwood fragrance
50g (1¾oz) blue poppy seeds

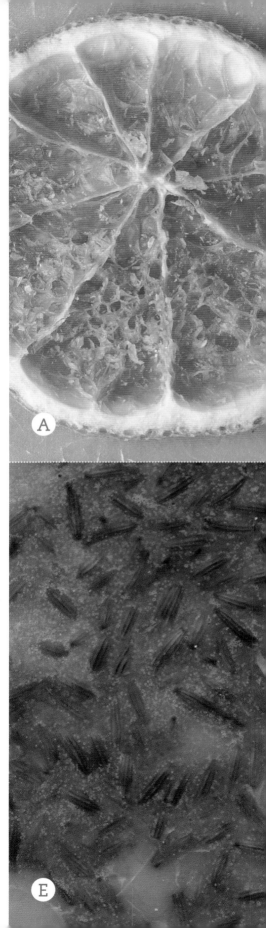

A

E

Juniper cake-slice soap

You will need
1kg (2¼lb) white melt-and-pour soap base
¼ tsp pink natural mineral colour
2½ tsp juniper essential oil
100g (3½oz) juniper berries

This soap cake is made like the lemon soap on pp.111–113, but in two stages. First, melt half the soap, adding the pink colour and half the essential oil. Pour it into a round container and let it set, spritzing it with surgical spirit to get rid of any bubbles. Melt the second half of the soap, adding the remaining scent. Spritz the base again, and pour on the second layer of soap. Add the juniper berries to the top, spritzing it one final time to get rid of any remaining bubbles. Once set, remove from the mould and cut into slices.

Moulded vanilla stars

You will need
1kg (2¼lb) white melt-and-pour soap base
¼–¾ tsp cream natural mineral colour
2½ tsp vanilla essential oil
30g (1oz) vanilla pods

These vanilla-scented stars are made in the same way as the lemon soap on pp.111–113, but the mixture is poured into individual moulds to set. Soap moulds are sold in craft shops, or you could use silicone cake moulds. Vanilla seeds are used instead of lemon peel granules as an exfoliant and for added scent. Vanilla pods can also be used to decorate the tops of the stars by placing them into the mould before the mixture is poured on top.

Cookie-cutter lavender hearts

You will need

1kg (2¼lb) white melt-and-pour soap base
¼–¾ tsp purple natural mineral colour
2½ tsp lavender essential oil
10g (¼oz) dried lavender

These heart-shaped soaps are made using the same method and quantity of ingredients as the Lemon soap on pp.111–113, swapping in the ingredients above. However, instead of cutting the soap into squares, they are cut with heart-shaped cookie cutters. The lavender buds will float to the top, creating an exfoliating layer.

See-through orange soap

You will need

1kg (2¼lb) clear melt-and-pour soap base
2½ tsp bergamot essential oil
9 dried orange slices

Although made in the same way as the lemon soap on pp.111–113, using a clear soap base and adding a dried orange slice inside the soap gives these soaps a fresh look. Make them by first melting half of the clear soap base, and adding half of the essential oil. Pour the mixture into a square mould, and add the orange slices evenly to the top. Allow this layer to set before melting the remaining half of the soap base and adding the remaining essential oil. Spritz the set layer with surgical spirit and add the melted soap mixture to the top. Spritz again to get rid of any bubbles and allow to set. Cut the soap into nine square bars.

Container
candles

A homemade candle can be made into an extra special gift by putting it in a pretty teacup or a handy travel-size tin. Add colour and fragrance to complement the container or the recipient.

To make a teacup candle you will need

Tools: double boiler (or large saucepan and heatproof bowl) • craft thermometer • heat-resistant mat or rack • metal spoon • 2 wooden skewers • 2 elastic bands *Materials:* teacup • soy wax flakes (the weight of wax in grams = the volume of water the container holds in ml) • wax dye • wick • wick sustainer

1

Boil water in the lower pan of a double boiler and add wax flakes to the top pan. Alternatively, use a heatproof bowl over a saucepan. Heat the wax, stirring occasionally.

2

When the wax has melted and reached a temperature of 70°C (158°F), take the pan off the heat and add the dye – 1g (1/16oz) for each 100g (3½oz) of wax. Stir until dissolved.

119

3

While the wax is heating, prepare the wick. Attach the wick sustainer (a metal tab) to a length of wick and place in the teacup. Secure the ends of the two skewers with elastic bands and insert the wick between them. Rest the skewers on the rim of the cup and pull the wick gently to ensure it is taut and centred in the cup.

4

Slowly pour the melted wax into the cup and tap it with a spoon to release air bubbles. Allow the candle to cool, add more wax if it has shrunk, then trim the wick when the candle has set.

Scented candles

There are two types of fragrance oil: candle fragrance oil (a synthetic blend) and essential/aromatherapy oil (extracted from plants and flowers, and 100% natural). Both types are stirred into the hot wax just before pouring. Try these different aromatherapy scents to enhance your mood:

Pine or clove
To increase energy

Lavender or neroli
To calm, soothe, and relax

Jasmine or bergamot
To uplift the mood and spirit

Cinnamon or eucalyptus
To promote concentration

Sandalwood or lemon
To relieve stress

Travel candles

Handy travel candles can be made in small tins or glass jars with lids.
Create them in the same way as the teacup candle (see pp.119–120).
If you are using different colours or scents, you will need to divide the
hot wax into batches before stirring in the dye or fragrance oil for each
tin. After the candle has set, decorate or label the container as desired.
These candles have each been decorated with beads threaded on a wire
and a label made out of thick foil and embossed from the other side.

Layered candles

To make these layered candles, follow the instructions for making the teacup candle (see pp.119–120). Divide the melted wax into batches – one for each colour you want – and stir in the dyes. With the wick in place, pour the first layer of coloured wax into the glass, tap to release air bubbles, and allow to set. When it is solid to the touch, reheat the next batch of wax and pour in, and repeat for each layer. Leave for 24 hours until fully set.

} *Tip: Produce darker shades of the same colour by increasing the quantity of dye used in each batch.*

Candles in ramekins

Ramekins – small dishes that are usually used for individual pudding portions – are ideal for making a set of candles to give as a gift. The ramekins can be washed and reused as long as the candles have been made with soy wax flakes. (Alternatively, pop them in a freezer for a few hours and the wax should drop out.) Use the method for making the teacup candle on pp.119–120.

Three-wick candle

This impressive three-wick candle can
be created in the same way as the teacup
candle (see pp.119–120), but you will need
another set of skewers to hold the third
wick (you should be able to get two wicks
into the first set). Multi-wick candles give
off more fragrance as well as more light.

*} Tip: Ceramic bowls
or long, narrow plant
containers can also be used
for multi-wick candles.*

Oilcloth
wash bag

Fill this wash bag with shredded tissue and cosmetics for the perfect pampering gift. The bag is made from oilcloth to make it water resistant, but you could use a sturdy cotton fabric or even quilted cotton for a different look.

To make an oilcloth wash bag you will need

Tools: rotary cutter and mat (or dressmaker's scissors) • sewing pins • sewing machine or needle
Materials: oilcloth • cotton lining fabric • 30cm (12in) zip • cotton sewing thread to match the lining fabric

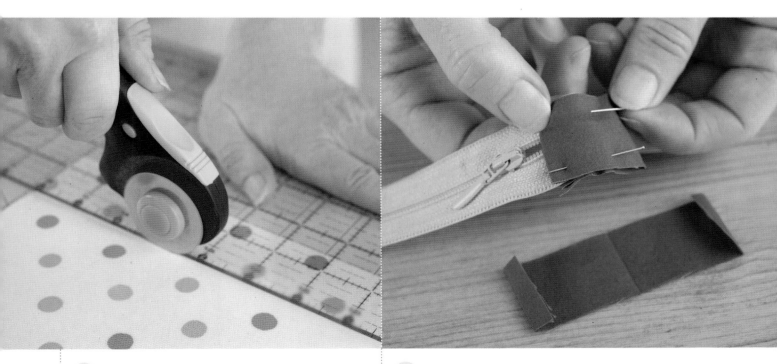

1

Cut two pieces of your chosen outer fabric and two pieces of lining, each 20 x 30cm (8 x 12in). Cut two more pieces of lining fabric, each 9 x 2.5cm (3½ x 1in).

2

Fold over 5mm (¼in) of each end of the small lining strips. Fold one piece over the end of the zip, pin in place, and stitch across all layers. Repeat for the other end.

3

Layer one piece of oilcloth, facing up, with the zip, facing down, and the lining, facing down. Pin. Then pin the other edge of the zip to the other oilcloth and lining pieces in the same way.

4

Stitch through all three layers along each side of the zip, using a long stitch and the correct zip foot for your machine. Make sure that you hold the layers not being stitched out of the way of the needle.

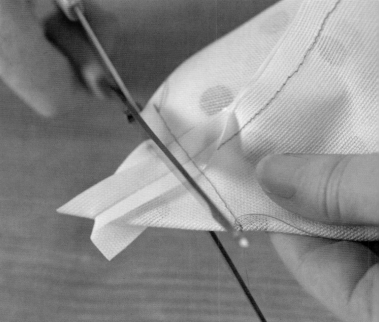

7

Ensure the zip is three-quarters open. Stitch around the edge of the lining and oilcloth, leaving a gap in the lining. When you come to the seams, flatten them to reduce bulk.

8

Shape all four corners by re-folding each corner so that the seam is now in the middle of the new corner. Fold open the seam and stitch across, 3cm (1¼in) up from the corner. Trim off the corner.

5

Use your finger to smooth along the line of the zip, pushing the fabric out. If needed, you can iron the seams on a very low setting, from the lining side protecting it with a tea towel.

6

Next, bring the right sides of the oilcloth and lining pieces together. Pin the two lining pieces together, leaving a 10cm (4in) gap at the bottom edge. You don't need to pin the oilcloth.

9

Reach through the gap in the lining to turn out the bag, pushing out the corners. If needed, iron on a very low setting from the inside, using a tea towel to protect the bag.

10

Finally, fold under the edges of the gap in the lining, and iron them so that they meet neatly. Then pin and stitch the lining closed either by hand or machine.

Follow instructions on pp.129–131 to make the juniper bath bomb. Make a rose bath bomb the same way, but using rose essential oil and adding rose petals.

Fizzy bath bombs

Bath bombs are solid balls that fizz and bubble as they dissolve, adding scent and colour to the bath water. They make wonderful gifts and are surprisingly easy to make with ingredients that are readily available at most supermarkets.

To make a juniper bath bomb you will need

Tools: sieve • 1 medium mixing bowl • 2 small mixing bowls • spoon • bath bomb mould

Materials: 155g (5½oz) bicarbonate of soda • 75g (2½oz) citric acid • ¼ tsp purple natural mineral colour • ½ tsp juniper essential oil • water in a spray bottle

Makes 1 bath bomb

1
Measure out the bicarbonate of soda and sieve it into the larger mixing bowl.

2
Add the citric acid to the bicarbonate of soda and mix well with your fingers until fully combined.

3

Split the mixture between the two smaller bowls. Add the colour to the first bowl and mix well with a spoon or your fingers, ensuring no lumps remain.

4

Add approximately half the fragrance to the first bowl and half to the second bowl. Mix each bowl well, again making sure that no lumps remain.

7

Add white mixture to the mould half, leaving a mound at the top. Repeat the process for the other mould half, this time starting with the white mixture.

8

Bring the two mould halves together, making sure that the two halves of the bath bomb are lined up exactly. Press the halves together.

5

Spray both bowls lightly with water and mix it in evenly with your fingers. Continue to spritz and mix until the mixture feels damp but not too moist.

6

Fill one of the mould halves halfway with the purple mixture. Gently press the mixture down into the mould with your fingers to remove any pockets of air.

9

Leave the bath bomb to set for approximately five minutes. Try not to move it at all during this time, as it can be very fragile before it is set.

10

Once set, first remove one of the mould halves. Then place your palm over the bath bomb and gently turn it over. Remove the other mould half.

Sweet dreams
eye mask

Sweet dreams are guaranteed with this eye mask, made using blackout fabric to ensure no light passes through. You could also put a little dried lavender inside before you sew up the mask, to add a lovely scent when the mask is used.

To make an eye mask you will need

Tools: dressmaker's scissors • sewing pins • sewing machine • sewing needle • safety pin

Materials: patterned cotton fabric • cotton lining fabric • blackout fabric • cotton sewing thread to match the binding and the main fabric • 50cm (20in) of 15mm (½in) bias binding in a matching colour • 40cm (16in) of 12mm (½in) elastic

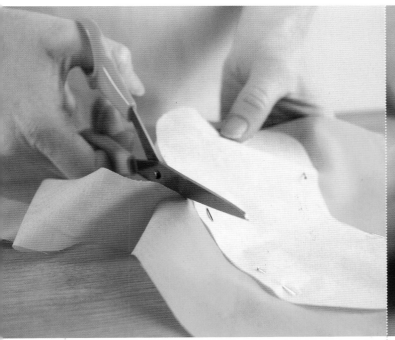

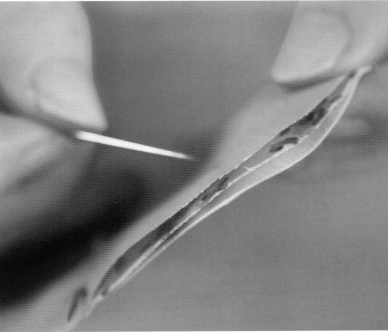

1

Photocopy or trace the eye mask template (see p.228). Cut one eye mask shape from the main fabric, one from the lining, and one from the blackout fabric.

2

Place the main fabric, right side up, on top of the blackout fabric. Place the lining fabric, right side down, on top of the main fabric. Pin all three layers together.

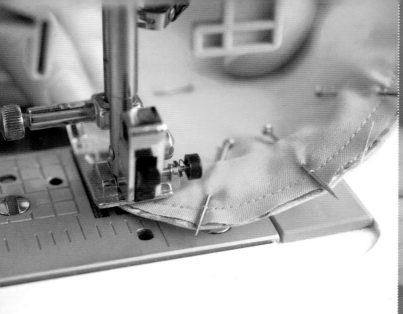

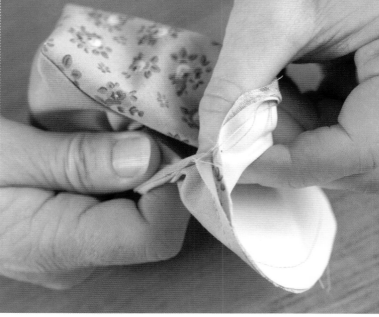

3

Stitch around the edge, beginning and ending so that you leave a 5cm (2in) gap along the straight top edge. Reverse stitch at the beginning and end to secure the stitching.

4

Trim the seam allowance all around the mask to remove the excess fabric and neaten the edge. Then turn the mask right side out. Iron it flat.

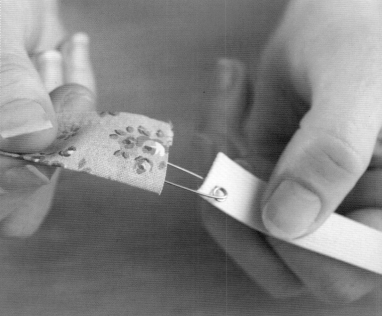

7

Cut out a 6.5 x 50cm (2½ x 20in) piece of fabric for the casing. Fold the piece in half lengthways, and fold the edges under again. Iron flat. Pin and stitch the long edge closed.

8

Attach a safety pin to one end of the elastic and a large straight pin to the other to stop the end slipping into the casing. Use the safety pin to help push the elastic through.

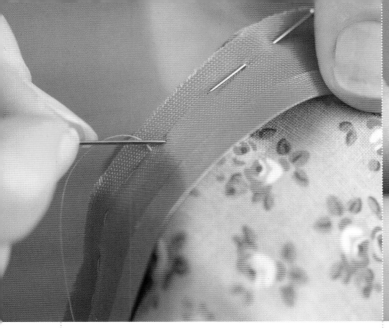

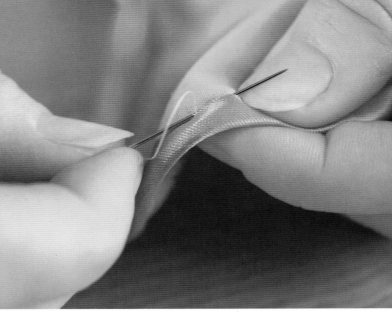

5

Open the bias binding and pin it onto the front of the mask, right side to right side, placing the pins on the fold line closest to the edge. Stitch along the fold line using a running stitch.

6

When you reach the end of the bias, fold the short edge under and stitch it over where you began for a neat finish. Then fold the binding over to the back of the mask and slip stitch in place.

9

Once the elastic is all the way through, stitch both ends of the elastic to the casing. Fold over the end of the strap to hide the raw edge, and handstitch to the back of the mask.

10

Flip the mask over, and stitch along the edge where the elastic meets the bias edging. Repeat Steps 9–10 for the other end of the strap to finish the mask.

Knotted scarf

Tempted by the balls of soft, luxurious wool in your local haberdashery shop? You can make this cosy scarf without knowing how to knit; simply knot strands of wool together to make this pretty macramé criss-cross design.

To make a knotted scarf you will need

Tools: scissors • 1cm (⅜in)-thick polystyrene foam board (or use a cork pin board) • sewing pins
Materials: 2 x 50g (3½oz) balls Super Chunky wool

1
Measure and cut the wool into 18 lengths, each about 3.8m (4yd).

2
Arrange the lengths of wool into six groups of three strands each. Wind the wool into bunches and tie loosely, leaving a 50cm (20in) tail; this will make the strands easier to work with.

 3

Take the first two bunches and tie them together with a double knot about 12cm (5in) from the top. Repeat with the other bunches, making three knotted sections.

4

Evenly space out the double bunches on a polystyrene foam board or cork pin board. Secure them to the board with a pin through the centre of each knot.

 7

Repeat Step 5 to complete the next row of knots. Pin through the new knots to keep the scarf secure and to help space out the knots correctly.

8

Then repeat Step 6. Continue to tie knots in this way until you reach the end of the foam board. Unpin the knots and move the scarf up the board. Repin the last row and continue to knot.

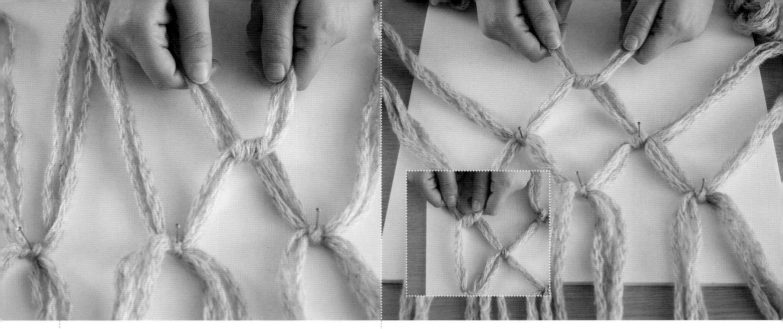

5

Working in bunches of two, knot together the second and third lengths from the left, about 5cm (2in) below the first knot. Repeat with the fourth and fifth lengths. Pin down.

6

Knot together the middle two lengths, again about 5cm (2in) below the previous knot. Then knot each of the sides, keeping the outermost length taut and ensuring the side knots line up with the middle. Pin.

9

When you are about 12cm (5in) from the end of the wool lengths, make a final three knots. Note that you will reach the end of the middle lengths sooner than the sides.

10

Cut all the strands to the same length, and the scarf is complete.

◀ Close-weave scarf

Once you have mastered the technique on pp.137–139, you could reduce the space between the knots and increase the number of bunches for a tighter and thicker finish. This scarf is made with eight bunches of wool, each made up of three strands.

} *Tip: When using two colours, choose the same type of yarn for both so the texture and weight matches.*

Colour-block scarf

Use different colours of wool to add interest to your scarf. Start by pinning the bunches to the board in the order you want them. This scarf is made with eight bunches of wool, each with two strands, and has two bunches of grey either side of four bunches of red.

Painted
silk scarf

It is surprisingly easy to make this beautiful, striped silk scarf. For this method, the silk needs to be suspended in air while it is being painted. If you don't have a silk painting frame, you can suspend it across an old picture frame.

To make a painted silk scarf you will need

Tools: silk painting frame (or medium-sized picture frame) • masking tape • pencil • mixing dishes • square-edged paintbrush
Materials: ready-made silk scarf • tube of water-soluble gutta resist • silk paints in your choice of colours

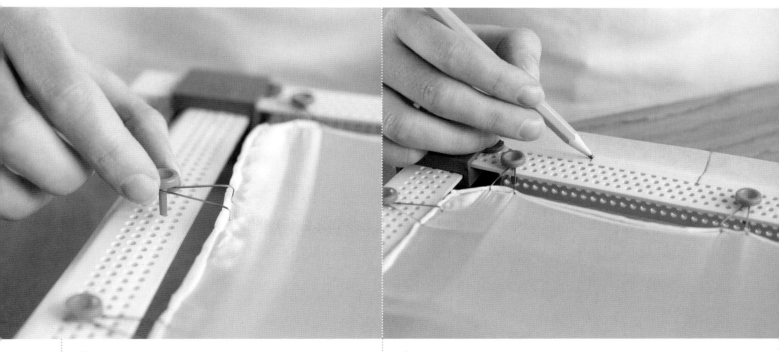

1
Fix the scarf to the silk painting frame. If you are using a picture frame, attach the scarf with masking tape and paint it in sections, moving it along as it dries.

2
Decide how you would like the white stripes on your scarf to be spaced. Stick masking tape down the side of the frame and draw a line for each stripe.

3

With a ruler as a guide, use gutta to draw a line at each marked interval. The gutta will keep the paint colours in each section from running into each other. Ensure that there are no breaks in the lines and that you continue each line all the way to the edge of the fabric (see inset).

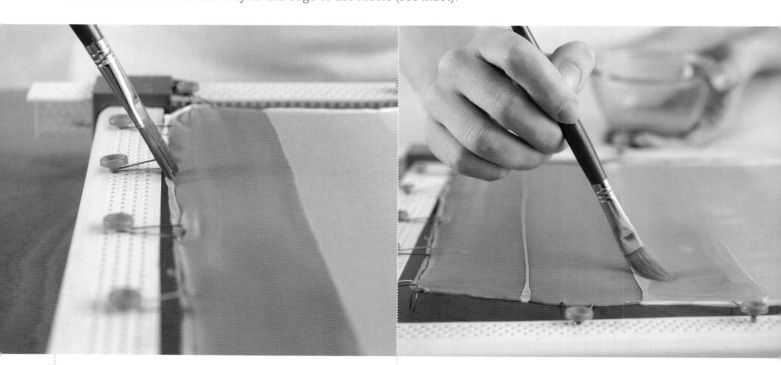

6

Starting with the left-most stripe (right-most if you're left-handed) and using a square-edged brush, paint the first section. Ensure you cover the scarf all the way to the edge.

7

Continue painting stripes in this way, switching colours and working across the scarf. Once finished, leave the scarf to dry.

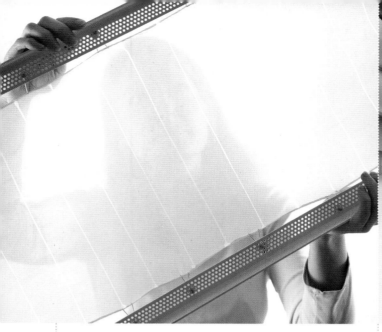

4

Let the gutta dry and then double-check that there are no breaks in the lines by holding the frame up to the light. Add more gutta to any breaks and allow to dry.

5

Mix your colours. Combine a few drops of each silk colour with 2 tablespoons of water and test the colour on a silk scrap. Adjust the intensity of the colours until you're happy with them.

8

Once the scarf has dried completely, remove it from the frame and, following your paint-manufacturer's instructions, iron it on a silk setting to fix the paints.

9

Using a wool and silk detergent, hand-wash the scarf to remove the gutta residue. This will leave behind white lines in the scarf. Leave the scarf to dry, and then iron again.

Customized
cushion

For the home

Customize a plain cushion cover with appliqué fabric shapes, buttons, and decorative stitches to make a stylish or funky cushion at a low cost – a perfect gift for a new home or for a child's bedroom.

To make a blossom cushion you will need

Tools: washable ink pen • tracing paper • steam iron • dressmaker's scissors • sewing pins • sewing machine • sewing needle • cotton sewing threads *Materials:* iron-on interfacing • brown cotton fabric • white cotton fabric • pink floral cotton fabric • green felt • cushion cover • 8 small white buttons and 4 large white buttons

1

Enlarge the blossom cushion templates on p.222 to fit your cushion. Trace all the shapes apart from the leaves onto iron-on interfacing.

2

Cut out the interfacing and iron each piece onto the chosen fabric for each: brown cotton for the bird and branch, white cotton for 12 petals, and pink floral cotton for 12 centres.

 3

Carefully cut out all
the interfaced shapes.

4

Trace the leaf template onto paper and cut it out.
Use the template to trace and cut out six leaves
from the felt. There is no need to iron these onto
interfacing as felt will not fray.

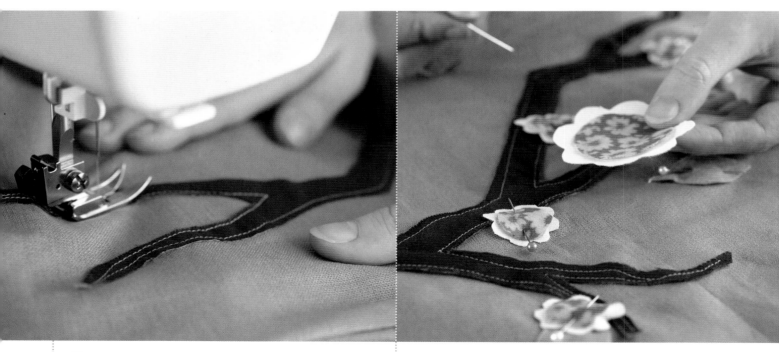

 6

Machine sew the branch and bird onto
the cushion using a contrasting colour
cotton thread, carefully sewing about
3–5mm (1/8–1/4in) from the edges.

7

Match the large, white flowers with the large,
pink centres and the small, white flowers with
the small, pink centres. Place the flowers and
leaves onto the cushion and pin in position.

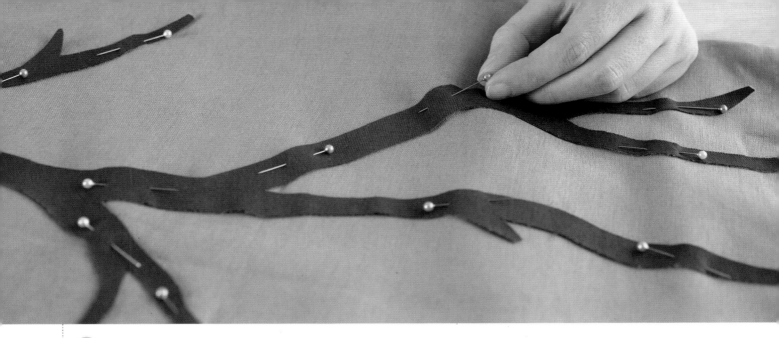

5

Place the cushion cover on a flat surface
and place the branch and bird in position.
Pin or use tacking stitches to secure.

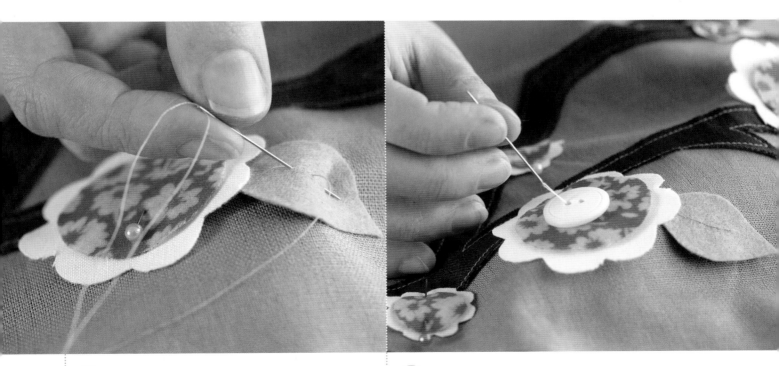

8

Tuck some of the leaves behind the flowers to
create a natural effect. Hand sew the leaves
on in a matching cotton down the centres,
using four or five backstitches to secure.

9

Sew large and small buttons into the centres
of the flowers, sewing through the cushion
cover to secure the flowers to the cover.

Castle cushion

Be as creative as you like with this castle. Start with the template on p.224 to create the basic shape. Use leather-effect fabric for the drawbridge and windows, and a favourite colour for the flag. The prince and princess are made from felt offcuts and are attached to the cushion by thin cord so they cannot be lost! You can make your own, or add ready-made fabric dolls. Remember to make a few pockets in the design for them to go into.

Tip: Use the templates on p.225 to make the dolls. Add yarn for hair and sew or draw the faces.

Skull and crossbones cushion

A fun skull motif will appeal to children of all ages, particularly those with a love of pirates! Find the template for this project on p.223. Cut out the skull and crossbone shapes from black felt and tack into position on the cushion cover Machine sew around the edge of the black shapes using white cotton. Cut out eyes and teeth from white felt and sew them by hand into position, onto the skull.

Guitar cushion

This is the perfect cushion for a teenager's room. Using the template on p.223, cut out the shapes for the guitar from black and white felt or suede-effect fabric. Tack and stitch the guitar body into place first, using contrast thread. Add the white board section, sewing it on with white thread. Add the black details, again using contrast thread. Use white ribbon for the strings, and stitch into position. A drum or a section of piano keys would also look effective.

Personalized journal

What better place to store notes and thoughts than in a handmade journal with a personalized cover? This technique demands precision – each stage leads on to the next, so if you're slightly "out", the journal may look misshapen.

To make a journal you will need

Tools: bone folder • craft knife • pencil • metal ruler • self-healing cutting mat • sewing needle
Materials: 6 sheets of heavy A3 white or cream paper • 1 sheet of A3 decorative paper • white thread

1
Making sure that the grain is running vertically, fold each piece of white or cream A3 paper in half so that the short edges meet. Smooth the crease with the bone folder.

2
Starting from the inside of the folded sheet, cut along the fold with the knife, stopping at a point just over halfway along the fold.

3

Fold each sheet of paper in half again, short edge to short edge. Crease then cut along the fold, stopping just after halfway. Fold the paper in half again, short edge to short edge, and crease.

4

Assemble the folded sheets in a pile of "stacks". To make the cover, first fold the decorative paper in half so that the long edges meet and press the crease down with the bone folder.

7

Use the ruler and the bone folder to crease the cover along the second pencil line you have just drawn. The area between the two creases will be the spine of your journal.

8

Measure the height of the cover, and divide this distance into five equal sections. Mark each section on the spine, and then use a craft knife to cut a slit through each line.

 5

Fold the paper in half again, this time so that the short edges meet. Smooth down the crease with the bone folder.

 6

Open the cover and draw a line down the crease. Press down gently on the pile of stacks and measure the height of the pile. Then measure the same distance to one side of the crease. Draw a line.

9

Use the ruler to draw lines on the pile of paper stacks to correspond with the slits in the cover.

 10

Open up each paper segment and prick the needle through each mark. There should now be four evenly spaced holes in each paper segment. Thread the needle.

155

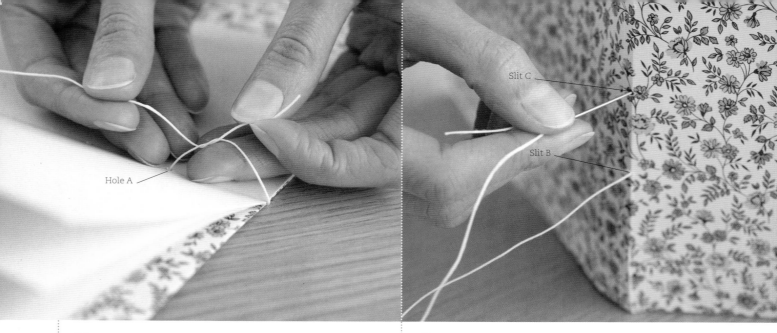

11

With one stack on top of the cover, push the needle through the first hole (hole A) and first slit (slit A) from the inside. Pass the thread around the top of the spine and tie a knot.

12

Pass the needle through the hole B from the inside and out through slit B. Run the thread along the spine and push the needle in through slit C and hole C to the inside.

15

Add a new stack and continue, securing and adding stacks. After the last stack, pass the needle around the top of the journal, and below one of the stitches. Knot on the inside.

16

Fold the decorative paper back over the stack and smooth it down, creasing the fold with your finger.

Hole D

Slit D

Hole 2D

Slit D

Hole D

 13

Push the needle out through hole D and slit D. Looping the thread around the bottom of the spine, push the needle through just hole D again. Tighten the thread.

 14

Add the next stack. Go through the first hole of the new stack (hole 2D) to the inside, then around the bottom of the spine and back through slit D and hole 2D. Continue, securing the second stack like the first.

 17

Now fold the paper under again to form the jacket. Repeat for the other side.

 18

Cut through the edges of the pages of the first stack. Repeat for all the other stacks.

Dot-decorated
ceramics

Painting ceramics by hand can seem a bit daunting, but this dot-decorating method is virtually foolproof. Almost any line-drawing can be turned into a dot painting, so once you have mastered the technique try out your own designs.

To make a dot-decorated vase you will need
Tools: scissors • ballpoint pen

Materials: ceramic vase • baby wipes or damp cloth • red transfer paper
• masking tape • black, food-safe ceramic pen or paint in a dispenser

1

Clean the vase to remove any loose dust or grease from the surface. Photocopy the vase template (see p.236) and reduce or enlarge it to fit.

2

Place a sheet of transfer paper behind the template and cut out the main dandelion motif. Then cut out the individual seeds.

 159

3

Tape the dandelion template to the front of your vase, with the transfer paper underneath. Position the seeds around the template and on one adjoining side.

4

Using a ballpoint pen, firmly trace the design onto the vase. Use solid lines across the dots as these show up best.

7

Using the template as a guide, complete the design with dots. Keep the spacing of the dots even and work quickly to avoid the paint pooling. Paint short, solid lines at the ends of the seeds and then fill in the dots.

 5

Remove the template and check that the lines are visible. If not, wipe away the trace lines and repeat the process, pressing down more firmly.

6

Use a ceramic paint pen or paint in a dispenser to draw the stem of the dandelion in one continuous line.

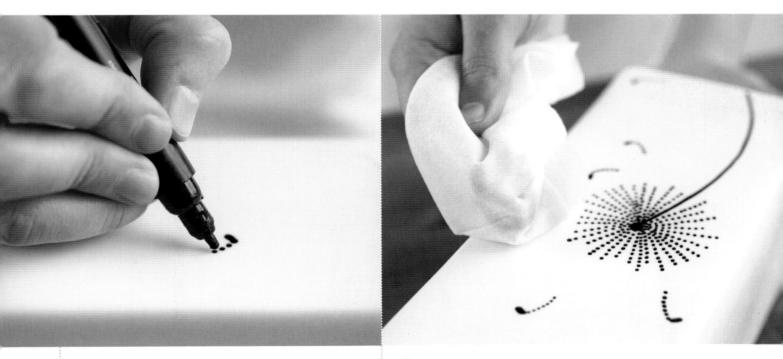

 8

Repeat Steps 4–7 to decorate the second side of the vase. Let the paint dry before repeating the whole process for the remaining two sides.

 9

When the paint is completely dry, use a baby wipe or damp cloth to wipe off the trace lines. Follow the paint manufacturer's instructions to set the paint.

Mug and coaster set

Create this delicately patterned mug and coaster set in exactly the same way as the vase (see pp.158–159) using the mug and coaster template (see p.237). When painting the dots, remember to work from left to right (right to left if you're left-handed) across the pattern to avoid smudging the dots you have already made.

Tip: Create a set of mugs using the same design in different colours — one for each family member.

Celebration bunting plate

As a rule, it is not safe to eat food from hand-painted ceramics (but do check the label on your paints). The dot-decorating method can be used to create stunning display plates though, and this bunting plate is the perfect gift to mark a celebration. Use the template (see p.237) to transfer the pattern to the plate. Draw the black lines, let them dry, then work across the pattern filling in the flags with coloured dots.

} Tip: Add a celebratory message or the recipient's name to the plate by painting a letter in each flag.

Mosaic
bowl

This calming, woodland-inspired mosaic bowl is created using the direct method, meaning that tiles are glued straight onto the object and then grouted. This will not produce a completely level surface, resulting in a tactile bowl.

To make a mosaic bowl you will need

Tools: tile nippers • rubber gloves • protective mask & goggles • grout spreader • sponge • lint-free cloth

Materials: wooden bowl • tesserae in different shades of green • flat-backed beads and 5mm millefiori • PVA glue • mosaic grout (either pre-mixed or made up following the manufacturer's instructions)

1

Draw a wavy line onto your bowl, about 4.5cm (1¾in) from the rim. Draw a second line roughly 1.5cm (⅝in) below this one. This will be the first accent line on your bowl.

2

Prepare your tiles by soaking or peeling off any backing sheets. Select the plain tiles and those for the accent lines, and place them in groups of the same colour and type.

3

Cut tiles for the accent lines. Wearing goggles, hold the tile between thumb and forefinger and, positioning nippers at the edge, gently squeeze. Repeat to cut into quarters.

4

Arrange the tiles and embellishments between your wavy lines. Vary iridescent and matt tiles, as well as round and rectangular ones to create a pattern.

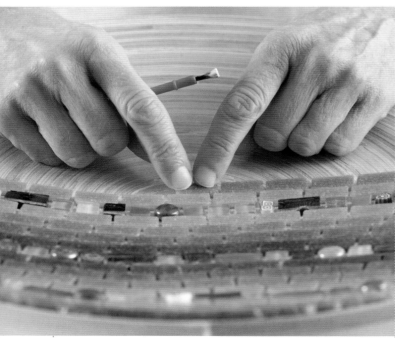

7

Complete one line at a time, increasing or decreasing the shade and adding accent lines at regular intervals. When complete, leave to dry overnight.

8

Wearing rubber gloves and a mask, apply the grout generously to the mosaic, working in different directions. Make sure to also grout around the outer edge of the bowl.

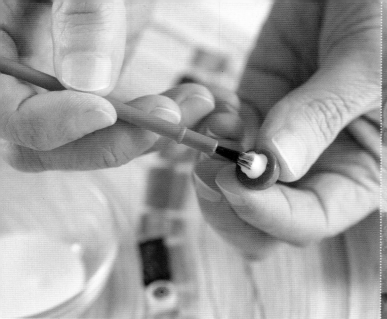

5

Move the pieces off the line, keeping their order. Add a dab of glue to the back of each piece and stick them to your bowl leaving even gaps between them.

6

For the lines of plain tiles, start with the lightest green tiles, and cut them in half (see Step 3). Glue them either side of the accent line, trimming them if necessary.

9

Use a damp sponge to carefully wipe away the excess grout. Leave for 20 minutes, then, before the grout is hard, wipe gently again.

10

When the grout is completely dry, use a lint-free dry cloth to wipe away any residue and polish the tiles to a shine.

Owl jewellery box

You will need

Wooden box
Glazed and unglazed ceramic tiles
Glass nuggets and beads
White grout
Felt for base

This pretty jewellery box is made using the same technique as the mosaic bowl on pp.165–167. Start by drawing the design on the box (see template p.234) and then seal the box with watered-down PVA glue. Start filling in the design, attaching the nuggets and whole tiles first. Cut the remaining tiles to size to complete the design. Finally, fill in the area around the design with randomly cut tiles – a technique known as crazy paving. Allow to dry and then grout the lid. Grout the box one side at a time, waiting for each side to dry before starting the next. Glue felt to the base to finish the box.

Flower garland mirror

You will need

Mirror with wide, flat, wooden frame
A selection of tiles and glass nuggets
White grout

Make this mirror in the same way as the mosaic bowl on pp.165–167. Draw on the design first (see template p.235) and seal the wooden frame with watered-down PVA glue if necessary. Create the flowers first, starting with a nugget and using tile nippers to shape the petals. Next, make the leaf garlands. Fill in the gaps with crazy paving (see above), and use tile halves to fill in the outer edge of the border. Cover the mirror with masking tape to protect it when grouting. Grout the frame, ensuring you create a straight edge around the mirror.

Round tea light holder

You will need

Ball-shaped, wooden tea light holder
Old crockery, broken into small pieces
Tiles and glass nuggets
White grout
Felt for the base

This tea light holder is made in the same way as the mosaic bowl (see pp.165–167), but using fragments of broken crockery. First, draw your design (see p.235) on the tea light holder and then seal it with watered-down PVA glue. Glue down the nuggets first, and then use tile nippers to shape the crockery pieces into petals. Next, add any whole tiles. Finally, fill in the area around the design with more crockery pieces. Work a small area at a time. Some tiles may have to be held in place using tape until they dry. Grout, allow to dry, and attach felt to the base to finish.

Seaside coasters

You will need

MDF squares
Tiles in a variety of colours
Grey grout

These seaside-inspired coasters have been made out of squares of MDF, using the technique described for the mosaic bowl on pp.165–167. Using either the template from p.234 or your own design, first draw guidelines onto the coaster in pencil. Fill in the design first, shaping the tiles to fit. Try to keep the tiles fairly flat, as you will need to be able to rest a glass or mug on the coaster when finished. Next, fill in the background using square tiles, shaping them to fit as necessary. Again, try to keep the tiles as flat as possible. Grout the coasters, not forgetting the edges, to finish.

Ribbon-bound
photo album

This wonderful album is bound to become a family treasure. Use thick, acid-free card for the pages to protect your photographs and thick, good-quality ribbon to ensure that the binding holds for years to come.

To make a ribbon-bound photo album you will need

Tools: craft knife • metal ruler • self-healing cutting mat • bookbinding needle

Materials: sheets of heavy white or cream paper • 3 x 15cm (5⅞in) lengths of ribbon • masking tape • 3 x 1m (40in) linen bookbinding thread • 2 sheets 2–3mm (1⁄16–1⁄8in) cardboard • 2 sheets decorative paper • glue • greaseproof paper

1
Find the grain of the paper by folding it over lengthways and widthways. The fold with least resistance tells you that the grain runs up and down.

2
With the grain running vertically, use the template (see p.232) to cut 18 rectangles to make 15 pages, two end papers, and one sewing template.

3

Transfer the hole markings to one sheet to use as your sewing template. One at a time, line up each of the 15 pages with the sewing template and pierce the needle through each mark.

4

Place one page at the edge of a table, the pierced side lined up with the table edge. Position the three lengths of ribbon between each set of holes, and tape them to the edge of the table.

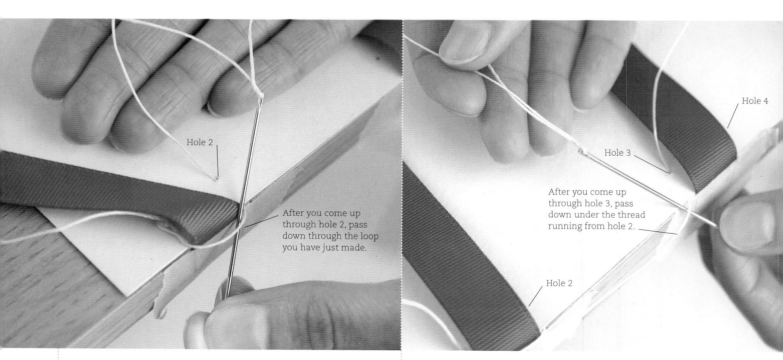

Hole 2

After you come up through hole 2, pass down through the loop you have just made.

Hole 4

Hole 3

After you come up through hole 3, pass down under the thread running from hole 2.

Hole 2

7

After you come up through the second hole, flip the ribbons over the paper. Pass down through the loop you have just made. Take care not to pull too tight, keeping all the loops slightly loose.

8

Next pass through hole 3, bottom to top, then under the thread running from hole 2. Pass through hole 4, bottom to top, and through the loop you have just made (see Step 7).

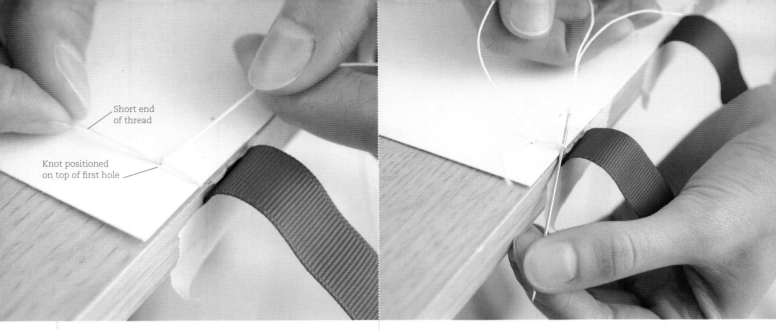

Short end
of thread

Knot positioned
on top of first hole

5

Flip the ribbons off the paper. Using a needle
and 1m (40in) thread, go through the first hole
from top to bottom. Loop around and tie a
double knot, positioning it on top of the hole.

6

Pass the needle underneath the loop you have
just made, right to left, and pull the thread
through. Pass under the ribbon, and through
the second hole, going from underneath to top.

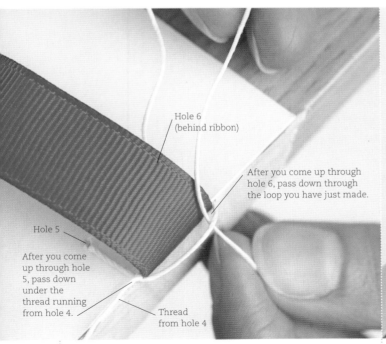

Hole 6
(behind ribbon)

After you come up through
hole 6, pass down through
the loop you have just made.

Hole 5

After you come
up through hole
5, pass down
under the
thread running
from hole 4.

Thread
from hole 4

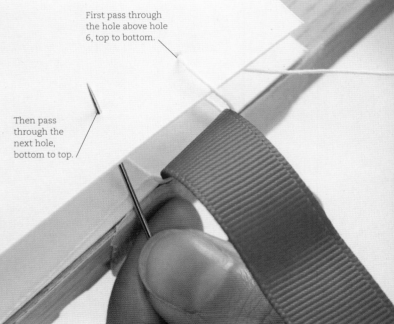

First pass through
the hole above hole
6, top to bottom.

Then pass
through the
next hole,
bottom to top.

9

Repeat for holes 5 and 6: pass up through
hole 5, bottom to top, and under the thread
running from hole 4; pass up through hole
6, and down through the loop.

10

Add the second page. Pass through the hole
above hole 6, top to bottom, across the ribbon,
and come up through the next hole. Repeat Steps
7–9 in reverse, but don't go through the last loop.

173

11

After you come up through the last hole on the second page, pass down through the last loop as well as the loop below it. Add the next page, and pass through the first two holes as in Step 10.

12

Repeat Steps 7–11 for the remaining 13 pages, always passing through both the last loop and the loop below it, securing the loops together in bunches of two. When you run out of thread, attach more with a weaver's knot.

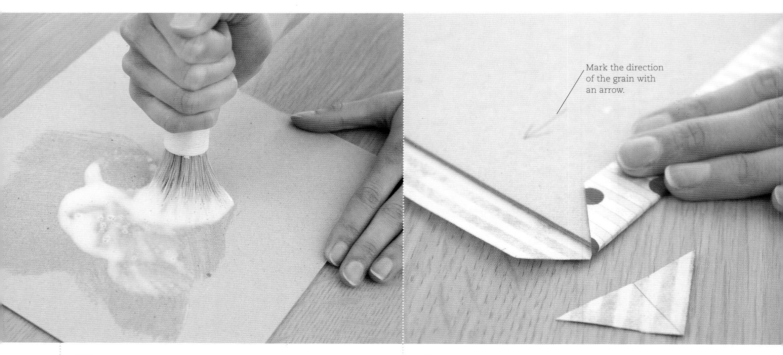

Mark the direction of the grain with an arrow.

14

Cut two cardboard covers, 3mm (⅛in) longer than the pages at the top, bottom, and one side. Cut two sheets of decorative paper, 2cm (¾in) longer on all sides than the boards. Spread glue on each board.

15

With the grain running vertically, place each board, glue side down, in the centre of one sheet of paper. Trim each corner diagonally and glue the edges over the board.

13

With the book closed, push the needle underneath the first page. Open the first page and pull the thread through. Next, push the needle through the first hole on the second page. Turn the page, pull the thread through, and tie a knot on the other side of the second page. Cut the thread.

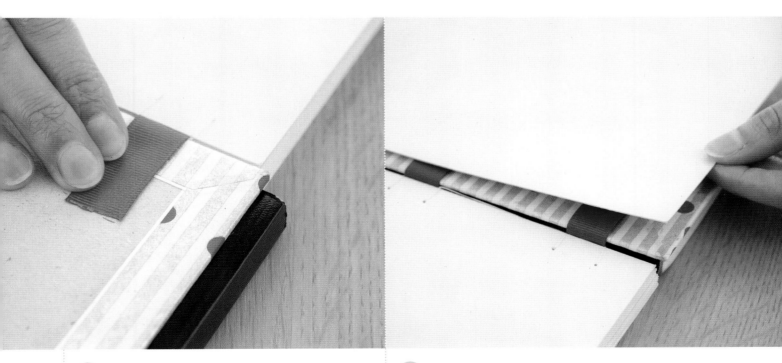

16

Place one cover on a book the same height as the stack of pages to hold it level and glue down the ribbon ends. Repeat for the other cover, trimming the ribbons if needed.

17

Glue the endpapers to the insides of each board to conceal the ribbons. Place greaseproof paper between both covers and first pages. Weigh down the album and let it dry overnight.

Rollaway gameboard

For the home

This draughts board has an integrated pocket for game pieces and it rolls up neatly, making it easy to store and ideal for travel. The patchwork top is cleverly made from fabric strips, saving you having to piece each square separately.

To make a rollaway gameboard you will need

Tools: dressmaker's scissors • sewing machine • sewing pins • iron

Materials: plain fabric in brown and cream • decorative fabric in two different designs • cotton sewing thread • interfacing • 3cm (1¼in) button • thin ribbon • buttons in 2 colours to use as draught pieces

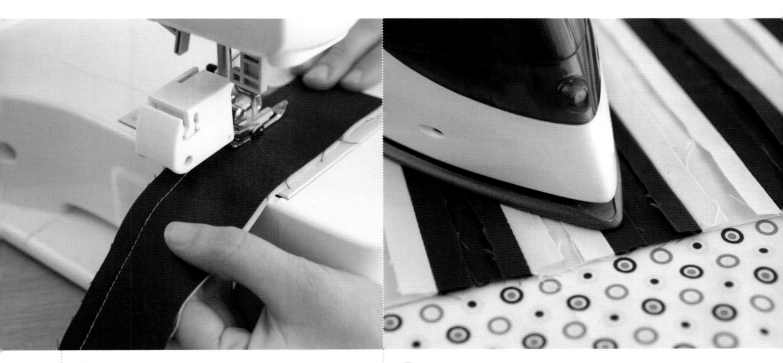

1
Use the chart in the Templates section (p.225) to measure and cut out the fabric pieces. Sew together one light and one dark strip with a 1cm (⅜in) seam allowance.

2
Sew a light strip to the other edge of the first dark strip. Add the remaining strips one at a time, alternating colours. Press all the seams open, forming a 29cm (12in) wide piece.

177

3

Mark lines across the strips every 5cm (2in).
Cut along the lines to make eight bands. Pin
the bands together, offsetting every other row
by one square to make a chequerboard.

4

Sew the strips together with a 1cm (⅜in)
seam allowance. Press open the seams. Trim
off the extra squares on either side to create
an 8 x 8 board, leaving the seam allowance.

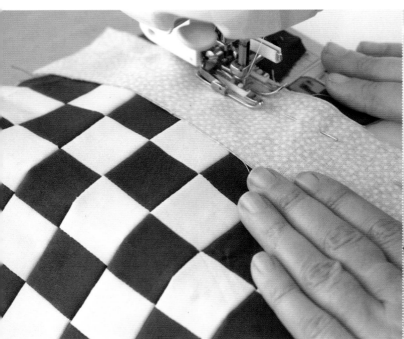

7

Place the two narrow strips of inner fabric
at two opposite sides of the board, right side
to right side. Pin, then sew with a 1cm (⅜in)
seam allowance. Press the seams open.

8

Sew the two remaining inner fabric panels
to the two remaining edges of the board
with a 1cm (⅜in) seam allowance. Press
the seams away from the board.

5

Apply interfacing to the wrong side of the 30 x 50cm (12 x 20in) piece of outer fabric and one of the 30 x 14cm (12 x 5¾in) pieces of inner fabric.

6

Fold over a 5mm (¼in) double hem at one end of the interfaced outer fabric and stitch. Do the same along one long edge of the interfaced inner fabric. These will form the pocket edges.

9

Place the right side of the outer fabric and the right side of the inner fabric together, making sure the pocket hems (see step 6) line up. Pin, then sew with 1cm (⅜in) seam allowance along three sides, leaving the pocket edges open.

10

Overstitch along the edge of the chequerboard closest to the pocket edges to form an interlined pocket. You can use the pocket to store the game pieces.

11

Sew a 3cm (1¼in) button in the middle of the outside of the non-pocket end, approximately 1.5cm (⅝in) from the edge. Thread a thin ribbon through the buttonhole.

12

Tie a knot in the ribbon behind the button. Wrap the ribbon around the rolled-up game, securing the counters inside. Secure the roll by winding the ribbon around the button.

All of these bags are made in the same way as the wave-patterned bag on pp.183–185. Turn to pp.186–187 for further instructions, ideas, and inspiration.

Stencilled bags

Turn plain canvas bags into unique and personal fashion statements with the use of paper stencils and fabric paint. Once you can stencil with confidence, why not try decorating a T-shirt or cushion cover?

To make the wave-patterned bag you will need

Tools: pencil • scalpel • cutting mat • iron • masking tape • plate or palette • sponge • hairdryer • kitchen towel

Materials: tracing paper • stencil paper or card • fabric bag • scrap paper or newspaper • fabric paint in two colours

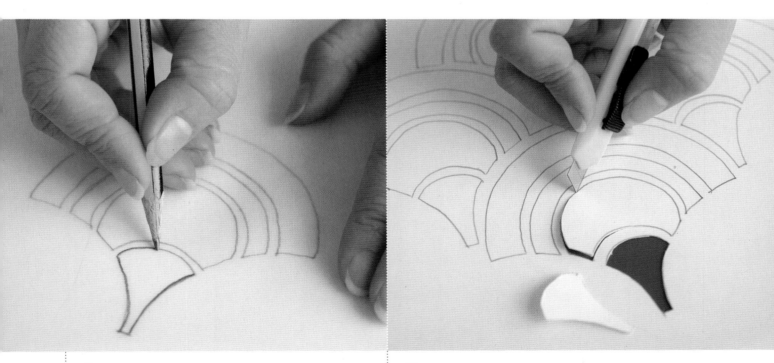

1

Trace the stencil template from p.238 on to tracing paper. Transfer it onto card by flipping the tracing paper over and drawing over the lines while pressing down firmly.

2

Use a scalpel to carefully cut the stencil shape out. If making a repeat pattern, you can cut out the stencil shape a number of times on one sheet, making sure to leave a border of paper.

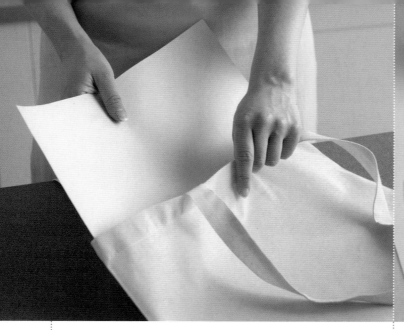

3

Prepare your fabric bag by ironing it, and line the inside with scrap paper or newspaper to stop any excess ink that may soak through the fabric from running through to the back of the bag.

4

Tape down the stencil. Pour some paint on a plate or palette. Dip a clean, dry sponge in the paint, dabbing off any excess. Then apply the paint with the sponge, starting from the centre and working out.

6

Use kitchen towel to blot your stencil and let it dry. You can also prepare more stencils, allowing you to move on with the design while you wait for the first stencil to dry.

7

Once your stencil and fabric paint are dry, reposition your stencil on the bag. Repeat the application process as many times as desired, leaving a few gaps for the second colour.

5

Remove your stencil and put it to one side to dry. Use a hairdryer to dry the paint onto the fabric, ensuring you blow dry the inside of your fabric bag as well as the front so the paint doesn't dry to the lining paper.

8

Once you've stencilled all of the design in one colour and it has dried, apply the second colour in the same way as the first, using a new stencil. Leave to dry overnight.

9

When the fabric paint has fully dried, iron the fabric for a minute or two to fix the paint to the material. You may wish to use a cloth to protect your iron.

Fluttering butterflies

This bag has been stencilled in the same way as the wave-patterned bag on pp.183–185, using the templates on p.239. Butterflies of different shapes and sizes are positioned at slight angles on the same diagonal line, making it look like they are all fluttering in the same direction. Creating the same stencil in different sizes, and overlapping some of the images, also adds a sense of depth to the scene.

The same colour paint has been used to create these butterflies, but you could try stencilling them in a variety of colours for a different look. Alternatively, wait for the design to dry and paint or stencil different coloured markings on the butterflies.

Stitched bag

This large-scale design looks like thread that has been stitched onto the bag, attached to a needle that has also been pushed through the fabric. The look is achieved by creating gaps in the stencil design where the item or object would be obscured by the fabric. Follow the instructions on pp.183–185 to create this look, using the stencils on p.238. Remember to cut separate stencils for different-coloured elements.

Have fun playing with the blank canvas provided by the bag by thinking of other designs that could be interacting with it in some way. For example, you could stencil on a belt going through belt loops, or a ribbon "threaded" through the bag.

Repeated chevrons

This deceptively simple idea results in a striking design with an element of optical illusion. Using the template on p.238, create a stencil, cutting several chevron shapes at equal distances to each other. Following the instructions for the wave-patterned bag on pp.183–185 and starting in the centre of your bag, stencil the pattern onto the bag and dry it. Reposition the stencil so that it continues the chevron pattern as shown, pointing the chevrons the opposite way for every other column, and taking care to keep all the stencilled figures evenly spaced.

Any evenly spaced, repeated pattern makes a striking design, so try this with circles or triangles for a different look. You could also try varying the colours, either according to a pattern or randomly.

Pencil illusion

At first glance it looks like these pencils are complete, but on closer inspection, you can see that only the tip and shaft of the pencil have been stencilled onto the bag. Your eye fills in the rest, completing the image with the background colour. This is a great technique to use for stencilled designs as it can be difficult to stencil very narrow lines or other details needed to complete an image. To make these pencils, use the stencil template on p.238 and follow the instructions for the wave-patterned bag on pp.183–185.

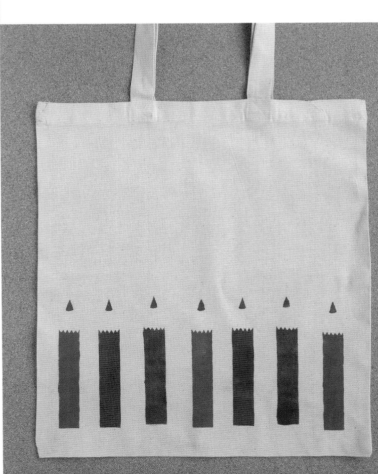

Make a sleeve for a device of any size by following the instructions for the tablet protector on pp.107–109. Choose the correct-size button to finish it off.

Phone and tablet protectors

Make a stylish and individual slipcase for a gadget-lover's phone, tablet, or laptop. These instructions are based on the individual device's measurements, and so can be used to make a cover for any make or model.

To make a tablet protector you will need

Tools: tape measure • dressmaker's scissors • iron • ruler • fabric marker • sewing pins • sewing machine or needle

Materials: cotton fabric for the shell • lining fabric • fleece fabric • medium-weight, fusible, woven interfacing • 15cm (5⅞in) round elastic • button • cotton sewing thread

1
Use a tape measure to measure around the length of the device. Divide this number by two, and then add 4.5cm (1¾in). Do the same for the width of the device.

2
Using the measurements from Step 1, draw and cut two rectangles from your chosen shell fabric. Then do the same for the lining fabric, fleece fabric, and fusible woven interfacing.

3

Iron one piece of fusible interfacing to the wrong side of each piece of shell fabric. With the wrong sides facing, lightly iron the lining fabric to the fleece fabric from the side of the lining.

4

Mark a sewing line 1cm (⅜in) from the edge along all four edges of one of the interfaced pieces, on the side of the interfacing. Do the same for one of the fleece and lining pieces, on the fleece side.

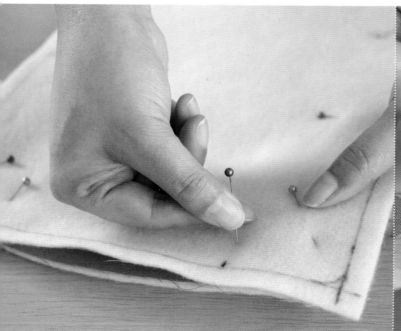

7

Pin the two padded lining pieces together, lining sides facing, marking a 12cm (4¾in) gap along the bottom edge. Sew as in Step 6, leaving a gap. Trim the seams and overstitch the edges.

8

Turn the shell right side out and press. Mark the centre of the top sewing line, mark down 5cm (2in), and sew on the button. Turn wrong side out, add a sewing line to the other side, and mark its centre for the elastic.

5

Round out the bottom corners of each of the pieces that you have drawn sewing lines on, using a button as a template, and drawing around the button.

6

Pin the two interfaced pieces together, right sides facing and top edges matching. Sew down one side, across the bottom, and up the other side, along the line. Trim the seams and overstitch the edges.

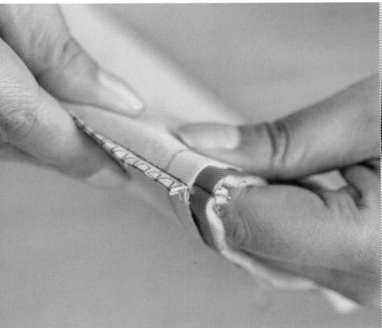

9

Turn the lining right side out. Slide it inside the outer piece. Insert the elastic loop between the two pieces as marked. Pin and sew around the sewing line, double-stitching over the elastic.

10

Trim the seam and overstitch the edges. Reach through the opening in the bottom lining to turn the cover right side out. Stitch closed the gap in the lining by hand. Press the cover.

Square
gift box

A gift box is the ideal way to present awkwardly shaped gifts. You can make this gift box exactly the required size by re-sizing the template. Use patterned card, or glue decorative paper to card before you start to create different looks.

To make a square gift box you will need

Tools: pencil • scalpel • cutting mat • ruler • blunt knife (or pair of scissors) • rubber
Materials: patterned card (or patterned paper glued onto card) • tracing paper • glue stick

1 Use a photocopier to re-size the box stencil on p.195. Using tracing paper and a pencil, transfer the template onto patterned card (or glue patterned paper to the back of the card).

2 Using a scalpel and a cutting mat, carefully cut out the shape you have drawn. Take care not to cut into the internal folding lines.

 3

Once you have cut out the entire shape, score all the folding lines using a ruler and blunt knife, or one side of a pair of scissors. This will make the box easier to assemble.

4

Fold the sides inwards along the scored lines, making sure that each crease is sharp. For a neat finish, rub out the pencil lines along the creases inside the box.

 5

Attach the three sides not adjacent to the lid to each other using the glue stick or double-sided sticky tape on the outside of the flaps. Hold in place until set.

 6

Fold in the flaps of the last remaining side, spread glue or attach tape to the patterned side of the flaps, and slot the side into place. Press the flaps down, and hold in place until set.

Square gift box template

Please enlarge to the required
size on a photocopier

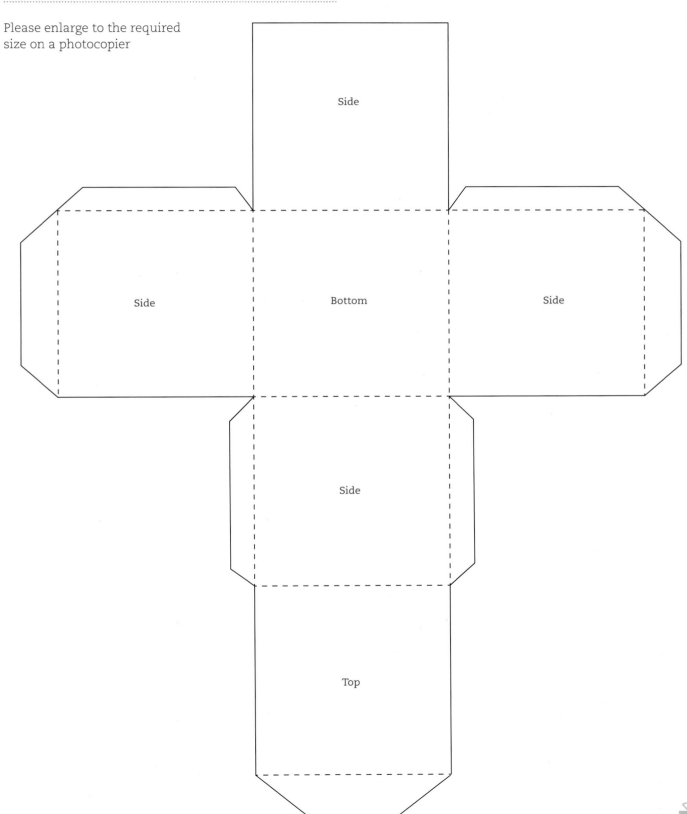

Side

Side

Bottom

Side

Side

Top

Decorating gift boxes

A few odds and ends (coloured paper, ribbons, tissue paper, and buttons) can turn plain wrapped parcels or plain boxes into beautiful, personalized gifts.

A. Gift tag and ribbon
Cut a luggage label shape from white card. Punch a hole in the corner and thread through with ribbon. Tie this ribbon around the box and glue the ends at the base of the box. Tie another ribbon in a different colour around the box.

B. Lots of dots
Layer sheets of tissue paper in different colours. Cut circles out of the layered sheets of tissue, cutting through all the layers. Using a needle and thread, sew a few small stitches through the centre of each stack of circles to secure and tie off at the back. Glue these to the top.

C. Button bow
Cut out four rectangles in two colours of patterned card. Cut a triangle out of one end of each. Glue to the top of the box, layered on top of one another. Cut out a bow-tie shape from patterned card. Fold the sides of the bow-tie shape around and under to meet at the back. Glue this to the box, press down, and glue in the middle to make the 3D bow shape. Glue on a button in the centre of the bow.

D. Button band
Cut out a strip of patterned card, long enough to wrap around the box. Sew on a variety of buttons using cream yarn. Wrap the strip around the box and glue at the bottom.

E. Floral wrap
Wrap a length of ribbon around the box and glue at the bottom. Cut out and glue another ribbon going the other way. Cut out flower shapes in different colours from tissue paper and layer on top of each other. Sew a few stitches to hold the flowers together. Stick the flowers on the box, where the ribbons meet. Add a few more smaller flowers made using the same method.

F. Rosette
Cut two lengths of ribbon and point the ends by cutting out a triangle. Glue these to the top of the box. Using pinking shears, cut circles from patterned card and decorative papers. Cut each circle smaller as you go and stack them up to make the rosette shape. Thread a button through the circles to hold them together then stick on the box.

Tip: All these ideas could be used on larger parcels or boxes. Or why not combine a few?

Homemade gift bags

Gift wrap

Follow this simple tutorial to turn any sheet of wrapping paper or gift wrap into a bespoke gift bag. For an even more personalized bag, use a sheet of paper printed with a message, or even a printout of a photograph.

To make a gift bag you will need

Tools: pencil • scissors • blunt knife (or pair of scissors) • glue stick • hole punch
Materials: tracing paper • wrapping paper or other printed or plain paper • card • ribbon

1
Re-size the template from pp.202–203 to the required size on a photocopier. Using tracing paper and a pencil, transfer the template onto the wrong side of your chosen paper.

2
Cut out the bag shape along the outer lines. Take care to not cut along any of the internal folding lines.

3

Score along the horizontal top and bottom folding lines, using a ruler and a blunt knife (or one side of a pair of scissors). Fold down the bottom and top flaps, making sure the creases are sharp.

4

Score along each of the vertical folding lines, going across the top and bottom flaps. Then fold the bag in along each of these lines in turn, again making sharp creases.

7

Fold the bottom of the bag as if you were wrapping a present. Fold one long side of the bottom tab in across the opening, creasing the sides sharply. Fold the sides in over the opening, again creasing sharply. Finally, fold in the remaining side to cover the opening, and glue or tape the base down.

5

Using a glue stick, spread glue evenly along the top flap. Smooth it down, holding it in place until it sticks. This will help the bag hold its shape.

6

Fold out the bottom flap. Spread glue along the outside of the side tab, and attach it to the inside of the opposite end, all the way along its length. Glue the other side tab over the seam.

8

Cut out a piece of card the size of the base of the bag, and place it in the bottom of the bag. This will strengthen the base.

9

Using a two-hole punch (or a single-hole punch), punch two holes on each long side of the bag, through the centre of the reinforced top fold. Add ribbon for handles.

Gift bag template

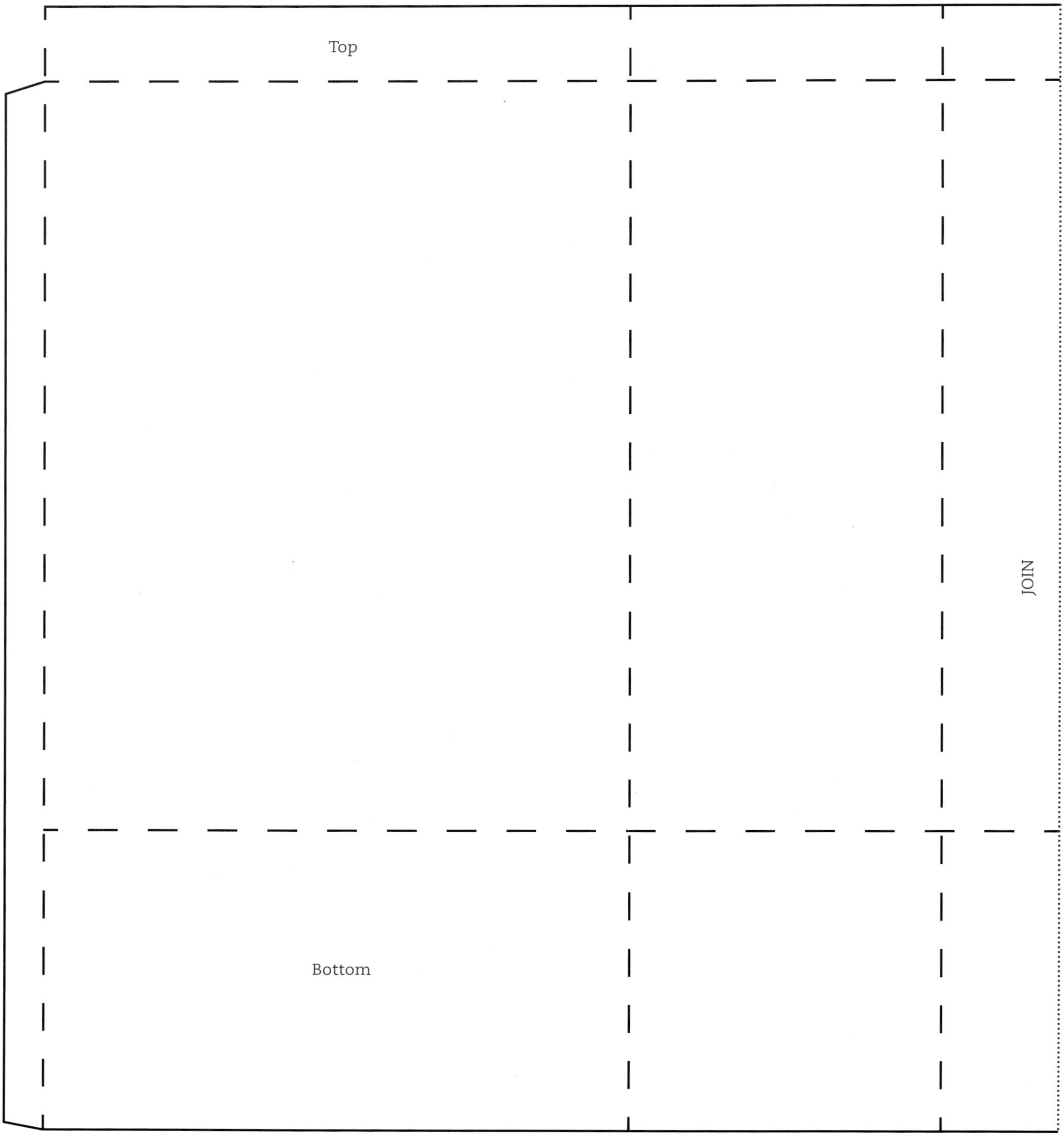

Top

JOIN

Bottom

JOIN

Side
tab

203

Printed
gift wrap

Gift wrap

Making your own gift wrap finishes off any gift with a personal touch. This stamped pattern of blocks of stripes is easy to create. Once you have mastered this technique, why not try creating your own shapes and patterns?

To make printed gift wrap you will need

Tools: scissors • glue

Materials: wood or balsa wood block • foam board • inkpad • sheets of white paper

1

To make a line stamp, start with a wooden block. Cut out strips of the desired width from foam board. Glue the strips to one side of a block and allow the glue to dry.

2

To make line-printed gift wrap, press the stamp on an inkpad and stamp in one corner of a sheet of paper. Continue stamping the paper, alternating the orientation of the stamp, until the paper is filled.

Simple silhouette

An even easier way to create an appliqué keepsake of your pet is to cut out a side-on silhouette from one fabric. Do this by enlarging a profile photograph on a photocopier to use as a template. You can make this floral pup using the template on p.227.

Appliqué pet portrait

Use the appliqué technique to create a stunning portrait of a beloved pet, perfect for decorating a cushion or displaying in a frame. Use the cat template provided, or make your own from a favourite photograph.

To make an appliqué pet portrait cushion cover you will need

Tools: iron • dressmaker's scissors • sewing needle • sewing pins • sewing machine

Materials: bonding web • black, grey, and white fabric • cushion cover • contrast cotton sewing thread for tacking • blue, pink, and black felt • black and white cotton sewing thread

1

Re-size the template (see p.226) to fit your cushion cover. Transfer the head piece on to bonding web, and iron it on to the reverse of your selected fabric.

2

Repeat the process for the back, chest, ear, and muzzle pieces. Then cut out each element. Note that the eyes and nose don't need to be faced.

207

3

Carefully peel off the backing paper from all the faced pieces.

4

Assemble the pieces on the cushion cover. Make sure the head piece overlaps the chest piece and the back piece. Iron in place.

7

Pin, then tack the pieces, except the eyes and nose, in place on the cushion cover. Remove the pins.

8

Sew around the outside of each of the tacked pieces about 5mm (¼in) from the edge, either by hand or with a sewing machine. Remove the tacking thread.

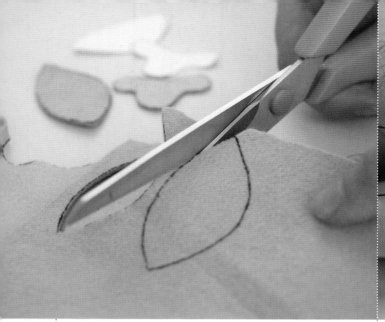

5

Trace the eyes, nose, and pupils on to coloured felt and cut them out.

6

Stitch pupils on to the eye pieces using tiny backstitches and black thread.

9

Tack the eyes and nose on to the cat's face and stitch around the edges of each piece. Remove the tacking thread.

10

Using the image on p.206 as a guide, sew guidelines for the whiskers and eyelashes using tacking thread. Stitch over them using topstitch. Remove the tacking threads.

Tartan
dog jacket

Keep a favourite dog warm and cosy all winter long with this easy-to-make, fleece-lined jacket. You can adjust the pattern to make it in any size. It fastens with Velcro, making it easy to put on and take off.

To make a tartan dog jacket you will need

Tools: tracing paper • dressmaker's scissors • sewing pins • sewing machine
Materials: tartan check fabric • wadding • interfacing • fleece fabric • cotton sewing threads
• Velcro • red grosgrain ribbon

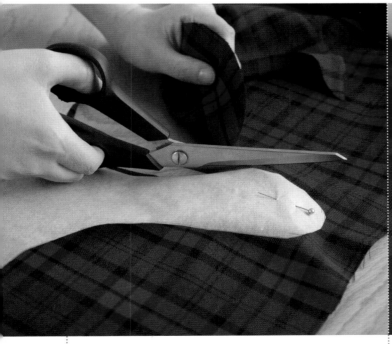

1

Using the template on pp.230–231, use tracing paper to make a pattern and adjust it to fit your dog. Cut out one jacket piece and one belly strap from each fabric.

2

Place the check fabric, right side out, on top of the wadding and interfacing. Pin all three layers together.

211

3

Machine sew along the lines of the check fabric using a long stitch, first in one direction and then the other. This quilts the jacket.

6

Machine sew around the edges of the jacket, joining the upper and lining pieces. Neaten the edges with a zigzag or overlock stitch.

7

Pin the grosgrain ribbon around the jacket as shown. Machine sew around the ribbon to attach. Fold the other half of the ribbon over the edge, and topstitch or hand stitch to attach.

4

Pin Velcro onto the lining and the quilted upper at the points marked on the template. Stitch the Velcro into place.

5

Pin the quilted upper and the fleece lining together, right sides out.

8

Make the belly strap in the same way as the jacket, attaching Velcro to the belly strap as indicated on the template. Pin the two sections as shown and stitch together.

Cat's playmat

For the cat who has everything! This mat will keep your feline friend busy and would also make a luxurious lining for a cat basket, or could be thrown over a favourite chair or sofa. For added appeal, fill the toys with catnip.

To make a cat playmat you will need

Tools: scissors • sewing pins • sewing machine • sewing needle • embroidery hoop *Materials:* metallic fabric in orange and silver • thin cord • stuffing • cotton sewing threads • white and black buttons • small bells • feathers • white embroidery thread • wadding • patterned cotton fabric • gingham fabric • orange bias binding • metal rings

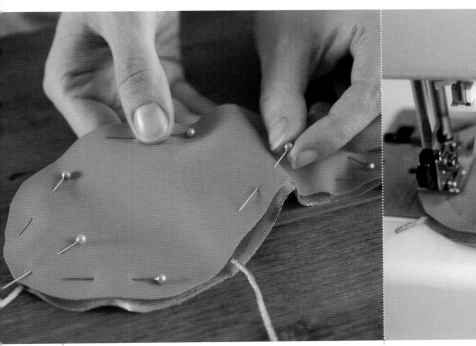

1

Using the template on p.229, cut two sides for each fish from two pieces of orange fabric held right sides together. Pin. Pin the end of 20cm (8in) thin cord to the mouth as shown.

2

Machine sew around the edges, 5mm (¼in) from the edge, securing the cord at the mouth. Leave a 2cm (¾in) gap, allowing the rest of the cord to pass through the gap.

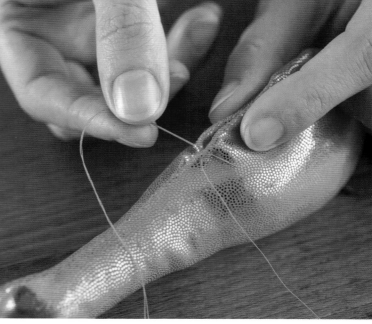

 3

Turn the fish right side out. You should have the long length of cord (the "fishing line") hanging from the mouth. Stitch several times through the cord to make it secure.

4

Push stuffing into the fish and sew the opening shut using neat overstitching and matching thread. Repeat to make another fish. Make a fish hook in the same way, using the silver metallic fabric.

 7

Cut a square of gingham fabric and a square of patterned fabric, each 70 x 70cm (27½ x 27½ in). Cut the wadding so it is about 3mm (⅛in) smaller all the way around than the fabric squares.

8

Place the gingham fabric in the embroidery hoop and tighten. Use the template on p.229 to draw a pencil outline of a fish skeleton and use chain stitch and white embroidery thread to go over the design.

5

Sew a white and black button either side of each fish head. Make sure they are attached securely. Alternatively, embroider eyes using embroidery thread.

6

Thread and knot a bell to the fishing line about 5cm (2in) from the fish's mouth. Using embroidery thread, tightly bind a feather to the fishing line, just above the bell.

9

Layer the fabrics – gingham, wadding, then patterned cotton – and pin together. Pin the bias binding around the edge and machine sew through it to sew the layers together.

10

Attach metal rings to two of the edges and one corner of the mat using cotton thread. Tie the fishes and hook securely to the rings.

Catnip mice

Filled with catnip, these little mice make a delightful gift that a cat literally cannot resist. This is a great project for using up offcuts and leftover pieces of material. Cotton fabrics work well, but why not also try tweed or leather?

To make a catnip mouse you will need

Tools: dressmaker's scissors • pencil • sewing pins • sewing machine • sewing needle
Materials: cotton fabric • felt fabric in two different colours • white wool yarn • wadding
• cotton sewing thread • dried catnip (optional) • black embroidery thread

1
Using the template on p.227, cut out two main body pieces from two pieces of fabric held right sides together. Cut out the base and ears from coloured felt.

2
Cut three lengths of wool to twice as long as you would like the tail to be and knot them together. Knot the short ends around a pencil and make a plait to use for the tail.

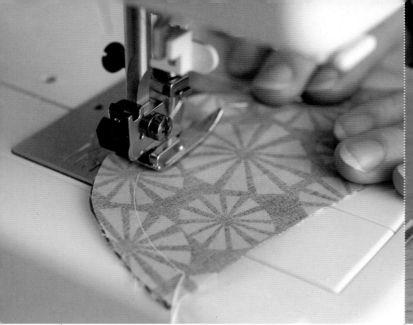

3

Pin the body pieces together, right side to right side. Start sewing 8mm (⅜in) in from the bottom edge. Sew around the curve, stopping 8mm (⅜in) from the end.

4

Tie off the ends and trim the excess fabric to make the seam less bulky once the mouse is turned right side out.

7

Trim off the excess fabric in the seams and turn the mouse right side out, pushing the nose out with your finger. If necessary, use a needle to pull out the tip from the outside.

8

Push small amounts of wadding into the mouse, ensuring that you fill the nose. When it is half stuffed, add dried catnip. Finish stuffing the mouse.

5

Pin the felt base to the long sides of the body pieces, so that the right side of each of the pieces is facing the felt base.

6

Starting from the back end (the slightly raised end) of the mouse, stitch all the way around the sides, attaching the top layer to the base, and stopping 2.5cm (1in) before the end.

9

Insert the tail underneath the back seam, pinning the seam closed. Using small stitches, carefully sew up the opening, securing the tail into position.

10

Bring one cut edge of the ear over the other so that the ear curves inward. Pin in place and stitch down, repeating for the other side. Embroider two black eyes onto the mouse.

Blossom cushion (pp.146-149)

Please enlarge to the required
size on a photocopier

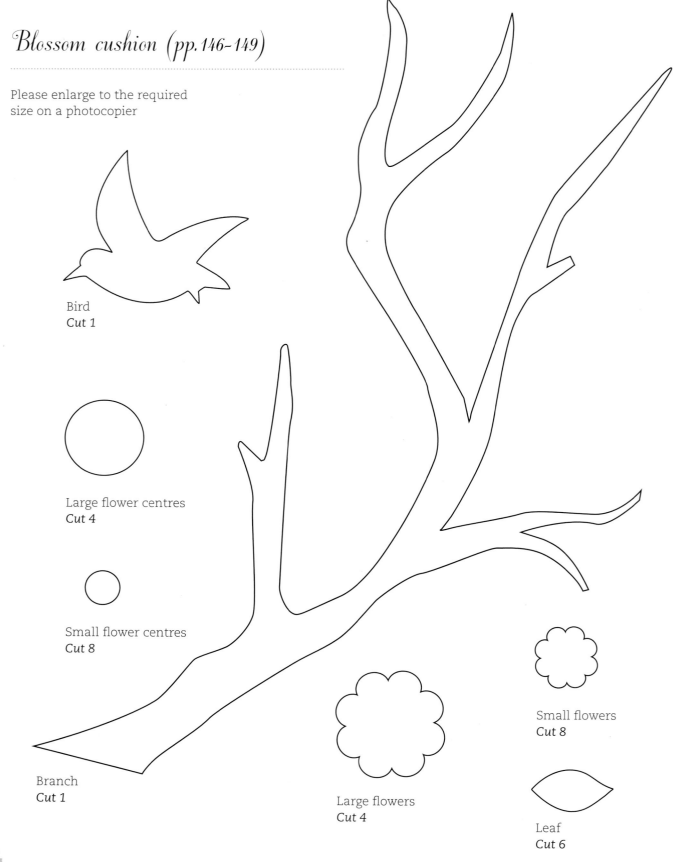

Bird
Cut 1

Large flower centres
Cut 4

Small flower centres
Cut 8

Branch
Cut 1

Large flowers
Cut 4

Small flowers
Cut 8

Leaf
Cut 6

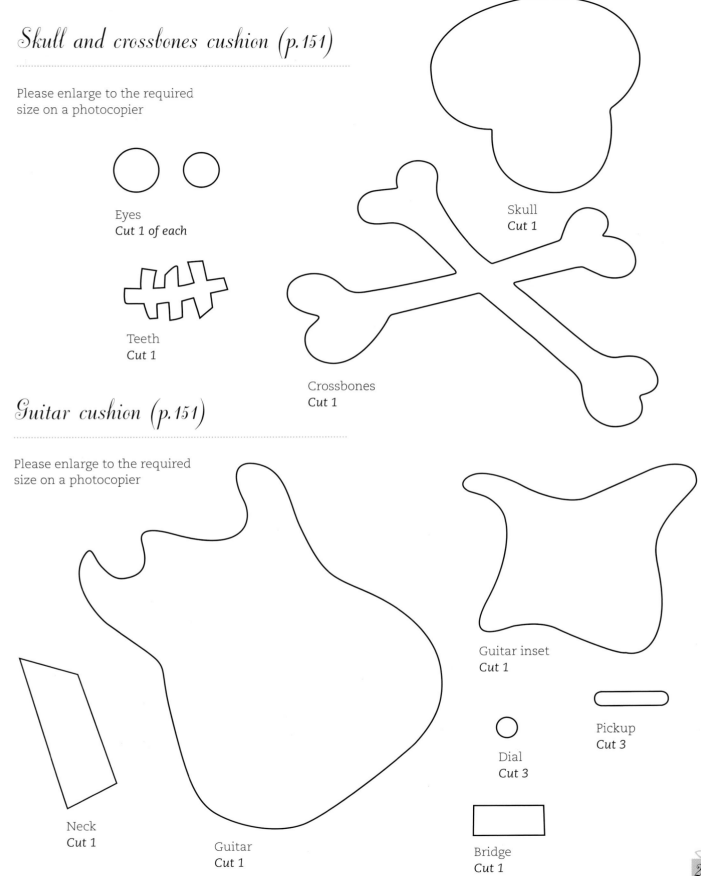

Skull and crossbones cushion (p.151)

Please enlarge to the required size on a photocopier

Eyes
Cut 1 of each

Teeth
Cut 1

Skull
Cut 1

Crossbones
Cut 1

Guitar cushion (p.151)

Please enlarge to the required size on a photocopier

Guitar inset
Cut 1

Dial
Cut 3

Pickup
Cut 3

Neck
Cut 1

Guitar
Cut 1

Bridge
Cut 1

Castle cushion (p.150)

Please enlarge to the required size on a photocopier

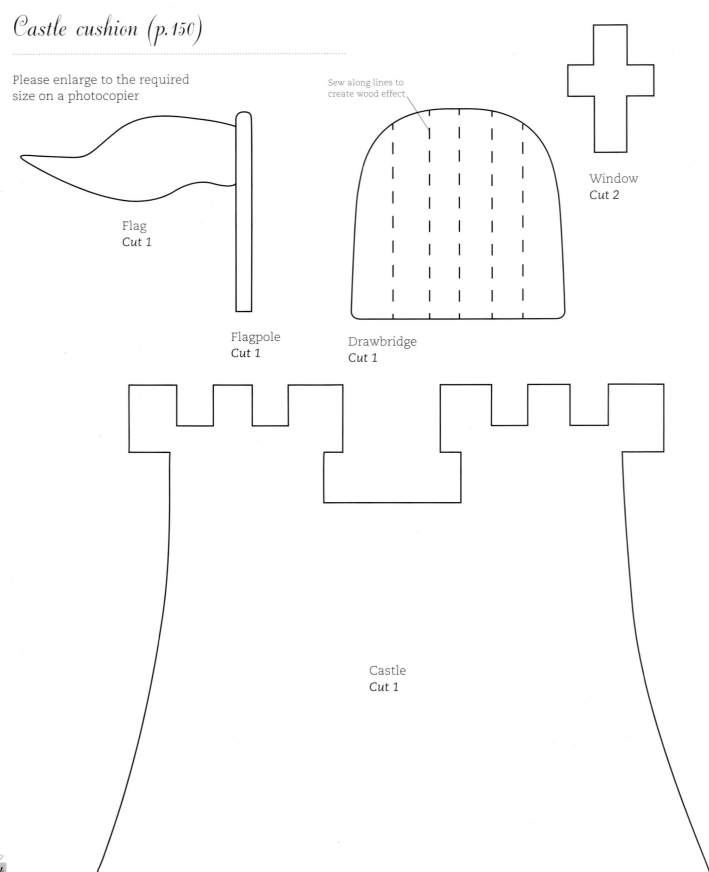

Flag
Cut 1

Flagpole
Cut 1

Sew along lines to create wood effect

Drawbridge
Cut 1

Window
Cut 2

Castle
Cut 1

Castle cushion dolls (p.150)

Please enlarge to the required
size on a photocopier

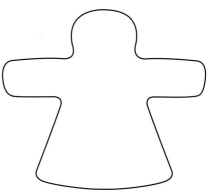

Prince's top
Cut 2
*If making the clothes out of felt, place pieces around doll and
sew together from the outside. If using other fabric, add a seam
allowance, sew together with right sides facing, and turn.*

Princess's dress
Cut 2

Body
Cut 2 for each doll.
*Sew together along
the edges, leaving a
gap. Turn, stuff, and
sew the gap closed.*

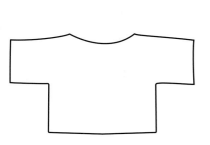

Fold here

Sew along line
through all layers
to make legs

Prince's trousers
Cut 1
Wrap around doll and sew in place.

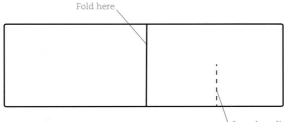

Crown
*Wrap around head
and sew in place.*

Rollaway gameboard (pp.176–181)

Type of fabric	Cut	Measurements in cm and in
Board: dark fabric	x 5	5 x 40cm (2 x 16in)
Board: light fabric	x 5	5 x 40cm (2 x 16in)
Outer fabric	x 1	30 x 50cm (12 x 20in)
Inner fabric	x 2	30 x 14cm (12 x 5¾in)
Inner fabric	x 2	5 x 27cm (2 x 10¾in)
Interfacing	x 1	30 x 50cm (12 x 20in)
Interfacing	x 1	30 x 14cm (12 x 5¾in)

Appliqué pet portrait (pp.207-209)

Please enlarge to the required
size on a photocopier

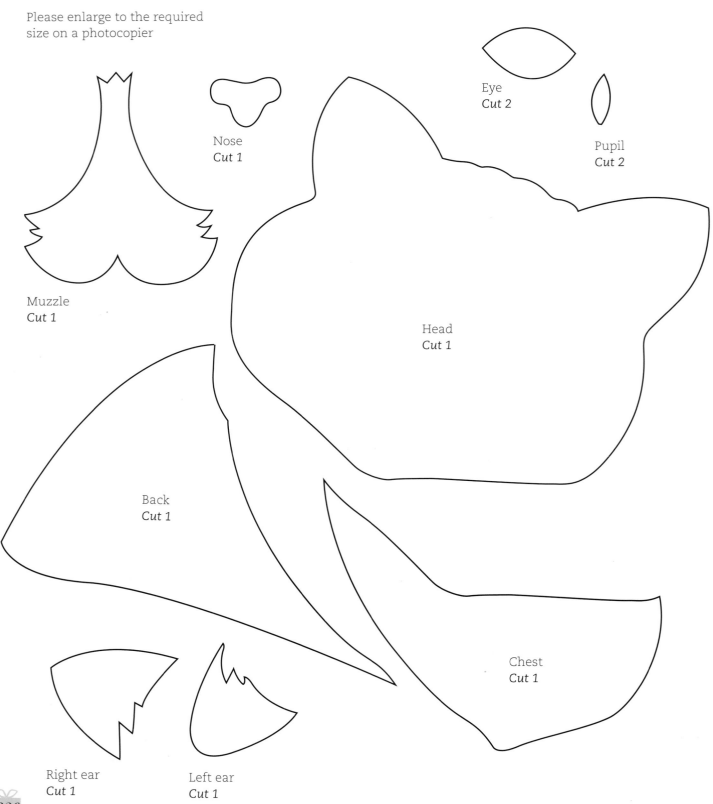

Nose
Cut 1

Eye
Cut 2

Pupil
Cut 2

Muzzle
Cut 1

Head
Cut 1

Back
Cut 1

Chest
Cut 1

Right ear
Cut 1

Left ear
Cut 1

Simple silhouette pet portrait (p.206)

Please enlarge to the required
size on a photocopier

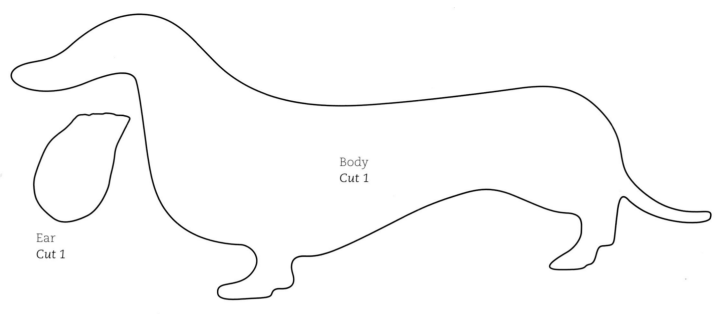

Body
Cut 1

Ear
Cut 1

Catnip mice (pp.218–221)

Please enlarge to the required
size on a photocopier

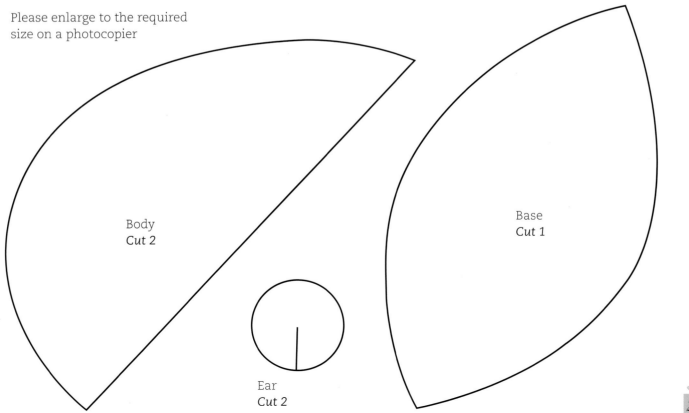

Body
Cut 2

Base
Cut 1

Ear
Cut 2

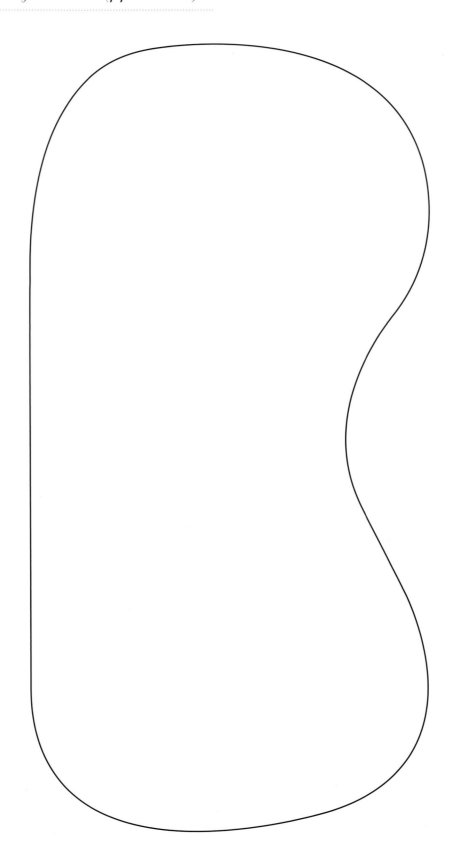

Cat's playmat (pp.214–217)

Please enlarge to the required
size on a photocopier

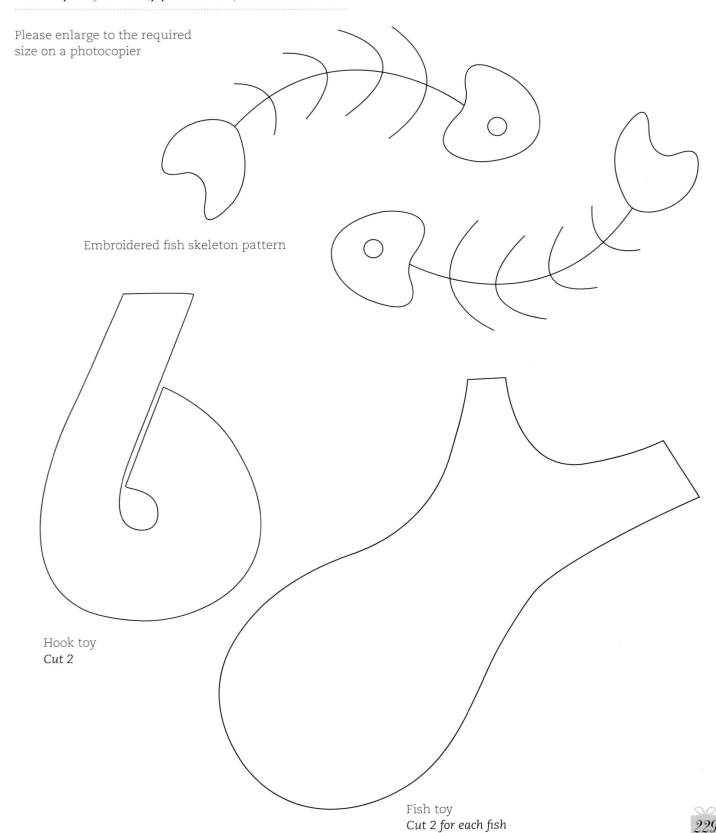

Embroidered fish skeleton pattern

Hook toy
Cut 2

Fish toy
Cut 2 for each fish

Tartan dog jacket (pp.210-213)

Please enlarge to the required
size on a photocopier

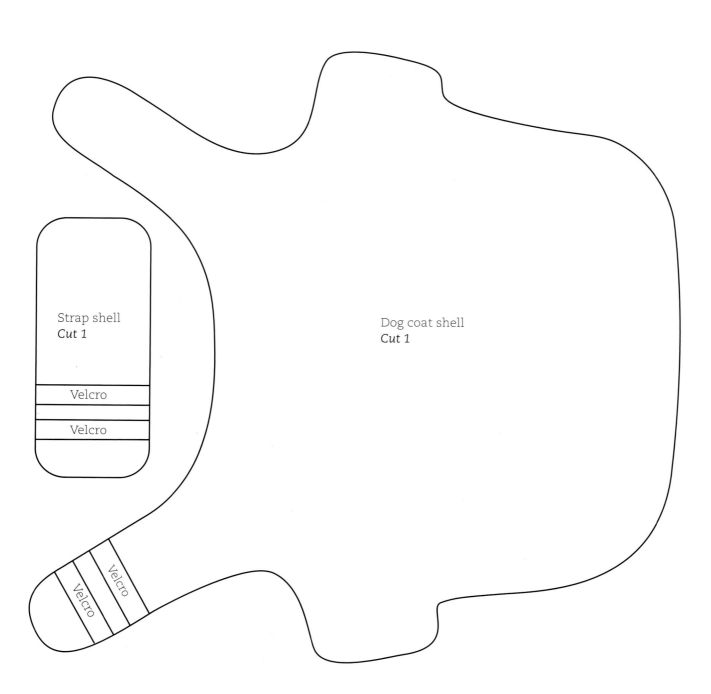

Strap shell
Cut 1

Velcro

Velcro

Dog coat shell
Cut 1

Velcro

Velcro

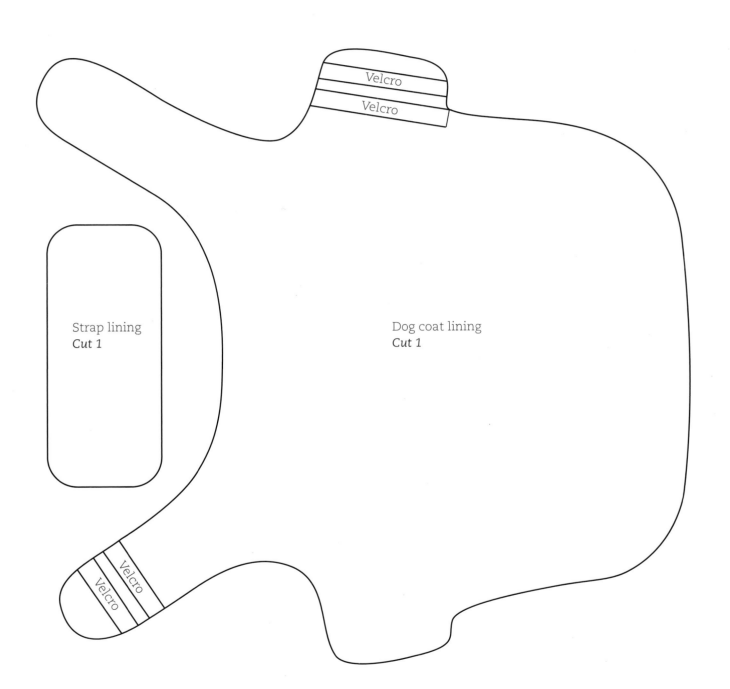

Velcro

Velcro

Strap lining
Cut 1

Dog coat lining
Cut 1

Velcro

Velcro

Ribbon-bound photo album (pp.170-175)

Please enlarge to the required
size on a photocopier

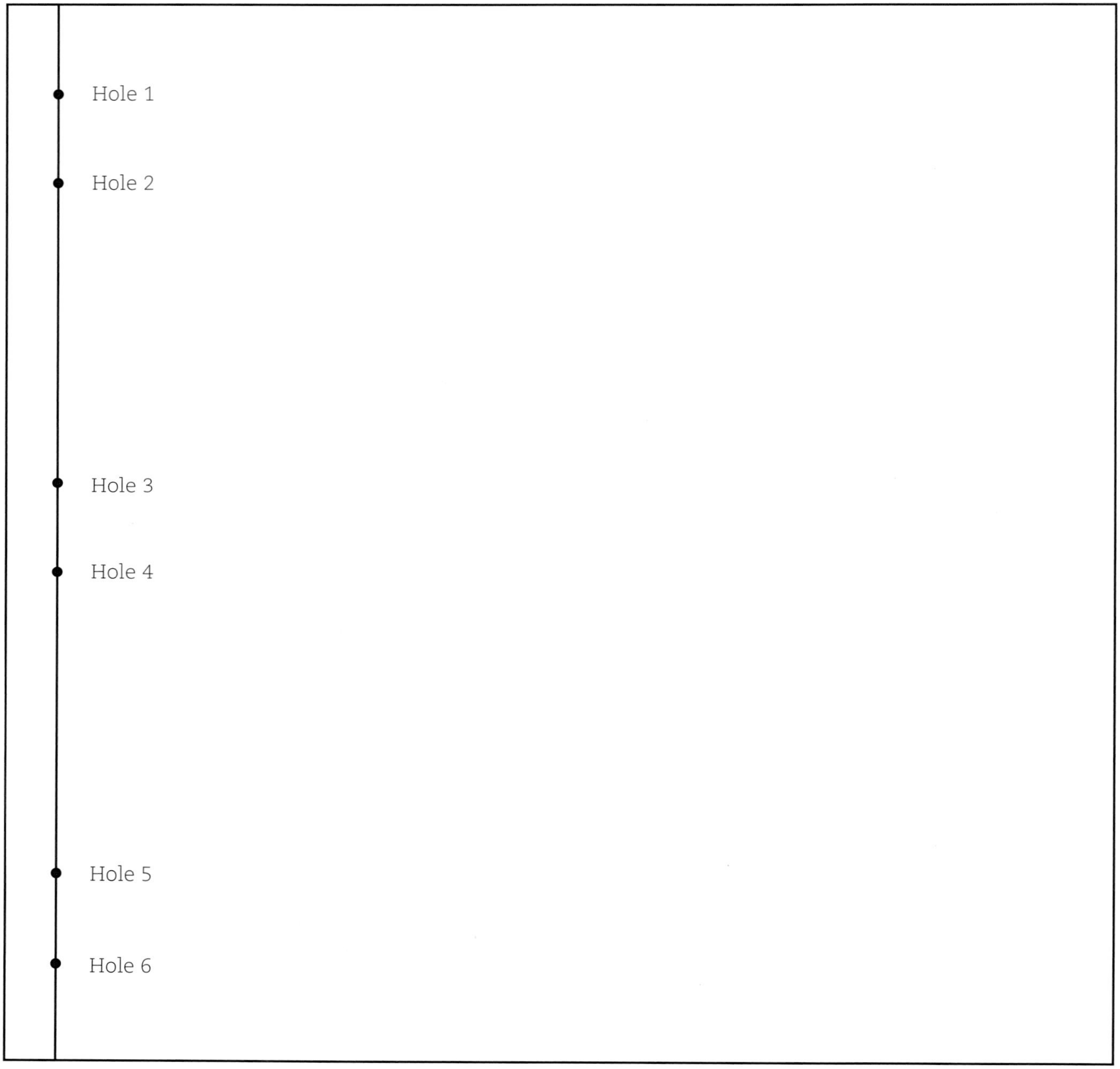

Hole 1

Hole 2

Hole 3

Hole 4

Hole 5

Hole 6

Silver clay jewellery (pp.88-93)

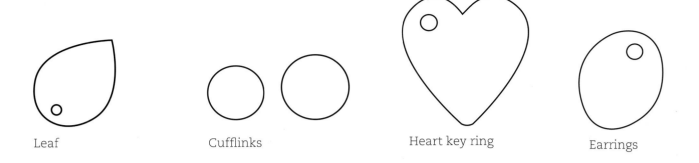

Leaf

Cufflinks

Heart key ring

Earrings

Embellished felt brooches (pp.84-87)

Bird

Wing

Heart

Owl

Face

Belly

Wing

Paisley

Mosaic seaside coasters (p.169)

Mosaic owl jewellery box (p.168)

Top of box

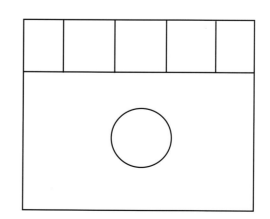

Side of box

Mosaic flower garland mirror (p.168)

Mosaic round tealight holder (p.169)

Please enlarge to the required
size on a photocopier

Dot-decorated mug and coaster set (p.162)

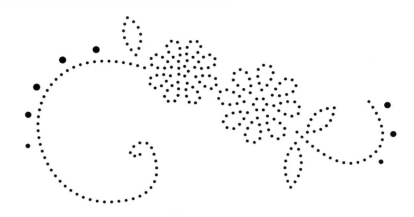

Dot-decorated bunting plate (p.163)

Please enlarge to the required
size on a photocopier

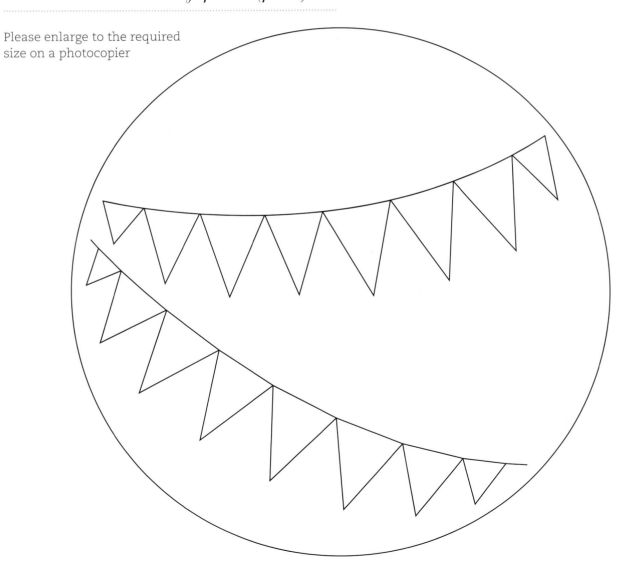

Stencilled bags (pp.182–187)

Please enlarge to the required
size on a photocopier

Stitched bag

Pencil illusion

Repeated chevrons

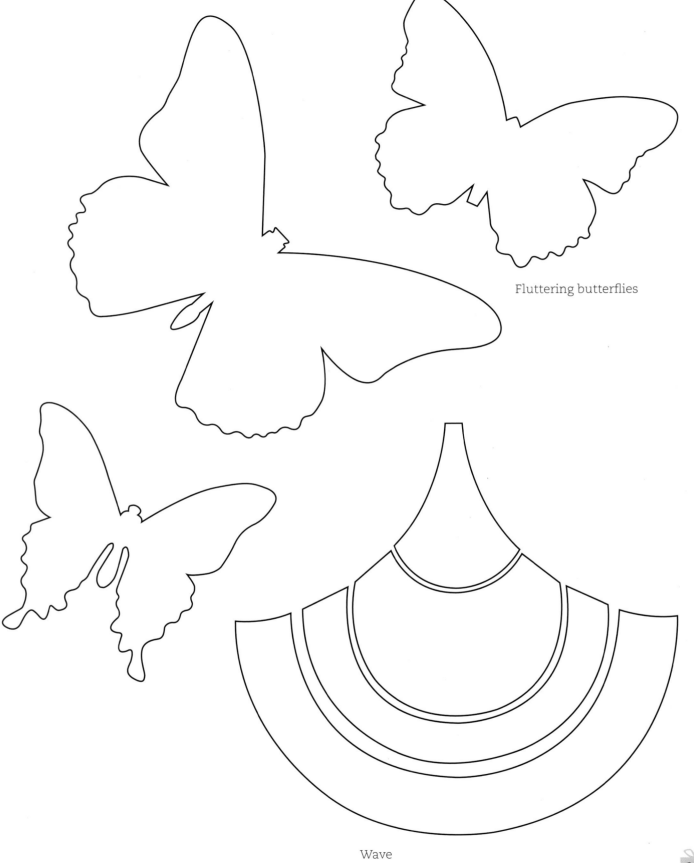

Fluttering butterflies

Wave

Crochet

This chapter is suitable for crocheters of all levels – those with no previous experience, crocheters hoping to improve their technique, or as an excellent reference for anyone with more advanced skills. Crochet guides you through basic techniques and stitches, covering the relevant abbreviations and symbols on the way.

If you're new to crochet, start by familiarizing yourself with the tools and materials. The pages that follow ease you into the essential skills you will need. For example, you will learn the techniques on how to hold the yarn and hook, how to make a slip knot, and how to create a foundation chain. You will then be taken through the most common crochet stitches as well as the "ins-and-outs" of reading crochet patterns.

Once you've mastered these basics, you are free to move through the sections, refining your skills, and practising the techniques that you enjoy the most. A section of beautiful projects to make will inspire you to put your newly honed skills to the test, with the added knowledge of how to finish your item by attaching hooks, eyes, and buttons.

TOOLS AND MATERIALS

To get started with crochet, have a look first at the wonderful variety of yarns available. Crochet can be used to create an astounding range of textiles, from sturdy textures suitable for coats to graceful, alluring lace. It requires very little equipment, so is probably the most economical needlework craft.

YARNS	Any yarn can usually be crocheted into an attractive textile using a small range of hook sizes, each of which produces a slightly looser or slightly tighter fabric that holds its shape well.

SMOOTH WOOL YARNS

‹‹ WOOL YARN WEIGHTS
Super-fine, fine, and lightweight wool yarns work best for crochet garments; the thicker yarns are only suitable for blankets. (A full explanation of yarn weights is given on page 245.)

SYNTHETIC YARNS
Many synthetic fibre yarns or synthetic and natural fibre mixes are very good imitations of pure wool. So if you are looking for a less expensive alternative to wool, try some of these out. They do not age as well as wool, but they are easy to care for.

SMOOTH COTTON YARNS

FINE-WEIGHT COTTON YARNS ››
This thicker yarn is a good weight for garments and accessories and will show the texture of stitch patterns clearly.

COTTON CROCHET THREADS ››
Traditionally, crochet was worked in cotton threads that were suitable for lace. Today cotton threads are still used for lace edgings and filet crochet (see pages 284–285 and pages 268–269).

MULTICOLOURED YARNS

"SOCK" YARN
"Sock" yarn is a spaced-dyed yarn originally designed for knitting socks – as the sock is knitted the yarn changes colour along its length and forms patterns. The fine-weight versions of this type of multicoloured yarn can be used for crochet as well, to produce interesting effects.

⪼ VARIEGATED YARN
Yarns flecked with different colours or dyed different colours along the length of one strand are useful for achieving multicoloured effects without needing to change yarn or colours.

TEXTURED AND NOVELTY YARNS

⪼ METALLIC THREAD
A fine, metallic thread is ideally suited to openwork crochet for evening shawls and scarves.

FINE MOHAIR YARN ⪼
This textured yarn will produce a tactile crocheted piece, partially obscuring the stitches.

TEXTURED NOVELTY YARNS
Highly textured yarns, such as bouclés and shaggy "fur" yarns are difficult to crochet with, so stick to simple double crochet when using them. They obscure the crochet stitches and produce an allover textured-effect fabric.

UNUSUAL YARNS

⪼ COLOURED WIRE
Thin 0.3mm (28 gauge) wire is flexible enough to work in crochet for jewellery.

STRING ⪼
Ideal for crocheting bags and containers, string is available in many colours and thicknesses.

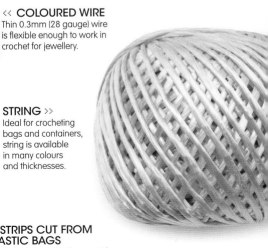

⪼ STRIPS CUT FROM PLASTIC BAGS
Crochet works well with unusual materials, such as strips of plastic, for making items with simple double crochet stitches.

FABRIC STRIPS ⪻
Fabric strips can be crocheted to produce household items and accessories.

YARN
PUT-UPS

A yarn "put-up" is a specific quantity of yarn packaged for sale. The most common put-ups for yarns are balls, hanks, and skeins. You can also buy bigger put-ups in cones, although these are more commonly sold for machine knitting than for crochet.

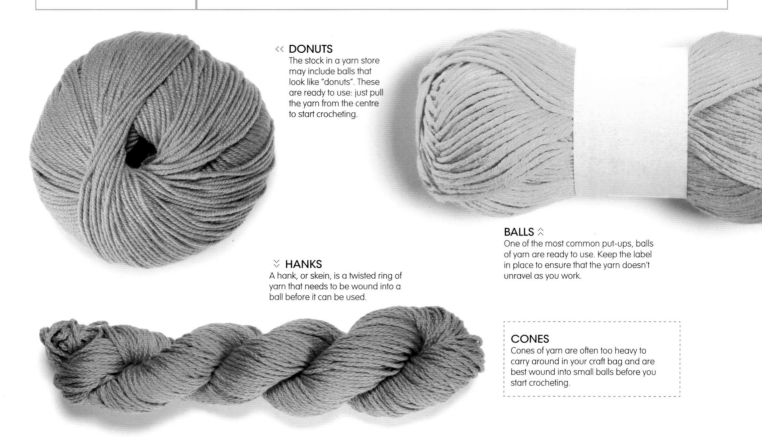

‹‹ DONUTS
The stock in a yarn store may include balls that look like "donuts". These are ready to use: just pull the yarn from the centre to start crocheting.

BALLS ⌃
One of the most common put-ups, balls of yarn are ready to use. Keep the label in place to ensure that the yarn doesn't unravel as you work.

⌄ HANKS
A hank, or skein, is a twisted ring of yarn that needs to be wound into a ball before it can be used.

CONES
Cones of yarn are often too heavy to carry around in your craft bag and are best wound into small balls before you start crocheting.

YARN
LABELS

Yarn put-ups are most commonly packaged with a label that provides you with all the information you need to crochet successfully. Before you buy, always read the label carefully to establish the type of yarn, suggested hook size, care instructions, and ball length.

READING A YARN LABEL ››
Decide whether you require an easy-care yarn and check the care instructions. Fibre content will indicate whether the yarn is synthetic or a synthetic mix, or 100 per cent natural, each giving a different effect as it ages. The ball length will enable you to calculate how many balls are required when you are substituting yarn (see opposite page). Check the dye-lot number if you are purchasing several balls, as variations in colour can occur across different dye-lots.

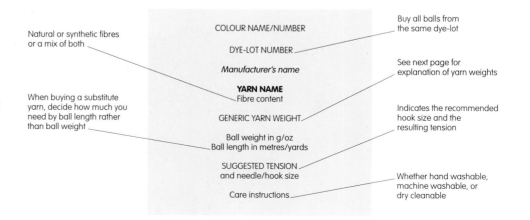

Natural or synthetic fibres or a mix of both

When buying a substitute yarn, decide how much you need by ball length rather than ball weight

COLOUR NAME/NUMBER

DYE-LOT NUMBER

Manufacturer's name

YARN NAME
Fibre content

GENERIC YARN WEIGHT

Ball weight in g/oz
Ball length in metres/yards

SUGGESTED TENSION
and needle/hook size

Care instructions

Buy all balls from the same dye-lot

See next page for explanation of yarn weights

Indicates the recommended hook size and the resulting tension

Whether hand washable, machine washable, or dry cleanable

YARN WEIGHTS

• **The yarn "weight"** refers to the thickness of a yarn. Some yarns are spun by manufacturers to fall into what are considered as "standard" yarn weights, such as US sport or worsted and UK double-knitting and aran. These standard weights have long histories and will probably be around for some time to come. However, even within these "standard" weights there is slight variation in thickness, and textured novelty yarns are not easy to categorize by thickness alone.

• **Visual yarn thickness** is only one indicator of a yarn-weight category. A yarn can look thicker than another yarn purely because of its loft, the air between the fibres, and the springiness of the strands. By pulling a strand between your two hands you can see how much it has by how much the thickness diminishes when the yarn is stretched. The ply is not an indication of yarn thickness.

Plies are the strands spun together around each other to form the yarn. A yarn with four plies can be very thick or very thin depending on the thickness of each individual ply.

• **In order to help crocheters** attempting to match like for like when looking for a substitute yarn for their pattern, the Craft Yarn Council of America has devised a table of yarn weights. This table (below) demonstrates how to find the perfect yarn substitute if you are unable to purchase the yarn specified in a crochet pattern. The very best indication of a yarn weight is the manufacturer's recommended tension and hook size for the yarn. (These recommendation will produce a fabric that is loose enough to be soft and flexible but not so loose that it loses its shape.) Two yarns with the same fibre content and the same recommended tension and hook size will be perfect substitutes for each other.

STANDARD YARN-WEIGHT SYSTEM

YARN WEIGHT SYMBOL & CATEGORY NAMES	0 LACE	1 SUPER FINE	2 FINE	3 LIGHT	4 MEDIUM	5 BULKY	6 SUPER BULKY
Types of yarns in category	Fingering, 10-count crochet thread	Sock, baby, fingering, UK "4-ply"	Sport, baby	Double knitting, light worsted	Worsted, afghan, aran	Chunky, craft, rug	Bulky, roving
Crochet tension ranges in dc to 10cm/4in	32–42 trebles	21–32 sts	16–20 sts	12–17 sts	11–14 sts	8–11 sts	5–9 sts
Recommended hook in metric size range	1.6–2.25mm	2.25–3.5mm	3.5–4.5mm	4.5–5.5mm	5.5–6.5mm	6.5–9mm	9mm and larger
Recommended hook in US size range	6 steel, 7 steel, 8 steel, B-1	B-1 to E-4	E-4 to 7	7 to I-9	I-9 to K-10½	K-10½ to M-13	M-13 and larger

GUIDELINES ONLY The above reflect the most commonly used tensions and hook sizes for specific yarn categories. The categories of yarn, tension ranges, and recommended hook sizes have been devised by the Craft Yarn Council of America (YarnStandards.com).

4mm (UK 8/ US G-6)

Recommended crochet hook size

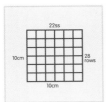

22ss
10cm
28 rows
10cm

Tension over a 10cm (4in) test square

SHADE/ COLOUR
520

Shade/colour number

DYE LOT NUMBER
313

Dye lot number

50g
NETT AT STANDARD CONDITION IN ACCORDANCE WITH BS984

Weight of ball or skein

100%
WOOL

Fibre content

CROCHET
HOOKS

If you are a beginner, start learning to crochet with a good-quality standard metal crochet hook. Once you know how to work the basic stitches with a lightweight wool yarn and a 4.5mm (US size 7) hook, branch out and try some other types of hooks in order to find the one that suits you best.

STANDARD METAL HOOK

Hook tip

Throat

Hook lip

Shank

Thumb rest

Handle

PARTS OF A CROCHET HOOK ⌇
The hook lip grabs the yarn to form the loops and the shank determines the size of the loop. The crochet handle gives weight to the tool and enhances a good grip.

ALTERNATIVE HOOK HANDLES

COMFORT HANDLE ⟩⟩
Hook handles come in different shapes. If you find the standard crochet hook uncomfortable to hold because it is too narrow, investigate hooks with alternative handles. This is a high-quality Japanese hook designed and refined especially for comfort and good grip.

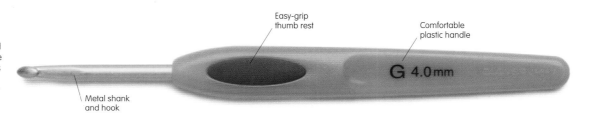

Easy-grip thumb rest

Comfortable plastic handle

Metal shank and hook

G 4.0 mm

HOOK TYPES

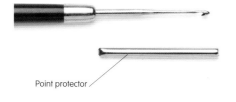

Point protector

⟨⟨ **LACE HOOK**
Because lace crochet hooks are so fine, ranging from 0.6mm (US size 14 steel) to 1.75mm (US size 5 steel), they are always manufactured in metal. Keep them with their metal point protectors in place to avoid accidents.

JUMBO HOOKS ⌇
The largest crochet hook sizes – from a 10mm (US size N-15) to a 20mm (US size S) are made in plastic. They are used for making thick crochet fabric very quickly.

⟨⟨ **METAL HOOKS**
Some ranges of aluminium hooks are available in bright colours – a different colour for each size, which is handy for picking up the right size at a glance.

HOOK SIZES

Crochet hooks are manufactured in the various sizes (diameters) listed in the hook conversion chart on the opposite page. The millimetre sizes are the diameters of the hook shank, which determines the size of the crochet stitches.

⟨⟨ **WOODEN HOOKS**
Hardwood and bamboo hooks are very attractive and lighter in weight than metal hooks. They also provide a good grip to prevent your fingers slipping when crocheting.

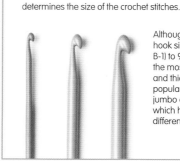

Although the middle range of hook sizes – from 2mm (US size B-1) to 9mm (US size M-13) – are the most commonly used, the finer and thicker hooks are also very popular for lace crochet and jumbo crochet. See page 15 for which hook size to use with the different yarn weights.

⟨⟨ **PLASTIC HOOKS**
Plastic hooks are not as precisely made as metal and wooden hooks, but they come in great colours, so are enjoyable to work with.

CONVERSION CHART

This chart gives the conversions between the various hook-size systems. Where there are no exact conversions possible the nearest equivalent is given.

EU METRIC	US SIZES	OLD UK
0.6mm	14 steel	
0.75mm	12 steel	
1mm	11 steel	
1.25mm	7 steel	
1.5mm	6 steel	
1.75mm	5 steel	
2mm		14
2.25mm	B-1	
2.5mm		12
2.75mm	C-2	
3mm		10
3.25mm	D-3	
3.5mm	E-4	9
3.75mm	F-5	
4mm	G-6	8
4.5mm	7	7
5mm	H-8	6
5.5mm	I-9	5
6mm	J-10	4
6.5mm	K-10½	3
7mm		2
8mm	L-11	
9mm	M-13	
10mm	N-15	
12mm	P	
15mm	Q (16mm)	
20mm	S (19mm)	

OTHER EQUIPMENT

To get started you only need a crochet hook and a blunt-ended yarn needle. You may have some of the other essentials in your sewing kit already.

THE ESSENTIALS

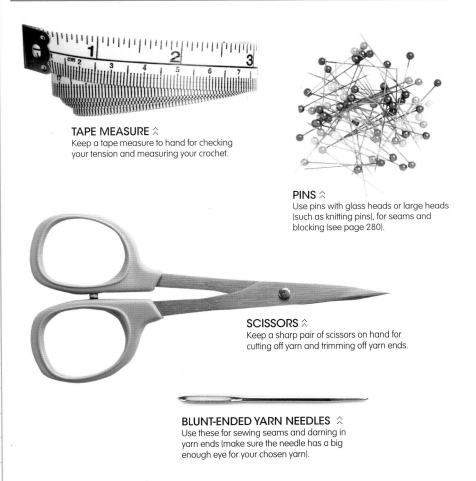

TAPE MEASURE ⚓
Keep a tape measure to hand for checking your tension and measuring your crochet.

PINS ⚓
Use pins with glass heads or large heads (such as knitting pins), for seams and blocking (see page 280).

SCISSORS ⚓
Keep a sharp pair of scissors on hand for cutting off yarn and trimming off yarn ends.

BLUNT-ENDED YARN NEEDLES ⚓
Use these for sewing seams and darning in yarn ends (make sure the needle has a big enough eye for your chosen yarn).

HANDY EXTRAS

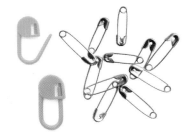

ROW COUNTER ⚓
These are useful for keeping track of where you are in your crochet. String on a length of cotton yarn and hang it around your neck – change it each time you complete a row.

YARN BOBBINS ⚓
Useful for holding short lengths of yarn for jacquard crochet.

STITCH MARKERS ⚓
These can be hooked onto the crochet to mark a specific row or a specific stitch in the row, or to mark the right-side of your crochet.

BASIC STITCHES

Learning to crochet takes a little longer than learning to knit because there are several basic stitches to master. But there is no need to learn all the stitches at once. With only chain stitches and double crochet at your disposal, you can make attractive striped blankets and cushion covers in luscious yarns.

GETTING STARTED

Before making your first loop, the slip knot (see opposite page), get to know your hook and how to hold it. First, review the detailed explanation of the parts of the hook on page 246. Then try out the various hook- and yarn-holding techniques below when learning how to make chain stitches. If you ever learned crochet as a child, you will automatically hold the hook the way you originally learned to, and you should stick to this whether it is the pencil or knife position.

HOLDING THE HOOK

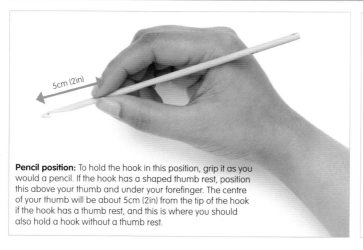

5cm (2in)

Pencil position: To hold the hook in this position, grip it as you would a pencil. If the hook has a shaped thumb rest, position this above your thumb and under your forefinger. The centre of your thumb will be about 5cm (2in) from the tip of the hook if the hook has a thumb rest, and this is where you should also hold a hook without a thumb rest.

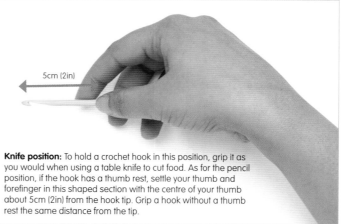

5cm (2in)

Knife position: To hold a crochet hook in this position, grip it as you would when using a table knife to cut food. As for the pencil position, if the hook has a thumb rest, settle your thumb and forefinger in this shaped section with the centre of your thumb about 5cm (2in) from the hook tip. Grip a hook without a thumb rest the same distance from the tip.

HOLDING THE YARN

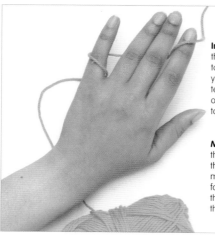

In order to control the flow of the yarn to your hook, you need to lace it around the fingers of your free hand. Both of the techniques shown here are only suggestions, so feel free to develop your own.

Method one: Start by winding the yarn around your little finger, then pass it under your two middle fingers and over your forefinger. With this method the forefinger is used to position the yarn.

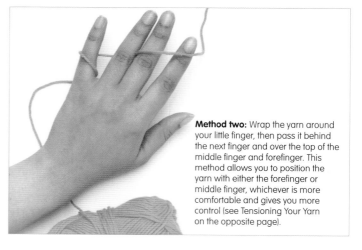

Method two: Wrap the yarn around your little finger, then pass it behind the next finger and over the top of the middle finger and forefinger. This method allows you to position the yarn with either the forefinger or middle finger, whichever is more comfortable and gives you more control (see Tensioning Your Yarn on the opposite page).

MAKING A SLIP KNOT

1 To make the first loop (called the slip knot) on your needle, begin by crossing the yarn coming from the ball over the yarn end (called the yarn tail) to form a circle of yarn.

Yarn coming from ball

Yarn tail

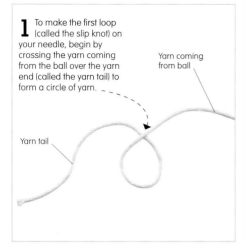

2 Insert the tip of the hook through the circle of yarn.

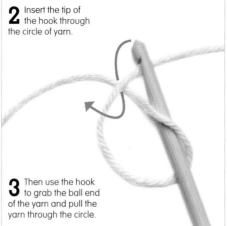

3 Then use the hook to grab the ball end of the yarn and pull the yarn through the circle.

4 This forms a loop on the hook and a loose, open knot below the loop.

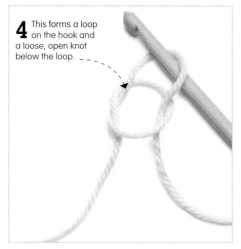

5 Pull both ends of the yarn firmly to tighten the knot and the loop around the shank of the hook.

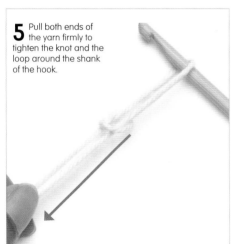

6 Make sure the completed slip knot is tight enough on the hook that it won't fall off but not so tight that you can barely slide it along the hook's shank.

Make sure loop is secure but slides easily

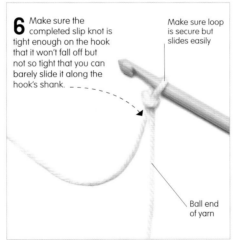

Ball end of yarn

7 The yarn tail on the slip knot should be at least 15cm (6in) long so it can be threaded onto a blunt-ended yarn needle and darned in later. However, a crochet pattern may instruct you to leave an extra-long yarn tail (called a long loose end) to use for seams or other purposes.

Extra-long yarn tail

TENSIONING YOUR YARN

1 With your slip knot on your hook, try out some yarn holding techniques. Wrap the yarn around your little finger and then lace it through your other fingers as desired, but so that it ends up over the tip of your forefinger (or your forefinger and middle finger).

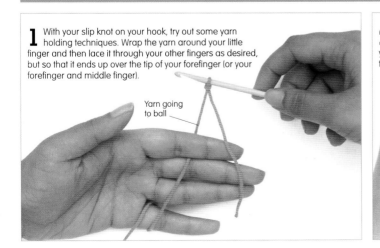

Yarn going to ball

2 As you crochet, grip the yarn tightly with your little finger and ring finger and release it gently as you form the loops. Use either your forefinger or your middle finger to position the yarn, and hold the base of the crochet close to the hook to keep it in place as the hook is drawn through the loops.

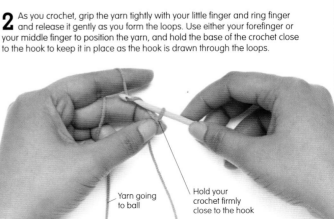

Yarn going to ball

Hold your crochet firmly close to the hook

# CHAIN STITCHES
Abbreviation = *ch*

Chain stitches are the first crochet stitches you need to learn because they form the base for all other stitches – called a foundation chain. They are used in combination with other basic stitches to create a vast array of crochet stitch patterns, both dense textured stitches and lacy ones. Practise chain stitches until you are comfortable holding a hook and releasing and tensioning yarn.

MAKING A FOUNDATION CHAIN

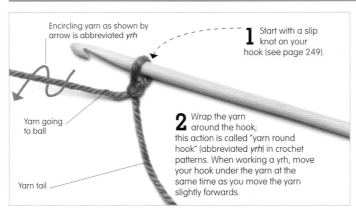

Encircling yarn as shown by arrow is abbreviated *yrh*

1 Start with a slip knot on your hook (see page 249).

Yarn going to ball

Yarn tail

2 Wrap the yarn around the hook; this action is called "yarn round hook" (abbreviated *yrh*) in crochet patterns. When working a yrh, move your hook under the yarn at the same time as you move the yarn slightly forwards.

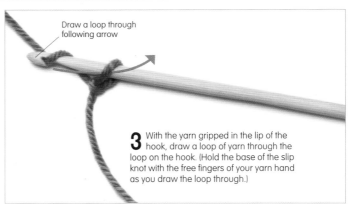

Draw a loop through following arrow

3 With the yarn gripped in the lip of the hook, draw a loop of yarn through the loop on the hook. (Hold the base of the slip knot with the free fingers of your yarn hand as you draw the loop through.)

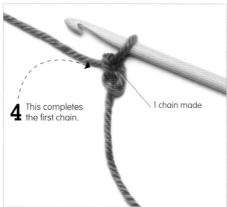

4 This completes the first chain.

1 chain made

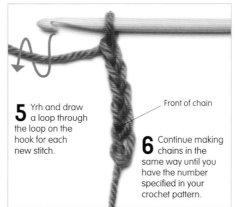

5 Yrh and draw a loop through the loop on the hook for each new stitch.

Front of chain

6 Continue making chains in the same way until you have the number specified in your crochet pattern.

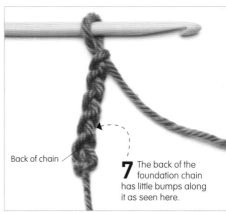

Back of chain

7 The back of the foundation chain has little bumps along it as seen here.

COUNTING CHAIN STITCHES

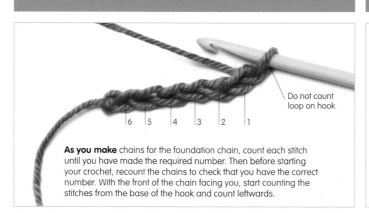

Do not count loop on hook

6 5 4 3 2 1

As you make chains for the foundation chain, count each stitch until you have made the required number. Then before starting your crochet, recount the chains to check that you have the correct number. With the front of the chain facing you, start counting the stitches from the base of the hook and count leftwards.

SIMPLE CHAIN STITCH NECKLACE

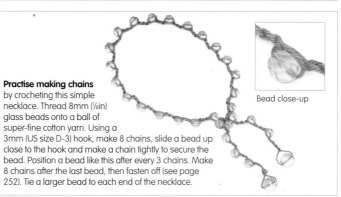

Bead close-up

Practise making chains by crocheting this simple necklace. Thread 8mm (⅓in) glass beads onto a ball of super-fine cotton yarn. Using a 3mm (US size D-3) hook, make 8 chains, slide a bead up close to the hook and make a chain tightly to secure the bead. Position a bead like this after every 3 chains. Make 8 chains after the last bead, then fasten off (see page 252). Tie a larger bead to each end of the necklace.

# SLIP STITCH
Abbreviation = *ss*

Slip stitches are the shortest of all the crochet stitches. Although they can be worked in rows, the resulting fabric is so dense that it is only really suitable for bag handles. However, slip stitches appear very frequently in crochet instructions – to join in new yarn (see page 257), to work invisibly along the top of a row to move to a new position (see page 279), and to join rounds in circular crochet.

WORKING SLIP STITCH AS A FABRIC

1 Make a foundation chain of the required length. To begin the first stitch, insert the hook through the second chain from the hook, passing the hook under only one strand of the chain. Then wrap the yarn around the hook (yrh).

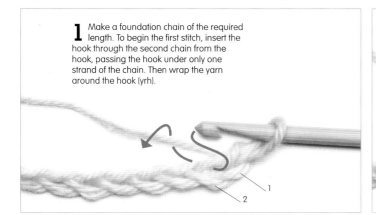

2 Holding the base of the chain firmly with the fingers of your left hand and tensioning the yarn (see page 249), draw a loop back through the chain and through the loop on the hook as shown by the large arrow.

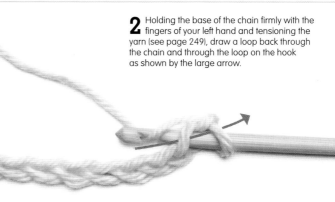

3 Continue across the foundation chain, working a slip stitch into each chain in the same way. Always work slip stitches fairly loosely for whatever purpose you are using them.

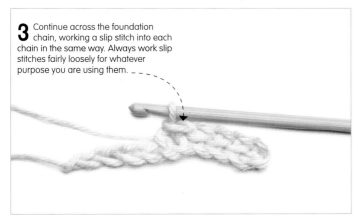

4 After the last stitch of the row has been completed, and if you want to work another row, turn your crochet to position the yarn at the right edge of the piece of crochet ready to begin the second row.

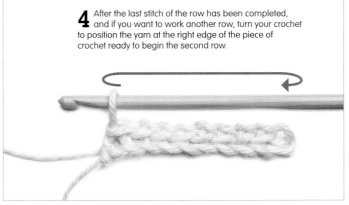

5 To begin a second row of slip stitches, make one chain stitch. This chain is called the turning chain.

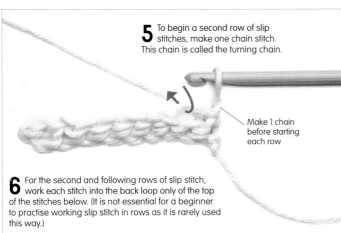

Make 1 chain before starting each row

6 For the second and following rows of slip stitch, work each stitch into the back loop only of the top of the stitches below. (It is not essential for a beginner to practise working slip stitch in rows as it is rarely used this way.)

USING SLIP STITCHES TO FORM A FOUNDATION RING

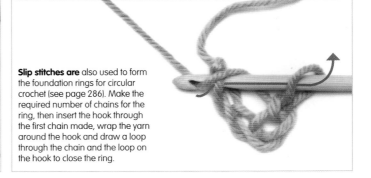

Slip stitches are also used to form the foundation rings for circular crochet (see page 286). Make the required number of chains for the ring, then insert the hook through the first chain made, wrap the yarn around the hook and draw a loop through the chain and the loop on the hook to close the ring.

FASTENING OFF
CHAINS AND SLIP STITCHES

Stopping your crochet when it is complete is called fastening off. As there is only one loop on your hook, the process is extremely simple, much quicker and easier than casting off stitches in knitting! Here is a visual aid for how to fasten off a length of chains or a row of slip stitches. The principle is the same for all stitches.

FASTENING OFF A LENGTH OF CHAINS

1 Remove the loop from the hook.

2 Pull out the loop to enlarge it so that it does not start to unravel.

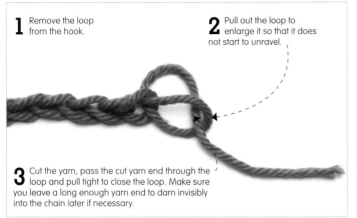

3 Cut the yarn, pass the cut yarn end through the loop and pull tight to close the loop. Make sure you leave a long enough yarn end to darn invisibly into the chain later if necessary.

FASTENING OFF SLIP STITCHES

Fasten off in the same way as for the chain stitches. Alternatively, you can use the hook to draw the cut end through the remaining loop as shown here by the large arrow.

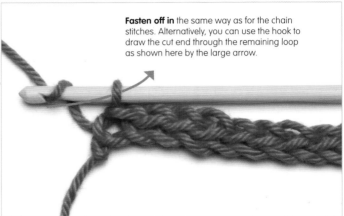

DOUBLE
CROCHET
Abbreviation = dc

Double crochet is the easiest crochet stitch to learn and the one crocheters use most frequently, either on its own or in combination with other stitches. Take your time learning and practising the stitch, because once you become proficient in double crochet the taller stitches will be much easier to master. It forms a dense fabric that is suitable for many types of garments and accessories. It is also the stitch used for toys and containers because it can be worked tightly to form a stiff, firm textile.

When double crochet is worked back and forth in rows, it looks identical on both sides. Worked in the round it looks different on the right and wrong sides, which you can see on page 286.

1 Make a foundation chain of the required length (see page 250).

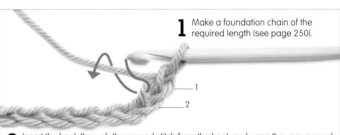

2 Insert the hook through the second stitch from the hook and wrap the yarn around the hook (yrh) following the large arrow. (You can insert the hook under one or two strands of the chain, but working under just one loop as shown here is easiest.)

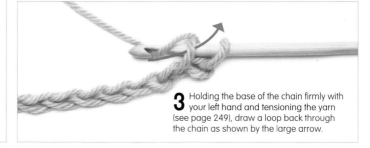

3 Holding the base of the chain firmly with your left hand and tensioning the yarn (see page 249), draw a loop back through the chain as shown by the large arrow.

4 There are now 2 loops on the hook. Next, yrh as shown by the large arrow.

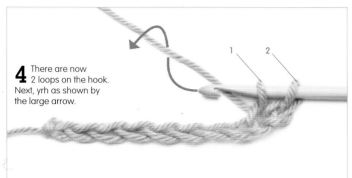

5 Draw a loop through both loops on the hook in one smooth action. As you use the yarn, allow it to flow through the fingers of your left hand while still tensioning it firmly.

6 This completes the first double crochet. The missed chain at the beginning of this first row does NOT count as a stitch on its own (in other words it is not counted when you count how many stitches are in the row and it is not worked into in the next row).

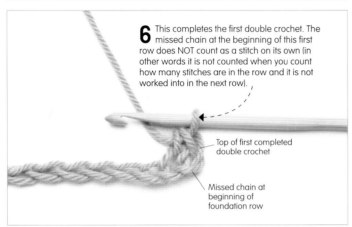

Top of first completed double crochet

Missed chain at beginning of foundation row

7 Continue across the foundation chain, working one double crochet into each chain in the same way.

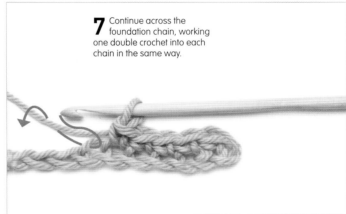

8 At the end of the row, turn your crochet to position the yarn at the right edge of the piece of crochet, ready to begin the second row.

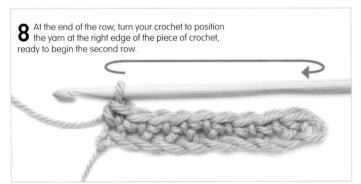

9 To begin the second row, make one chain stitch. This chain is called the turning chain, and it brings the work up to the height of the double crochet stitches that will follow.

1-chain turning chain does NOT count as first stitch of row

10 Work the first double crochet into the top of the first stitch in the row below. Work a double crochet into the top of each of the remaining double crochets in the row below.

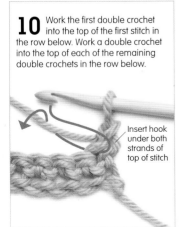

Insert hook under both strands of top of stitch

11 At the end of the row, work the last stitch into the top of the last double crochet of the row below. Work following rows as for the second row.

12 When you have completed your crochet, cut the yarn leaving a long loose end – at least 15cm (6in) long.

13 Remove the hook from the remaining loop, pass the yarn end through the loop and pull tight to close it. Fastening off like this is done the same way for all crochet stitches.

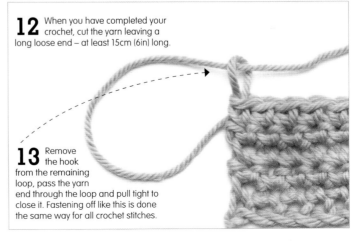

HALF TREBLE
CROCHET
Abbreviation = htr

After slip stitches and double crochet, half treble crochet comes next in order of stitch heights. It is firm like double crochet and fairly dense, but produces a slightly softer texture, which makes it ideal for warm baby garments. Don't attempt to learn how to work half trebles until you make double crochet stitches with confidence.

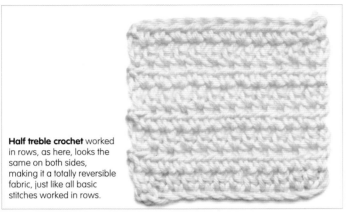

Half treble crochet worked in rows, as here, looks the same on both sides, making it a totally reversible fabric, just like all basic stitches worked in rows.

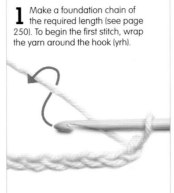

1 Make a foundation chain of the required length (see page 250). To begin the first stitch, wrap the yarn around the hook (yrh).

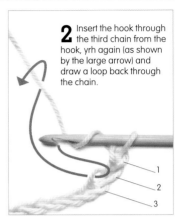

2 Insert the hook through the third chain from the hook, yrh again (as shown by the large arrow) and draw a loop back through the chain.

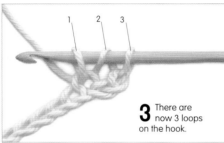

3 There are now 3 loops on the hook.

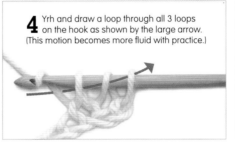

4 Yrh and draw a loop through all 3 loops on the hook as shown by the large arrow. (This motion becomes more fluid with practice.)

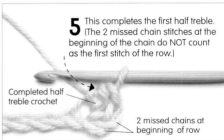

5 This completes the first half treble. (The 2 missed chain stitches at the beginning of the chain do NOT count as the first stitch of the row.)

Completed half treble crochet

2 missed chains at beginning of row

6 Work one half treble crochet into each chain in the same way. Remember to start each half treble by wrapping the yarn around the hook before inserting it through the chain.

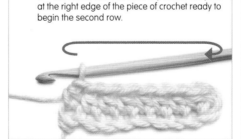

7 After working a half treble crochet into the last chain, turn the work to position the yarn at the right edge of the piece of crochet ready to begin the second row.

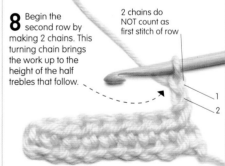

8 Begin the second row by making 2 chains. This turning chain brings the work up to the height of the half trebles that follow.

2 chains do NOT count as first stitch of row

9 Yrh and work the first half treble into the top of the first stitch in the row below.

Insert hook under both strands of top of stitch

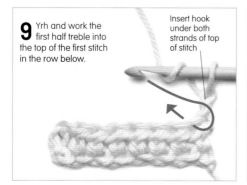

10 Work a half treble into each of the remaining half treble crochets in the row below. Work the following rows as for the second row.

Top of last half treble crochet of previous row

Leave an end at least 15cm (6in) long, so it can be darned in later

11 When the crochet is complete, cut the yarn. Remove the hook from the remaining loop, pass the yarn end through the loop and pull tight to close the loop and fasten off securely.

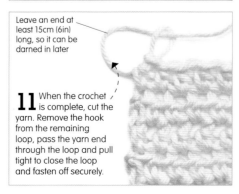

TREBLE CROCHET
Abbreviation = tr

Treble crochet produces a more open and softer crochet fabric than the denser double and half treble crochet. Because treble crochet is a tall stitch, the fabric grows quickly as you proceed, which makes it the most popular of all crochet stitches.

As you work treble crochet in rows, you will see that it looks identical on the front and the back.

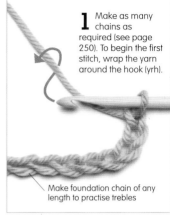

1 Make as many chains as required (see page 250). To begin the first stitch, wrap the yarn around the hook (yrh).

Make foundation chain of any length to practise trebles

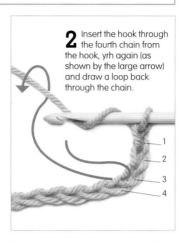

2 Insert the hook through the fourth chain from the hook, yrh again (as shown by the large arrow) and draw a loop back through the chain.

1
2
3
4

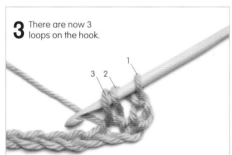

3 There are now 3 loops on the hook.

3 2 1

4 Yrh and draw a loop through the first 2 loops on the hook.

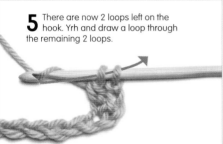

5 There are now 2 loops left on the hook. Yrh and draw a loop through the remaining 2 loops.

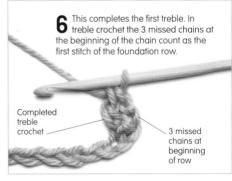

6 This completes the first treble. In treble crochet the 3 missed chains at the beginning of the chain count as the first stitch of the foundation row.

Completed treble crochet

3 missed chains at beginning of row

7 Work one treble crochet into each chain in the same way. Remember to start each stitch with a yrh before inserting the hook through the chain.

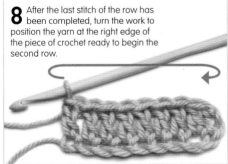

8 After the last stitch of the row has been completed, turn the work to position the yarn at the right edge of the piece of crochet ready to begin the second row.

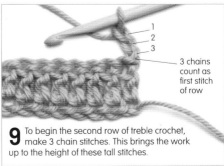

9 To begin the second row of treble crochet, make 3 chain stitches. This brings the work up to the height of these tall stitches.

1
2
3
3 chains count as first stitch of row

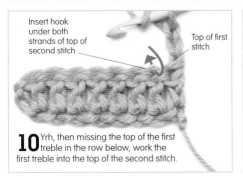

10 Yrh, then missing the top of the first treble in the row below, work the first treble into the top of the second stitch.

Insert hook under both strands of top of second stitch

Top of first stitch

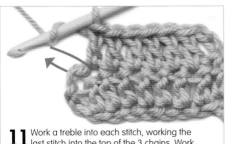

11 Work a treble into each stitch, working the last stitch into the top of the 3 chains. Work the following rows in the same way.

DOUBLE TREBLE
CROCHET
Abbreviation = dtr

Worked in a very similar way to treble crochet, double treble crochet stitches are approximately one chain length taller because the stitch is begun with two wraps instead of only one (see page 258). Double trebles are often used in lace crochet and in crochet motifs.

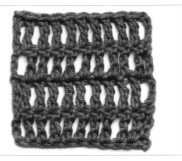

Identical on the front and the back, double treble crochet worked in rows is even softer than treble crochet. It also grows more quickly because the stitches are taller but not that much slower to work.

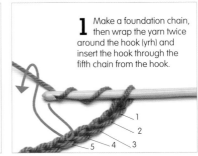

1 Make a foundation chain, then wrap the yarn twice around the hook (yrh) and insert the hook through the fifth chain from the hook.

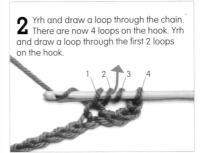

2 Yrh and draw a loop through the chain. There are now 4 loops on the hook. Yrh and draw a loop through the first 2 loops on the hook.

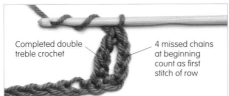

3 There are now 3 loops remaining. Yrh and draw a loop through the first 2 loops on the hook.

4 There are 2 loops remaining. Yrh and draw a loop through these 2 loops.

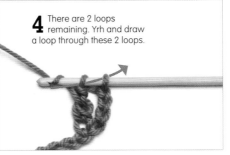

Completed double treble crochet

4 missed chains at beginning count as first stitch of row

5 This completes the first double treble. As for all tall crochet stitches, the missed chain stitches at the beginning of the foundation chain count as the first stitch of the foundation row.

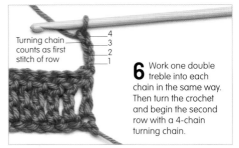

Turning chain counts as first stitch of row

6 Work one double treble into each chain in the same way. Then turn the crochet and begin the second row with a 4-chain turning chain.

Top of first stitch

7 Miss the top of the first double treble in the row below and work the first double treble into the top of the second stitch.

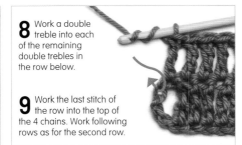

8 Work a double treble into each of the remaining double trebles in the row below.

9 Work the last stitch of the row into the top of the 4 chains. Work following rows as for the second row.

TRIPLE TREBLE
CROCHET
Abbreviation = trtr

Stitches taller than double trebles are all worked in the same way as double trebles, except that more wraps are wound around the hook before the stitch is begun and they require taller turning chains. Once you can work triple trebles easily, you will be able to work quadruple and quintuple trebles without much effort.

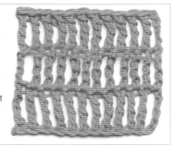

Triple treble crochet worked in rows looks the same on both sides of the fabric. Notice how airy the crochet texture becomes as the basic stitches get taller.

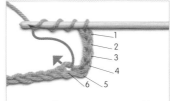

1 Wrap the yarn 3 times around the hook and insert the hook through the sixth stitch from the hook.

5 missed chains count as first stitch of row

2 Work the loops off the hook two at a time as for double trebles. Remember to wrap the yarn three times around the hook before starting each stitch. Start following rows with 5 chains.

BEGINNER'S
TIPS

It is important to learn how to count stitches so you can make sure you retain the same number as your crochet grows. Two other essential techniques are how to join in a new ball of yarn and how to darn in yarn ends when your piece of crochet is complete.

COUNTING CROCHET STITCHES

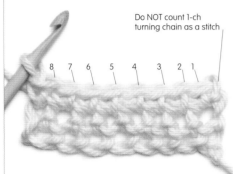

Do NOT count 1-ch turning chain as a stitch

8 7 6 5 4 3 2 1

Counting double crochet stitches: With the front of the last row facing, count the top of each stitch. If you are losing stitches as your crochet grows, then you are probably failing to work into the last stitch in the row below; if you are gaining stitches, you may have worked twice into the same stitch.

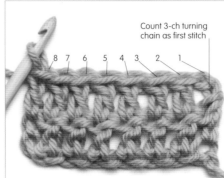

Count 3-ch turning chain as first stitch

8 7 6 5 4 3 2 1

Counting trebles: With the front of the last row facing, count the turning chain as the first stitch, then count the top of each treble. If you are losing stitches as your crochet grows, you are probably failing to work into the top of the turning chain; if you are gaining stitches, you may be working into the first treble of the row, instead of missing it.

JOINING IN NEW YARN

Method one: Always join on a new yarn at the beginning of a row if possible. Simply drop the old yarn and pull the new yarn through the loop on the hook, then begin the row in the usual way. Darn in the yarn ends later.

New yarn

Old yarn

Method two: This method is suitable for both stripes and plain crochet fabrics. First, fasten off the old yarn. Then place a slip knot on the hook, insert the hook through the first stitch of the row and draw a loop through the top of the stitch and the loop on the hook.

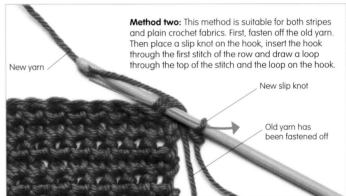

New yarn

New slip knot

Old yarn has been fastened off

DARNING IN YARN

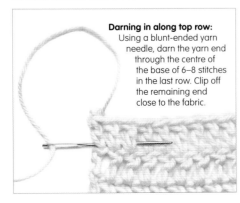

Darning in along top row: Using a blunt-ended yarn needle, darn the yarn end through the centre of the base of 6–8 stitches in the last row. Clip off the remaining end close to the fabric.

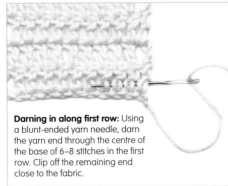

Darning in along first row: Using a blunt-ended yarn needle, darn the yarn end through the centre of the base of 6–8 stitches in the first row. Clip off the remaining end close to the fabric.

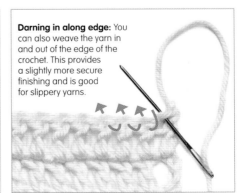

Darning in along edge: You can also weave the yarn in and out of the edge of the crochet. This provides a slightly more secure finishing and is good for slippery yarns.

BASIC STITCHES
IN SYMBOLS AND ABBREVIATIONS

Crochet row instructions can be written out with abbreviations or using symbols for the stitches. There is a more detailed explanation for reading stitch pattern instructions on page 262, but directions for the basic stitches are given here in both symbols and abbreviations. This provides an introduction to crochet instructions and a quick reference for how to work crochet fabrics with basic stitches.

STITCH HEIGHTS

The diagram below shows all the basic stitches in symbols and illustrates approximately how tall the stitches are when standing side by side. A double crochet is roughly one chain tall, a half treble crochet two chains tall, a treble crochet three chains tall, and so on. These heights determine the number of turning chains you need to work at the beginning of each row for each of the basic stitches. Also provided here is a reference for which chain to work into when working the first stitch into the foundation chain.

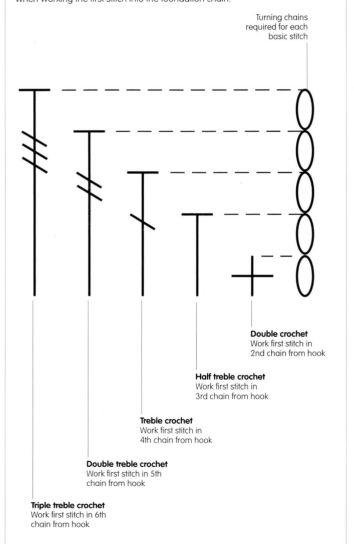

Turning chains required for each basic stitch

Double crochet
Work first stitch in 2nd chain from hook

Half treble crochet
Work first stitch in 3rd chain from hook

Treble crochet
Work first stitch in 4th chain from hook

Double treble crochet
Work first stitch in 5th chain from hook

Triple treble crochet
Work first stitch in 6th chain from hook

DOUBLE CROCHET INSTRUCTIONS

Crochet symbol instructions, especially for the basic stitches, are super-easy to understand. Roughly imitating the size and shape of the stitch, the symbols are read from the bottom of the diagram upwards. To get used to very simple crochet instructions, try working double crochet following the written directions and the symbol diagram at the same time (see page 263 for abbreviations list), then try this with the other basic stitches as well.

DOUBLE CROCHET IN ABBREVIATIONS
Make any number of ch.
Row 1 1 dc in 2nd ch from hook, 1 dc in each of rem ch to end, turn.
Row 2 1 ch (does NOT count as a st), 1 dc in each dc to end, turn.
Rep row 2 to form dc fabric.

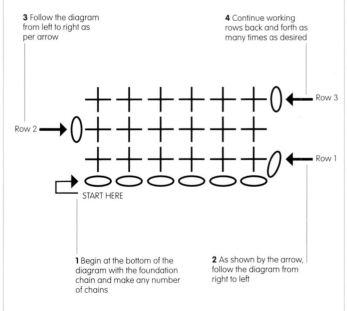

3 Follow the diagram from left to right as per arrow

4 Continue working rows back and forth as many times as desired

Row 3

Row 2

Row 1

START HERE

1 Begin at the bottom of the diagram with the foundation chain and make any number of chains

2 As shown by the arrow, follow the diagram from right to left

HALF TREBLE CROCHET INSTRUCTIONS

The symbol for half treble is a vertical line with a horizontal bar at the top, and it is about twice as tall as the double crochet symbol, just like the stitch is in real life. Read the written instructions for this basic stitch (below) and look at the chart at the same time. The direction of each arrow indicates whether to read the chart from left to right or right to left.

HALF TREBLE CROCHET IN ABBREVIATIONS
Make any number of ch.
Row 1 1 htr in 3rd ch from hook, 1 htr in each of rem ch to end, turn.
Row 2 2 ch (does NOT count as a st), 1 htr in each htr to end, turn.
Rep row 2 to form htr fabric.

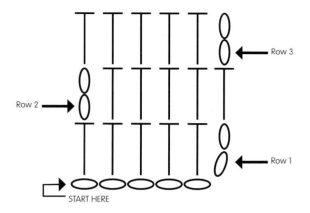

TREBLE CROCHET INSTRUCTIONS

The treble symbol has a short diagonal line across its "waist". The diagram shows clearly how the 3-chain turning chain counts as the first stitch of each row.

TREBLE CROCHET IN ABBREVIATIONS
Make any number of ch.
Row 1 1 tr in 4th ch from hook, 1 tr in each or rem ch to end, turn.
Row 2 3 ch (counts as first tr), miss first tr in row below, *1 tr in next tr; rep from * to end, then work 1 tr in top of 3-ch at end, turn.
Rep row 2 to form tr fabric.

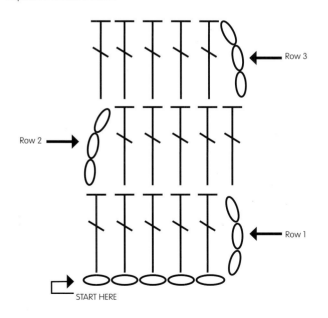

DOUBLE TREBLE CROCHET INSTRUCTIONS

Two short diagonal lines cross the "waist" of the double treble symbol, echoing the two diagonal yarn strands on the stitch itself.

DOUBLE TREBLE CROCHET IN ABBREVIATIONS
Make any number of ch.
Row 1 1 dtr in 5th ch from hook, 1 dtr in each of rem ch to end, turn.
Row 2 4 ch (counts as first dtr), miss first dtr in row below, *1 dtr in next dtr; rep from * to end, then work 1 dtr in top of 4-ch at end, turn.
Rep row 2 to form dtr fabric.

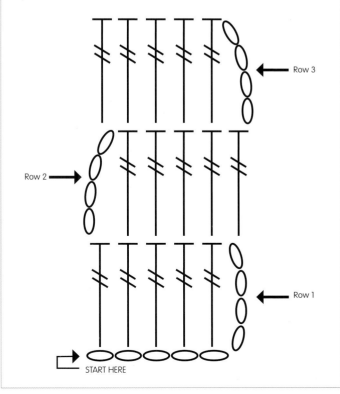

STITCH TECHNIQUES

The basic crochet stitches can be combined together in various ways to create endless textures and sculptured effects. Not all the vast range of crochet stitch techniques can be included, but the most commonly used are explained here in detail. When attempting the stitch patterns on pages 264–265, refer back to these step-by-step instructions to see more clearly how to achieve the textures.

SIMPLE TEXTURES

The simplest and most subtle crochet textures are created by working into various parts of the stitches or between the stitches in the row below. Before trying out any of these techniques, learn about the parts of the stitches so you can identify them easily.

PARTS OF STITCHES

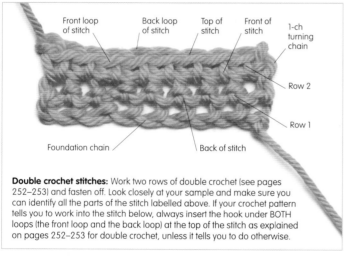

Double crochet stitches: Work two rows of double crochet (see pages 252–253) and fasten off. Look closely at your sample and make sure you can identify all the parts of the stitch labelled above. If your crochet pattern tells you to work into the stitch below, always insert the hook under BOTH loops (the front loop and the back loop) at the top of the stitch as explained on pages 252–253 for double crochet, unless it tells you to do otherwise.

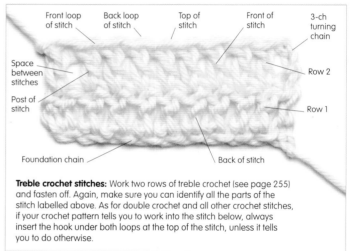

Treble crochet stitches: Work two rows of treble crochet (see page 255) and fasten off. Again, make sure you can identify all the parts of the stitch labelled above. As for double crochet and all other crochet stitches, if your crochet pattern tells you to work into the stitch below, always insert the hook under both loops at the top of the stitch, unless it tells you to do otherwise.

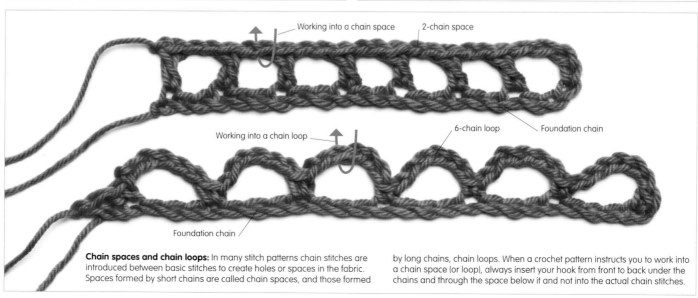

Chain spaces and chain loops: In many stitch patterns chain stitches are introduced between basic stitches to create holes or spaces in the fabric. Spaces formed by short chains are called chain spaces, and those formed by long chains, chain loops. When a crochet pattern instructs you to work into a chain space (or loop), always insert your hook from front to back under the chains and through the space below it and not into the actual chain stitches.

WORKING INTO THE BACK OF A DOUBLE CROCHET

Working into only the back loops of the stitches in every row of double crochet creates a deep ridged effect. The ridges are formed by the unworked loops.

WORKING INTO THE FRONT OF A DOUBLE CROCHET

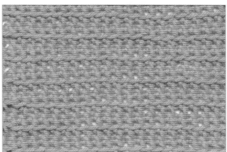

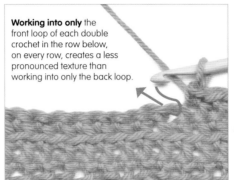

Working into only the front loop of each double crochet in the row below, on every row, creates a less pronounced texture than working into only the back loop.

WORKING INTO THE BACK OF A TREBLE CROCHET

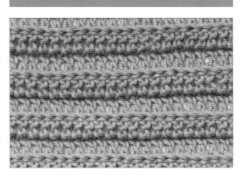

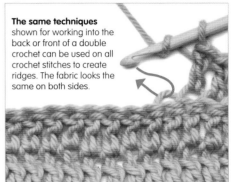

The same techniques shown for working into the back or front of a double crochet can be used on all crochet stitches to create ridges. The fabric looks the same on both sides.

WORKING INTO SPACES BETWEEN STITCHES

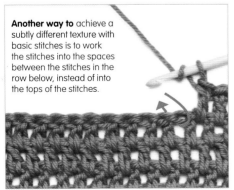

Another way to achieve a subtly different texture with basic stitches is to work the stitches into the spaces between the stitches in the row below, instead of into the tops of the stitches.

WORKING INTO A CHAIN SPACE

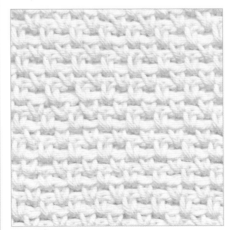

Tweed stitch illustrates the simplest of all textures created by working into a chain space. Here double crochet stitches are worked in the 1-chain spaces between the stitches in the row below instead of into the tops of the stitches.

Tweed stitch pattern
Because it is such a popular stitch and a perfect alternative for basic double crochet, the pattern for it is given here. (See page 263 for abbreviations.) Start with an even number of chains.
Row 1 1 dc in 2nd ch from hook, *1 ch, miss next ch, 1 dc in next ch; rep from * to end, turn.
Row 2 1 ch (does NOT count as a stitch), 1 dc in first dc, 1 dc in next 1-ch sp, *1 ch, 1 dc in next 1-ch sp; rep from * to last dc, 1 dc in last dc, turn.
Row 3 1 ch (does NOT count as a stitch), 1 dc in first dc, *1 ch, 1 dc in next 1-ch sp; rep from * to last 2 dc, 1 ch, miss next dc, 1 dc in last dc, turn.
Rep rows 2 and 3 to form patt.

FOLLOWING SIMPLE STITCH PATTERNS

Working a project from a crochet pattern for the first time can seem difficult for a beginner, especially if an experienced crocheter is not at hand as a guide. The best way to prepare for a crochet pattern is first to practise crocheting rectangles of various stitch patterns using simple stitch techniques. This is a good introduction to following abbreviated written row instructions and symbol diagrams.

UNDERSTANDING WRITTEN INSTRUCTIONS

As long as you are confident that you know how to work all the basic stitches as described on pages 248–249, there is nothing stopping you progressing on to the simple textured stitch patterns on pages 264–265. Simply consult the list on the opposite page for the meanings of the various abbreviations and follow the written row instructions one step at a time.

Begin by making the required number of chains for the foundation chain, using your chosen yarn and one of the hook sizes recommended for this yarn weight on page 245. Crochet a swatch that repeats the pattern only a few times to test it out. (If you decide to make a blanket or cushion cover with the stitch

later, you can adjust the hook size before starting it to obtain the exact flexibility of fabric you desire.)

Work each row of the stitch pattern slowly and mark the right side of the fabric (if there is one) as soon as you start, by tying a contrasting coloured thread to it. Another good tip is to tick off the rows as you complete them or put a sticky note under them so you don't lose your place in the pattern. If you do get lost in all the stitches, pull out all the rows and start from the foundation-chain again.

UNDERSTANDING STITCH SYMBOL DIAGRAMS

Crochet stitch patterns can also be given in symbols (see opposite page). These diagrams are usually even easier to follow than directions with abbreviations because they create a visual reference of approximately how the finished stitch will look. Each basic stitch on the chart is represented by a symbol that resembles it in some way. The position of the base of each stitch symbol indicates which stitch or chain space it is worked into in the row below. If the symbols are joined at the base, this means that they are worked into the same stitch in the row below.

The beginning of the foundation chain will be marked as your starting point on the diagram. Read each row on the diagram either from right to left or left to right following the direction of the arrow. Although you can consult the

written instructions for how many chains to make for a foundation chain and how to repeat the stitch repeat across a row (or a row repeat up the fabric), it is easy to work these out yourself from the diagram once you become proficient in reading diagrams. But to begin with, work from the written instructions and use the diagram as a visual aid. Once you have completed the first few rows of the pattern, you can dispense with the written instructions all together and continue with the diagram as your sole guide. If the stitch is an easy one, you will very quickly be able to work it without looking at any instructions at all.

This symbol diagram for the open shell stitch (see page 270) is a good introduction to working from a symbol diagram. Start at the bottom of the diagram and follow it row by row with the aid of the numbered tips.

OPEN SHELL STITCH

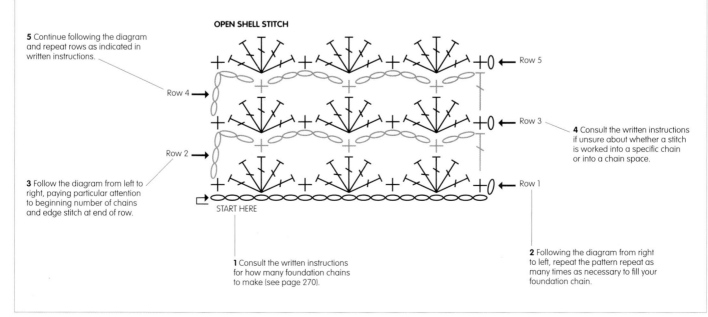

5 Continue following the diagram and repeat rows as indicated in written instructions.

Row 4

Row 2

3 Follow the diagram from left to right, paying particular attention to beginning number of chains and edge stitch at end of row.

START HERE

1 Consult the written instructions for how many foundation chains to make (see page 270).

Row 5

Row 3

Row 1

4 Consult the written instructions if unsure about whether a stitch is worked into a specific chain or into a chain space.

2 Following the diagram from right to left, repeat the pattern repeat as many times as necessary to fill your foundation chain.

CROCHET ABBREVIATIONS

These are the abbreviations most commonly used in crochet patterns. The abbreviations for the basic stitches are listed first and the other abbreviations found in crochet patterns follow. Any special abbreviations in a crochet pattern will always be explained in the pattern.

Abbreviations for basic stitches
Note: The names for the basic crochet stitches differ in the UK and the US. This book uses UK crochet terminology, so if you have learned to crochet in the US, be sure to take note of the difference in terminology.

ch	chain
ss	slip stitch
dc	double crochet (US single crochet – sc)
htr	half treble (US half double crochet – hdc)
tr	treble (US double crochet – dc)
dtr	double treble (US treble crochet – tr)
trtr	triple treble (US double treble crochet – dtr)
qtr	quadruple treble (US triple treble crochet – trtr)
quintr	quintuple treble (US quadruple treble – quadtr)

Other abbreviations
alt	alternate
beg	begin(ning)
cm	centimetre(s)
cont	continu(e)(ing)
dc2tog	see Crochet Terminology

dc3tog	see Crochet Terminology
dec	decreas(e)(ing)
foll	follow(s)(ing)
g	gram(s)
htr2tog	see Crochet Terminology
htr3tog	see Crochet Terminology
in	inch(es)
inc	increas(e)(ing)
m	metre(s)
mm	millimetre(s)
oz	ounce(s)
patt(s)	pattern(s)
rem	remain(s)(ing)
rep	repeat(s)(ing)
RS	right side
sp	space(s)
st(s)	stitch(es)
tog	together
tr2tog	see Crochet Terminology
tr3tog	see Crochet Terminology
WS	wrong side
yd	yard(s)
yrh	yarn round hook (US yarn over hook – yo)

* Repeat instructions after asterisk or between asterisks as many times as instructed.
[ ] Repeat instructions inside square brackets as many times as instructed.

CROCHET TERMINOLOGY

The following terms are commonly used in crochet patterns. Many crochet terms are the same in the UK and the US, but where they differ, the US equivalent is given in parentheses. Turn to the pages indicated for how to work the various increases, decreases, or stitch techniques listed.

bobble: Several stitches worked into the same stitch in the row below and joined together at the top.
cluster: Several stitches worked into different stitches in the row below, but joined together at the top.
dc2tog (work 2 dc together): See page 48. (US sc2tog)
dc3tog (work 3 dc together): [Insert hook in next st, yrh and draw a loop through] 3 times, yrh and draw through all 4 loops on hook – 2 sts decreased. (US sc3tog)
fasten off: Cut the yarn and draw the yarn tail through the remaining loop on the hook (see page 22).
foundation chain: The base of chain stitches that the first row of crochet is worked onto.
foundation row: The first row of a piece of crochet (the row worked onto the foundation chain) is sometimes called the foundation row.
htr2tog (work 2 htr together): [Yrh and insert hook in next st, yrh and draw a loop through] twice, yrh and draw through all 5 loops on hook – 1 st decreased. (US hdc2tog)
htr3tog (work 3 htr together): [Yrh and insert hook in next st, yrh and draw a loop through] 3 times, yrh and draw

through all 7 loops on hook – 2 sts decreased. (US hdc3tog)
miss a stitch: Do not work into the stitch, but go on to the next stitch. (US "skip" a stitch).
shell: Several stitches worked into the same stitch in the previous row or into the same chain space.
pineapple: A bobble made with half trebles; also called a puff stitch.
popcorn: A type of bobble.
puff stitch: See pineapple.
tr2tog (work 2 tr together): See page 49. (US dc2tog)
tr3tog (work 3 tr together): [Yrh and insert hook in next st, yrh and draw a loop through, yrh and draw through first 2 loops on hook] 3 times, yrh and draw through all 4 loops on hook – 2 sts decreased. (US dc3tog)
turning chain: The chain/s worked at the beginning of the row (or round) to bring the hook up to the correct height for working the following stitches in the row.

CROCHET STITCH SYMBOLS

These are the symbols used in this book, but crochet symbols are not universal so always consult the key with your crochet instructions for the symbols used in your pattern.

Basic stitches

⬭	= ch
••	= ss
+	= dc
T	= htr
	= tr
	= dtr
	= trtr
	= qtr
	= quintr

Special stitches and stitch combinations

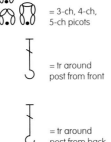
= 3-ch, 4-ch, 5-ch picots

= tr around post from front

= tr around post from back

= dc2tog

= dc3tog

= htr2tog

= htr3tog

= tr2tog

= tr3tog

= 2 dc in same st

✗ = 3 dc in same st

= 2 htr in same st

= 3 htr in same st

Shells, cluster, bobbles, popcorns

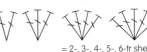
= 2-, 3-, 4-, 5-, 6-tr shells

= 2-, 3-, 4-, 5-, 6-tr clusters

= 3-, 4-, 5-tr bobbles

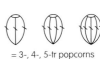
= 3-, 4-, 5-tr popcorns

SIMPLE TEXTURES
STITCH PATTERNS

Selected for how easy they are to work, these stitch patterns cover an array of crochet textures, including those made using the techniques explained on pages 260–261. Although crochet is often identified with lacy openwork fabrics, there are also lots of solid textures like these to choose from. Quick to work and easy to memorize after the first few rows, the following stitches would make lovely cushion covers, baby blankets, or throws. They all look good on both sides of the fabrics and two are completely reversible (see Special Notes).

CROCHET RIB STITCH

CROCHET DIAGRAM

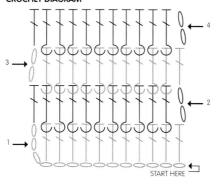

CROCHET INSTRUCTIONS
Make a multiple of 2 ch.
Row 1 1 tr in 4th ch from hook, 1 tr in each of rem ch, turn.
Row 2 2 ch (counts as first st), miss first tr, *1 tr around post of next tr from front, 1 tr around post of next tr from back; rep from * to end, 1 tr in top of turning ch at end, turn.
Rep row 2 to form patt.

SIMPLE CROSSED STITCH

CROCHET DIAGRAM

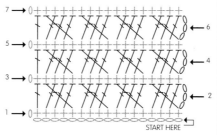

CROCHET INSTRUCTIONS
Make a multiple of 4 ch, plus 2 extra.
Row 1 1 dc in 2nd ch from hook, 1 dc in each of rem ch, turn.
Row 2 (RS) 3 ch (counts as first tr), miss first dc, 1 tr in each of next 3 dc, yrh and insert hook from front to back in first dc (the missed dc), yrh and draw a long loop through (extending the loop that so it reaches back to position of work and does not squash 3-tr group just made), [yrh and draw through first 2 loops on hook] twice – called long tr–, *miss next dc, 1 tr in each of next 3 dc, 1 long tr in last missed dc; rep from * to last dc, 1 tr in last dc, turn.
Row 3 1 ch (does NOT count as a st), 1 dc in each tr to end (do NOT work a dc in 3-ch turning chain), turn.
Rep rows 2 and 3 to form patt.

CLOSE SHELLS STITCH

CROCHET DIAGRAM

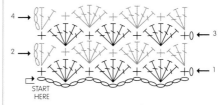

CROCHET INSTRUCTIONS
Make a multiple of 6 ch, plus 2 extra.
Row 1 1 dc in 2nd ch from hook, *miss next 2 ch, 5 tr in next ch, miss next 2 ch, 1 dc in next ch; rep from * to end, turn.
Row 2 3 ch (counts as first tr), 2 tr in first dc, *miss next 2 tr, 1 dc in next tr, 5 tr in next dc (between shells); rep from *, ending last rep with 3 tr in last dc (instead of 5 tr), turn.
Row 3 1 ch (does NOT count as a st), 1 dc in first tr, 5 tr in next dc (between shells), miss next 2 tr, 1 dc in next tr; rep from *, working last dc in top of 3-ch at end, turn.
Rep rows 2 and 3 to form patt.

SPECIAL NOTES

• Both written and symbol instructions are given for all the Simple Textures Stitch Patterns. To get started, beginners should follow the written instructions for the first few rows, referring to the symbols for clarification. See page 263 for a list of crochet abbreviations and basic stitch symbols. If a special symbol is used in a diagram, this symbol is explained in the accompanying key. A complete explanation of how to read a crochet symbol diagram is included on page 262.

• Where there is no right side or wrong side marked in the instructions of a stitch, it looks exactly the same on both sides of the fabric. The crochet rib stitch and the close shells stitch (opposite) are examples of this – they are completely reversible.

SIMPLE BOBBLE STITCH

CROCHET DIAGRAM

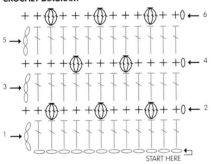

START HERE

CROCHET INSTRUCTIONS

Note: bobble = [yrh and insert hook in specified st, yrh and draw a loop through, yrh and draw through first 2 loops on hook] 4 times all in same st (5 loops now on hook), yrh and draw through all 5 loops on hook.
Make a multiple of 4 ch, plus 3 extra.
Row 1 (WS) 1 tr in 4th ch from hook, 1 tr in each of rem ch, turn.
Row 2 (RS) 1 ch (does NOT count as a st), 1 dc in each of first 2 tr, *1 bobble in next tr, 1 dc in each of next 3 tr; rep from * to last 2 tr, 1 bobble in next tr, 1 dc in next tr, 1 dc in top of 3-ch at end, turn.
Row 3 3 ch (counts as first tr), miss first dc and work 1 tr in each st to end, turn.
Row 4 1 ch (does NOT count as a st), 1 dc in each of first 4 tr, *1 bobble in next tr, 1 dc in each of next 3 tr; rep from *, ending with 1 dc in top of 3-ch at end, turn.
Row 5 Rep row 3.
Rep rows 2–5 to form patt, ending with a patt row 5.

CLUSTER AND SHELL STITCH

CROCHET DIAGRAM

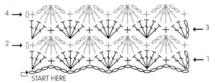

START HERE

CROCHET INSTRUCTIONS

Note: cluster (also called dc5tog) = over next 5 sts (which include 2 tr, 1 dc, 2 tr) work [yrh and insert hook in next st, yrh and draw a loop through, yrh and draw through first 2 loops on hook] 5 times (6 loops now on hook), yrh and draw through all 6 loops on hook.
Make a multiple of 6 ch, plus 4 extra.
Row 1 (RS) 2 tr in 4th ch from hook, miss next 2 ch, 1 dc in next ch, *miss next 2 ch, 5 tr in next ch, miss next 2 ch, 1 dc in next ch: rep from * to last 3 ch, miss next 2 ch, 3 tr in last ch, turn.
Row 2 1 ch (does NOT count as a st), 1 dc in first tr, *2 ch, 1 cluster over next 5 sts, 2 ch, 1 dc in next tr (centre tr of 5-tr group); rep from *, working last dc of last rep in top of 3-ch at end, turn.
Row 3 3 ch (counts as first tr), 2 tr in first dc, miss next 2 ch, 1 dc in next st (top of first cluster), *5 tr in next st, miss next 2 ch, 1 dc in next st (top of next cluster); rep from *, ending with 3 tr in last dc, turn.
Rep rows 2 and 3 to form patt.

SHELLS AND CHAINS

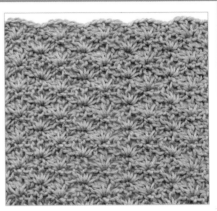

CROCHET DIAGRAM

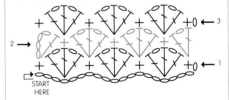

START HERE

CROCHET INSTRUCTIONS

Make a multiple of 6 ch, plus 2 extra.
Row 1 (RS) 1 dc in 2nd ch from hook, *miss next 2 ch, work [1 tr, 1 ch, 1 tr, 1 ch, 1 tr] all in next ch, miss next 2 ch, 1 dc in next ch; rep from * to end, turn.
Row 2 4 ch (counts as 1 tr and a 1-ch sp), 1 tr in first dc, miss next tr, 1 dc in next tr (centre tr of shell), *work [1 tr, 1 ch, 1 tr, 1 ch, 1 tr] all in next dc (between shells), miss next tr, 1 dc in next tr (centre tr of shell); rep from *, ending with [1 tr, 1 ch, 1 tr] in last dc, turn.
Row 3 1 ch (does NOT count as a st), 1 dc in first tr, *work [1 tr, 1 ch, 1 tr, 1 ch, 1 tr] all in next dc, miss next tr, 1 dc in next tr (centre tr of shell); rep from *, working last dc of last rep in 3rd of 4-ch made at beg of previous row, turn.
Rep rows 2 and 3 to form patt.

SPECIAL NOTES

• Refer to page 263 for a complete list of crochet abbreviations and an explanation of all the most commonly used crochet symbols. The written instructions explain how many chains to start with and which rows to repeat to form the pattern. So if working from the diagram, be sure to read the written instructions first for guidance.

• Make a test swatch of your chosen stitch pattern before starting to make a cushion cover, baby blanket, or throw from any of these textured stitches. Try out various yarns to see which suits your purpose. Tightly spun yarns are the best for showing off the sculptural aspects of textured stitches. Keep in mind that dense crochet textures need not be stiff and unyielding. If your sample swatch is not soft and pliable enough, try working another swatch with a larger hook size to loosen up the fabric a little. For baby blankets, super-fine cotton, or washable wool yarns are the most baby friendly.

POPCORN PATTERN STITCH

CROCHET DIAGRAM

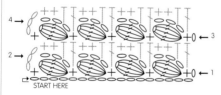

START HERE

CROCHET INSTRUCTIONS

Note: popcorn = 5 tr all in same st, carefully remove loop from hook and insert it through top of first tr of this 5-tr group, pull loop (the one removed from hook) through first tr.

Make a multiple of 4 ch, plus 2 extra.

Row 1 (RS) 1 dc in 2nd ch from hook, *3 ch, 1 popcorn in same place as last dc, miss next 3 ch, 1 dc in next ch; rep from * to end, turn.

Row 2 3 ch (counts as first tr), *work [2 dc, 1 htr] all in next 3-ch sp, 1 tr in next dc; rep from * to end, turn.

Row 3 1 ch (does NOT count as a st), 1 dc in first tr, *3 ch, 1 popcorn in same place as last dc, miss next 3 sts, 1 dc in next tr; rep from *, working last dc of last rep in top of 3-ch at end, turn.

Rep rows 2 and 3 to form patt.

SIMPLE PUFF STITCH

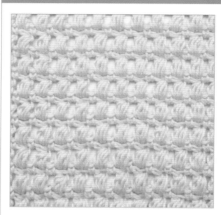

CROCHET DIAGRAM

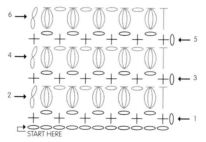

START HERE

KEY

 4-htr puff stitch

CROCHET INSTRUCTIONS

Note: puff stitch = [yrh and insert hook in st] 4 times all in same st (9 loops now on hook), yrh and draw through all 9 loops on hook to complete 4-htr puff stitch.

Make a multiple of 2 ch.

Row 1 (RS) 1 dc in 2nd ch from hook, *1 ch, miss next ch, 1 dc in next ch; rep from * to end, turn.

Row 2 2 ch (counts as first htr), 1 puff st in first 1-ch sp, *1 ch, 1 puff st in next 1-ch sp; rep from *, ending with 1 htr in last dc, turn.

Row 3 1 ch (does NOT count as a st), 1 dc in first htr, *1 ch, 1 dc in next 1-ch sp; rep from *, working last rep in top of 2-ch at end, turn.

Rep rows 2 and 3 to form patt.

SIMPLE TEXTURE STITCH

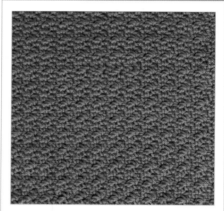

CROCHET DIAGRAM

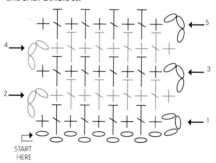

START HERE

CROCHET INSTRUCTIONS

Make a multiple of 2 ch.

Row 1 (RS) 1 dc in 4th ch from hook, *1 tr in next ch, 1 dc in next ch; rep from * to end, turn.

Row 2 3 ch (counts as first tr), miss first dc, *1 dc in next tr, 1 tr in next dc; rep from *, ending with 1 dc in top of 3-ch at end, turn.

Rep row 2 to form patt.

OPENWORK

Whether worked with fine threads for lace collars, pillow edgings, and tablecloths or with soft wools for shawls, throws, and scarves, openwork crochet has an enduring appeal. As illustrated by the easy techniques on this page and the next, these airy lace textures are produced by working chain spaces and chain loops between the basic stitches.

SIMPLE LACE TECHNIQUES

A few of the openwork stitch patterns on pages 270–271 are explained here to provide an introduction to some popular openwork crochet techniques – chain loops, shells, and picots. Refer to the instructions for the stitches when following the steps.

CHAIN LOOP MESH

1 After working the first row of chain loops into the foundation chain as explained (see page 270), work the 5-chain loops of the following rows into the loops below, joining them on with a dc as shown here.

2 Remember to work the last dc of each row into the space inside the turning chain made at the beginning of the previous row. If you forget this, your lace will become narrower.

SHELL MESH STITCH

1 On the shell row of this stitch (see page 270) start each shell with a dc in a chain loop. Then work all the tr of the shell into a single dc as shown.

2 Complete the shell with a dc worked into the following chain loop. Then work a chain loop and join it to the next chain loop with a dc as shown.

Dc at sides of shell secure it to mesh row below

3 Continue alternating shells and chain loops to complete the shell row.

Partial shell

Full shell

4 Work mesh and shell rows alternately, working partial shells at ends on alternate shell rows.

PICOT NET STITCH

1 In this stitch pattern (see page 270), work 4 chains for each picot. Close the picot-ring by working a slip stitch in the fourth chain from the hook as shown.

2 Work 3 dc between each of the picots in each picot row as shown.

3 After each picot row, work a 2-chain space above each picot and a tr between the picots as shown.

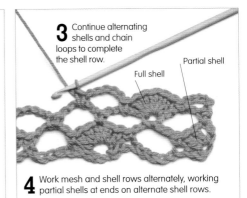
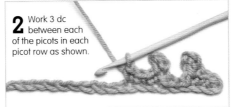
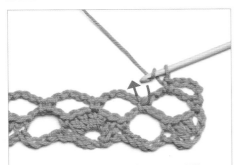

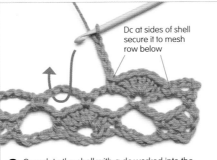

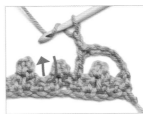

FILET CROCHET

Filet crochet is the easiest of all the openwork techniques. Once you learn how to work the simple structure of the open filet mesh and the solid filet blocks, all you need to do is follow a simple chart to form the motifs and repeating patterns.

MAKING BASIC FILET MESH

When working the foundation chain for the basic filet mesh, there is no need to start with an exact number of chains, just make an extra long chain and unravel the unused excess later when finishing your crochet.

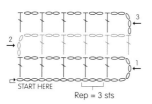

Filet mesh in symbols and words: The diagram provides the best explanation of how filet mesh is worked. If in doubt, work a mesh from the written pattern as follows:

Make a multiple of 3 ch (3 ch for each mesh square needed), plus 5 extra (to form the right side edge and top of the first mesh square of the first row).
Row 1 1 tr in 8th ch from hook, *2 ch, miss next 2 ch, 1 tr in next ch; rep from * to end.
Row 1 5 ch, miss first tr, 1 tr in next tr, *2 ch, 1 tr in next tr; rep from * working last tr in 3rd ch from last tr in row below.

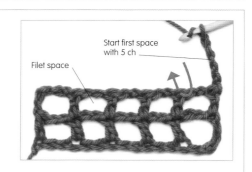

Start first space with 5 ch

Filet space

MAKING FILET BLOCKS

The pattern motifs on filet crochet are created by filling in some of the mesh squares and leaving others empty. In other words, the designs are built up with solid squares and square holes. Having learned how to work the filet mesh, understanding how to fill them in to form blocks is easy.

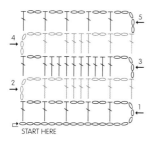

Filet blocks in symbols: The diagram illustrates how the blocks are made – instead of working 2 chains to form an empty square, work 2 trebles fill in the square. An individual block consists of a treble on each side and 2 trebles in the centre. To work a block above a filet space, work the 2 centre trebles into the 2-chain space. To work a block above another block, work a treble into each of the trebles below.

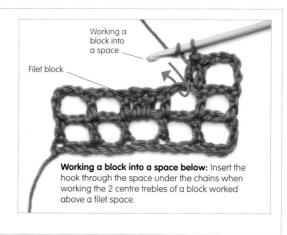

Working a block into a space

Filet block

Working a block into a space below: Insert the hook through the space under the chains when working the 2 centre trebles of a block worked above a filet space.

READING FILET CHARTS

This chart on the right shows the simple motif in the block symbol diagram above. Although actual filet charts are bigger and have elaborate patterns (see page 269), the principle is the same as for this tiny chart. Each square on the chart represents either a filet space or a filet block.

To start working from a chart, make 3 chains for each of the squares along the bottom row of the chart, plus 5 chains extra. (You can work the chart stitch-repeat as many times as desired.) Working the chart from the bottom upwards, make the blocks and spaces on the chart, while reading the first row and all following odd-numbered rows from right to left, and the even-numbered rows from left to right.

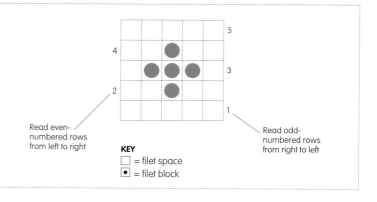

Read even-numbered rows from left to right

Read odd-numbered rows from right to left

KEY
☐ = filet space
⊡ = filet block

FILET STITCH
PATTERNS

Follow the instructions on the opposite page to work filet crochet from these charts. The best yarn to use for filet lace is a super-fine cotton yarn and a suitably small size crochet hook (see recommended hook sizes on page 245). Because filet crochet is reversible, it makes great curtains. It can also be used for edgings or insertions along the ends of pillowcases and hand towels.

SPECIAL NOTE AND SYMBOL KEY

• Repeat the charted motifs as many times as desired widthwise, and work across the stitches in rows until the chart is complete. To continue the pattern upwards, start at row 1 again.

KEY
☐ = filet space
⊡ = filet block

FLOWERS AND CIRCLES

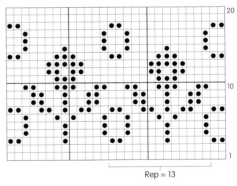

CROCHET CHART

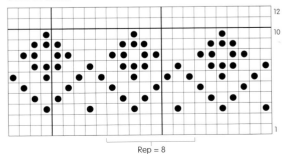

Rep = 13

DIAMONDS BORDER

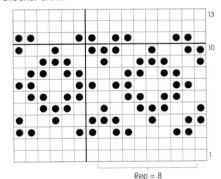

CROCHET CHART

Rep = 8

ZIGZAG BORDER

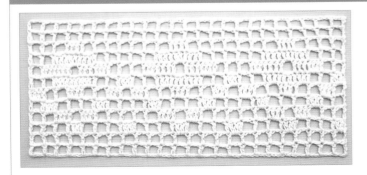

CROCHET CHART

Rep = 8

SIMPLE OPENWORK STITCH PATTERNS

Openwork crochet stitches are always popular because of their lacy appearance and because they are quicker to work than solid crochet textures. They also drape gracefully due to their airy construction. Any of these easy stitch patterns would make an attractive shawl or scarf. Why not make small samples of the stitches to try them out? Then work your favourite in a range of yarns to see which texture you prefer (see Special Notes on page 272). A glance at the symbol diagram will reveal which basic stitches and simple stitch techniques are involved.

CHAIN LOOP MESH

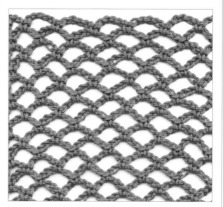

CROCHET DIAGRAM

CROCHET INSTRUCTIONS
Make a multiple of 4 ch, plus 2 extra.
Row 1 1 dc in 6th ch from hook, *5 ch, miss next 3 ch, 1 dc in next ch; rep from * to end, turn.
Row 2 *5 ch, 1 dc in next 5-ch loop; rep from * to end, turn.
Rep row 2 to form patt.

PICOT NET STITCH

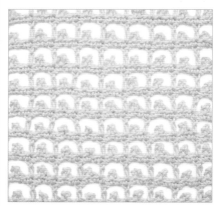

CROCHET DIAGRAM

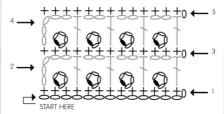

CROCHET INSTRUCTIONS
Make a multiple of 3 ch, plus 2 extra.
Row 1 (RS) 1 dc in 2nd ch from hook, 1 dc in next ch, *4 ch, 1 ss in 4th from hook – called 1 picot –, 1 dc in each of next 3 ch; rep from * omitting 1 dc at end of last rep, turn.
Row 2 5 ch (counts as 1 tr and a 2-ch sp), miss first 3 dc (which includes 2 dc before picot and 1 dc after picot), 1 tr in next dc, *2 ch, miss next 2 dc (which includes 1 dc on each side of picot), 1 tr in next dc; rep from * to end, turn.
Row 3 1 ch (does NOT count as a st), 1 dc in first tr, *work [1 dc, 1 picot, 1 dc] all in next 2-ch sp, 1 dc in next tr; rep from * working last dc of last rep in 3rd ch from last tr, turn.
Rep rows 2 and 3 to form patt.

OPEN SHELL STITCH

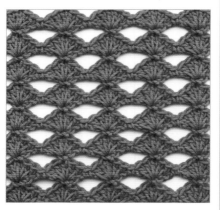

CROCHET DIAGRAM

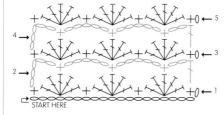

CROCHET INSTRUCTIONS
Make a multiple of 6 ch, plus 2 extra.
Row 1 (RS) 1 dc in 2nd ch from hook, *miss next 2 ch, 5 tr in next ch, miss next 2 ch, 1 dc in next ch; rep from * to end, turn.
Row 2 5 ch (counts as first tr and a 2-ch sp), 1 dc in centre tr in of first shell, *5 ch, 1 dc in centre tr of next shell; rep from *, ending with 2 ch, 1 tr in last dc, turn.
Row 3 1 ch (does NOT count as a st), 1 dc in first tr, *5 tr in next dc, 1 dc in next 5-ch loop; rep from * working last dc of last rep in 3rd ch from last dc, turn.
Rep rows 2 and 3 to form patt.

• Both written and symbol instructions are given for all the Simple Openwork Stitch Patterns. To get started, beginners should follow the written instructions for the first few rows, referring to the symbols for clarification. See page 263 for a list of crochet abbreviations and basic stitch symbols. A complete explanation of how to read a crochet symbol diagram is included on page 262.

• The written instructions explain how many chains to start with. So if working from the diagram, consult the written instructions to make the foundation chain. When working a very wide piece, such as a blanket, it is difficult to count and keep track of the number of foundation chains being made. In this case, you can make a chain a few centimetres longer than the correct approximate length and then unravel the excess later.

ARCHED MESH STITCH

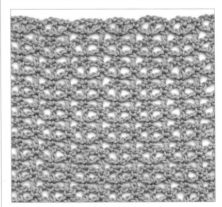

CROCHET DIAGRAM

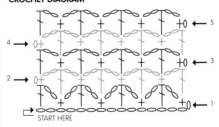

START HERE

CROCHET INSTRUCTIONS
Make a multiple of 4 ch.
Row 1 1 dc in 2nd ch from hook, 2 ch, miss next ch, 1 tr in next ch, *2 ch, miss next ch, 1 dc in next ch, 2 ch, miss next ch, 1 tr in next ch; rep from * to end, turn.
Row 2 1 ch (does NOT count as a st), 1 dc in first tr, 2 ch, 1 tr in next dc, *2 ch, 1 dc in next tr, 2 ch, 1 tr in next dc; rep from * to end, turn.
Rep row 2 to form patt.

BANDED NET STITCH

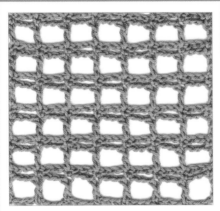

CROCHET DIAGRAM

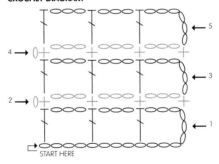

START HERE

CROCHET INSTRUCTIONS
Make a multiple of 4 ch, plus 2 extra.
Row 1 (RS) 1 tr in 10th ch from hook, 3 ch, miss next 3 ch, 1 tr in next ch; rep from * to end, turn.
Row 2 1 ch (does NOT count as a st), 1 dc in first tr, *3 ch, 1 dc in next tr; rep from *, ending with 3 ch, miss next 3 ch, 1 dc in last ch, turn.
Row 3 6 ch (counts as 1 tr and a 3-ch sp), miss first dc and first 3-ch sp, 1 tr in next dc, *3 ch, 1 tr in next dc; rep from * to end, turn.
Rep rows 2 and 3 to form patt.

SHELL MESH STITCH

CROCHET DIAGRAM

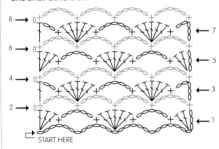

START HERE

CROCHET INSTRUCTIONS
Make a multiple of 12 ch, plus 4 extra.
Row 1 (RS) 2 tr in 4th ch from hook, *miss next 2 ch, 1 dc in next ch, 5 ch, miss next 5 ch, 1 dc in next ch, miss next 2 ch, 5 tr in next ch; rep from *, ending last rep with 3 tr (instead of 5 tr) in last ch, turn.
Row 2 1 ch (does NOT count as a st), 1 dc in first tr, *5 ch, 1 dc in next 5-ch loop, 5 ch, 1 dc in 3rd tr of next 5-tr shell; rep from * working last dc of last rep in top of 3-ch at end, turn.
Row 3 *5 ch, 1 dc in next 5-ch loop, 5 tr in next dc, 1 dc in next 5-ch loop; rep from *, ending with 2 ch, 1 tr in last dc, turn.
Row 4 1 ch (does NOT count as a st), 1 dc in first tr, *5 ch, 1 dc in 3rd tr of next 5-tr shell, 5 ch, 1 dc in next 5-ch loop; rep from * to end, turn.
Row 5 3 ch (counts as first tr), 2 tr in first dc, *1 dc in next 5-ch loop, 5 ch, 1 dc in next 5-ch loop, 5 tr in next dc; rep from * ending last rep with 3 tr (instead of 5 tr) in last dc, turn.
Rep rows 2–5 to form patt.

SPECIAL NOTES

• Lacy shawls and scarves look best worked in super-fine to lightweight yarns of various textures. Always make a swatch with your chosen yarn before beginning to make a project with one of these openwork stitch patterns. Gossamer mohair-mix yarns will work with the very simplest stitches, but to show off intricate laces, use a smooth, tightly twisted wool or cotton yarn.

• Notice how the symbol diagrams for a stitch pattern usually show more rows than appear in the accompanying written instructions. This is done on purpose so that the build-up of the rows is completely clear to the crocheter. With simple openwork patterns like these, once you have completed all the rows of the diagram you will probably have committed the pattern to memory and will not have to refer to the instructions again.

BLOCKS LACE

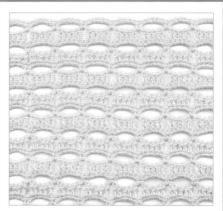

CROCHET DIAGRAM

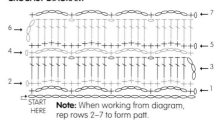

Note: When working from diagram, rep rows 2–7 to form patt.

CROCHET INSTRUCTIONS
Make a multiple of 5 ch, plus 2 extra.
Row 1 (RS) 1 dc in 2nd ch from hook, *5 ch, miss next 4 ch, 1 dc in next ch; rep from * to end, turn.
Row 2 1 ch (does NOT count as a st), 1 dc in first dc, *5 dc in next 5-ch loop, 1 dc in next dc; rep from * to end, turn.
Row 3 3 ch (counts as first tr), miss first dc, 1 tr in each of next 5 dc, *1 ch, miss next dc, 1 tr in each of next 5 dc; rep from * to last dc, 1 tr in last dc, turn.
Row 4 1 ch (does NOT count as a st), 1 dc in first tr, *5 ch, 1 dc in next 1-ch sp; rep from * working last sc of last rep in top of 3-ch at end, turn.
Rep rows 2–4 to form patt.

FANS STITCH

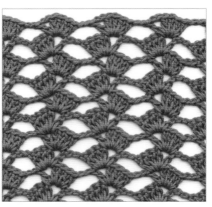

CROCHET DIAGRAM

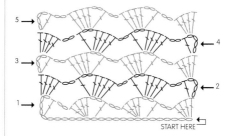

START HERE

CROCHET INSTRUCTIONS
Make a multiple of 7 ch, plus 4 extra.
Row 1 1 tr in 5th ch from hook, 2 ch, miss next 5 ch, 4 tr in next ch, *2 ch, 1 tr in next ch, 2 ch, miss next 5 ch, 4 tr in next ch; rep from * to end, turn.
Row 2 4 ch, 1 tr in first tr, *2 ch, miss next 2-ch sp and work [4 tr, 2 ch, 1 tr] all in following 2-ch sp; rep from * to last 2-ch sp, miss last 2-ch sp and work 4 tr in 4-ch loop at end, turn.
Rep row 2 to form patt.

TIARA LACE

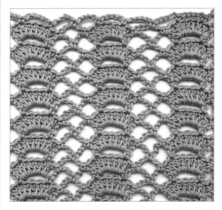

CROCHET DIAGRAM

START HERE

CROCHET INSTRUCTIONS
Make a multiple of 12 ch.
Row 1 (WS) 1 dc in 2nd ch from hook, *5 ch, miss next 3 ch, 1 dc in next ch; rep from *to last 2 ch, 2 ch, miss next ch, 1 tr in last ch, turn.
Row 2 (RS) 1 ch (does NOT count as a st), 1 dc in first st, miss next 2-ch sp, 7 tr in next 5-ch loop, 1 dc in next 5-ch loop, *5 ch, 1 dc in next 5-ch loop, 7 tr in next 5-ch loop, 1 dc in next 5-ch loop; rep from *, ending with 2 ch, 1 dtr in last dc, turn.
Row 3 1 ch (does NOT count as a st), 1 dc in first dtr, 5 ch, 1 dc in 2nd of next 7-tr shell, 5 ch, 1 dc in 6th tr of same shell, *5 ch, 1 dc in next 5-ch loop, 5 ch, 1 dc in 2nd of next 7-tr shell, 5 ch, 1 dc in 6th tr of same shell; rep from *, ending with 2 ch, 1 dtr in last dc, turn.
Rep rows 2 and 3 to form patt.

COLOURWORK

One-colour crochet has its charms, but using your creative imagination to combine colours is both more challenging and more rewarding. All of the crochet colourwork techniques are easy to master and worth experimenting with. Start by crocheting simple stripes, see below, before moving onto more decorative flower patterns (see page 283).

SIMPLE STRIPES	Stripes worked in basic stitches have more potential for creativity than most crocheters realize. The only techniques you need to learn is how and when to change colours to start a new stripe, and how to carry the yarns up the side edge of the crochet.

CHANGING COLOURS

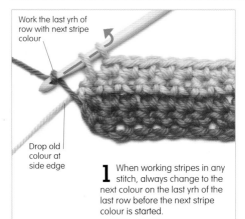

Work the last yrh of row with next stripe colour

Drop old colour at side edge

1 When working stripes in any stitch, always change to the next colour on the last yrh of the last row before the next stripe colour is started.

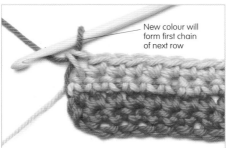

New colour will form first chain of next row

2 Drawing through the last yrh of the row completes the last stitch. The new colour is now on the hook ready to start the next stripe on the next row; this is so that the first turning chain in the next stripe is in the correct colour.

CARRYING COLOURS UP SIDE EDGE

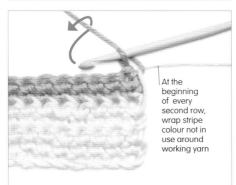

At the beginning of every second row, wrap stripe colour not in use around working yarn

If a colour is not needed for more than 2 rows, wrap it around the other colour to secure it. If it is not needed for more than 8 rows, cut it off and rejoin it later.

STRIPE COMBINATIONS

Smooth wool and fuzzy mohair stripe: The repeated double crochet stripe sequence here is two rows of a smooth wool yarn and two rows of a fuzzy mohair yarn, so each colour can simply be dropped at the side of the work and picked up when it is needed again.

Three-colour stripe: This double crochet stripe has a repeated sequence of two rows of each of three colours. Wrap the working yarn around the colours not in use on every second row to keep them snug against the edge. When changing colours, pull in the new colour firmly but not too tightly or it will pucker the edge.

Double crochet and treble crochet stripe: Each of the two stripes in this design is 2 rows tall. One stripe is worked in double crochet and the other in treble crochet. Adding in the taller trebles gives the crochet fabric a softer texture.

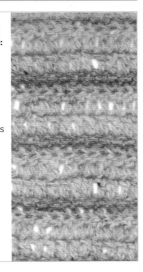

FOLLOWING A CROCHET PATTERN

Followed step by step and slowly, crochet patterns are not as difficult to work from as they appear. The guides here for a simple accessory and a garment give many tips for how to approach your first crochet patterns. This section also includes other techniques needed for working from a crochet pattern – simple increases and decreases for shaping garments, finishings such as edgings and button loops, and blocking and seams.

SIMPLE ACCESSORY PATTERNS

A beginner should choose an easy accessory pattern for a first crochet project. A striped cushion cover is given here as an example. Follow the numbered tips of the guide to familiarize yourself with the parts of a simple pattern.

1 Check the size of the finished item. If it is a simple square like this cushion, you can easily adjust the size by adding or subtracting stitches and rows.

2 It is best to use the yarn specified. But if you are unable to obtain this yarn, choose a substitute yarn as explained on page 245.

7 Make a tension swatch before starting to crochet and change the hook size if necessary (see opposite page).

8 Instructions for working a piece of crocheted fabric always start with how many chains to make for the foundation chain and which yarn or hook size to use. If there is only one hook size and one yarn, these may be absent here.

9 Consult the abbreviations list with your pattern for the meanings of abbreviations (see page 263).

13 The back of a cushion cover is sometimes exactly the same as the front or it has a fabric back. In this case, the stripes are reversed on the back for a more versatile cover.

14 After all the crocheted pieces are completed, follow the Finishing (or Making Up) section of the pattern.

STRIPED CUSHION COVER

Size of finished cushion
40.5 x 40.5cm (16 x 16in)

Materials
7 x 25g/⅞oz (110m/120yd) balls of branded Scottish Tweed 4-Ply in Thatch 00018 **(A)**
4 x 25g/⅞oz (110m/120yd) balls of branded Scottish Tweed 4-Ply in Skye 00009 **(B)**
3.5mm (US size E-4) crochet hook
Cushion pad to fit finished cover

Tension
22 sts and 24 rows to 10cm (4in) over double crochet using 3.5mm (US size E-4) hook or size necessary to achieve correct tension. To save time, take time to check tension.

Front
Using 3.5mm (US size E-4) hook and A, make 89 ch.
Row 1 1 dc in 2nd ch from hook, 1 dc in each of rem ch, turn. 88 dc.
Row 2 1 ch (does NOT count as a st), 1 dc in each dc to end, turn.
Rep row 2 throughout to form dc fabric.
Always changing to new colour with last yrh of last dc of previous row, work in stripes as follows:
26 rows more in A, 8 rows B, [8 rows A, 8 rows B] twice, 28 rows A.
Fasten off.

Back
Work as for Front, but use B for A, and A for B.

Finishing
Darn in loose ends.
Block and press lightly on wrong side, following instructions on yarn label.
With wrong sides facing, sew three sides of back and front together. Turn right-side out, insert cushion pad, and sew remaining seam.

3 Always purchase the same total amount in metres/yards of a substitute yarn; NOT the same amount in weight.

4 If desired, select different colours to suit your décor; the colours specified are just suggestions.

5 Alter the hook size if you cannot achieve the correct tension with the specified size (see 8 left).

6 Extra items needed for your project will usually be listed under Materials or Extras.

10 Work in the specified stitch pattern, for the specified number of rows or cm/in.

11 Colours for stripes are always changed at the end of the previous row before the colour change so the first turning chain of the new stripe is in the correct colour (see page 273).

12 Fastening off completes the crochet piece.

15 See page 257 for how to darn in loose ends.

16 Make sure you look at the yarn label instructions before attempting to press any piece of crochet. The label may say that the yarn cannot be pressed or it can be pressed only with a cool iron. (See page 280 for blocking tips.)

17 See pages 280 and 281 for seaming options. Take time with seams on crochet, and when working your very first seams, get an experienced crocheter to help you.

GARMENT PATTERNS

Garment instructions usually start with the Skill Level, followed by the Sizes, Materials, and finally the instructions. Most important for achieving a successful garment – or other fitted items such as hats, mittens, gloves, and socks – is choosing the right size and making a tension swatch.

TIPS

● **Choose a skill level** that suits your crochet experience. If in doubt or if you haven't crocheted for many years, stick to an Easy or Beginner's level until you are confident you can go to the next level.

● **White is a good colour** to use for your first crocheted sweater because the stitches are so easy to see clearly. But if you do choose white yarn, be sure to wash your hands every time you start crocheting; and when you stop, put away the yarn and sweater in a bag to keep it from becoming soiled.

● **Avoid black** or other very dark yarn for a first crocheted sweater, as the stitches are very difficult to distinguish, even for an accomplished crocheter.

● **Purchase yarn balls** that have the same dye-lot number (see pages 244–245).

● **Have a set** of hook sizes at hand if you are starting to crochet sweaters. When checking tension (see below), you will need other sizes in order to alter your hook size if necessary.

● **Always make the pieces** in the order given in the instructions, whether you are crocheting a garment, accessory or toy. On a garment, the back is usually crocheted first, followed by the front (or fronts if it is a cardigan or jacket), and lastly the sleeves. Pockets that are integrated into the fronts are crocheted before the fronts and those applied as patches are worked last.

● **It is not advisable** to attempt to alter sweater patterns. They are carefully designed for the back, front/s and sleeves to fit together precisely. For example, altering an armhole length will mean the sleeve head will not fit into it in the right way. The total length of the sleeve or sweater are sometimes adjustable, however, at the points specified in the pattern – usually right before the armhole shaping on the body and before the sleeve head shaping on the sleeve. But only adjust lengths where your instructions suggest it.

CHOOSING A GARMENT SIZE

Crochet garment sizes are usually listed as specific bust/chest sizes or in generic terms as Small, Medium, Large. (Children's sweater sizes are given in ages and chest sizes.) The best advice is not to stick strictly to choosing your preferred size by these criteria. Decide instead how you want the garment to fit you – how close-fitting or loose-fitting it should be. If you are planning to crochet a sweater, find one in your wardrobe that is comfortable and flattering and has a fabric weight and shape similar to the garment you are going to crochet. Smooth out the sweater and measure the width. Find the same, or closest, width to this on the sweater diagram of your crochet pattern – this is the size for you.

Make a photocopy of your pattern and circle or highlight all the figures that apply to your size throughout the pattern, starting with the number of balls of yarn to purchase, followed by the number of chains in the foundation chain for the sweater back, the length to the armhole, and so on. The figure for the smallest size is given first and all the figures for the larger sizes follow in parentheses. Where there is only one figure given in the instructions – be it a measurement, the number of rows, or the number of stitches – this figure applies to all sizes. Before starting your crochet, always check your tension.

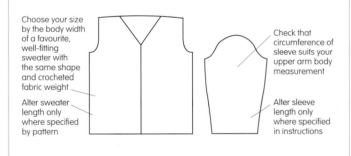

Choose your size by the body width of a favourite, well-fitting sweater with the same shape and crocheted fabric weight

Alter sweater length only where specified by pattern

Check that circumference of sleeve suits your upper arm body measurement

Alter sleeve length only where specified in instructions

MEASURING TENSION

It is essential to check your tension (stitch size) before beginning a crochet pattern. Not everyone crochets stitches with exactly the same tightness or looseness, so you may well need to use a different hook size to achieve the stitch size required by your pattern.

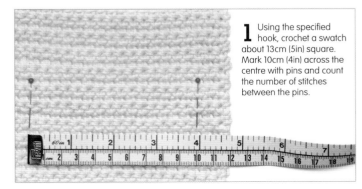

1 Using the specified hook, crochet a swatch about 13cm (5in) square. Mark 10cm (4in) across the centre with pins and count the number of stitches between the pins.

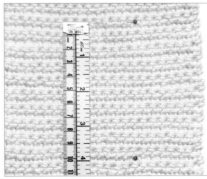

2 Count the number of rows to 10cm (4in) in the same way. If you have fewer stitches and rows than you should, try again with a smaller hook size; if you have more, change to a larger hook size. Use the hook size that best matches the correct tension. (Matching the stitch width is much more important than matching the row height.)

SHAPING
CROCHET

To move from making simple squares and rectangles, a crocheter needs to know how to increase and decrease the number of stitches in the row to make shaped pieces. The most commonly used simple shaping techniques are provided here.

DOUBLE CROCHET INCREASES

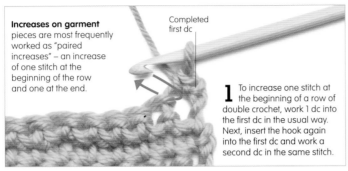

Increases on garment pieces are most frequently worked as "paired increases" – an increase of one stitch at the beginning of the row and one at the end.

Completed first dc

1 To increase one stitch at the beginning of a row of double crochet, work 1 dc into the first dc in the usual way. Next, insert the hook again into the first dc and work a second dc in the same stitch.

2 This completes the increase. Continue across the row, working 1 dc into each dc in the usual way.

2 dc worked into same stitch

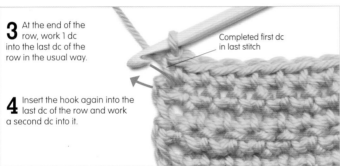

3 At the end of the row, work 1 dc into the last dc of the row in the usual way.

Completed first dc in last stitch

4 Insert the hook again into the last dc of the row and work a second dc into it.

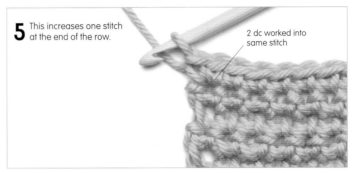

5 This increases one stitch at the end of the row.

2 dc worked into same stitch

TREBLE CROCHET INCREASES

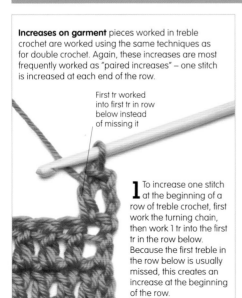

Increases on garment pieces worked in treble crochet are worked using the same techniques as for double crochet. Again, these increases are most frequently worked as "paired increases" – one stitch is increased at each end of the row.

First tr worked into first tr in row below instead of missing it

1 To increase one stitch at the beginning of a row of treble crochet, first work the turning chain, then work 1 tr into the first tr in the row below. Because the first treble in the row below is usually missed, this creates an increase at the beginning of the row.

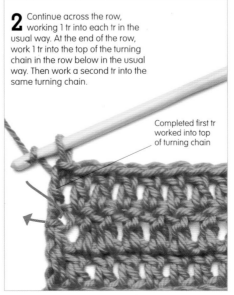

2 Continue across the row, working 1 tr into each tr in the usual way. At the end of the row, work 1 tr into the top of the turning chain in the row below in the usual way. Then work a second tr into the same turning chain.

Completed first tr worked into top of turning chain

3 This completes the one stitch increase at the end of the row as shown.

2 tr worked into same chain

STEP INCREASE AT BEGINNING OF ROW

1 Increases are also frequently worked in crochet so that they form little steps at the edge. As an example, to add a 3-stitch step increase at the beginning of a row of double crochet, begin by making 4 chains as shown here. (Always make one chain more than the number of extra double crochets required.)

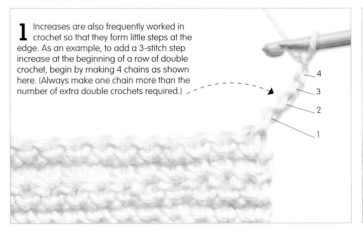

2 Work the first dc into the second chain from the hook. Then work 1 dc into each of the remaining 2 chains. This creates a 3-dc increase at the beginning of the row.

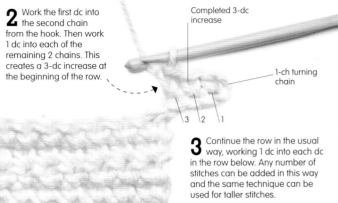

Completed 3-dc increase

1-ch turning chain

3 Continue the row in the usual way, working 1 dc into each dc in the row below. Any number of stitches can be added in this way and the same technique can be used for taller stitches.

STEP INCREASE AT END OF ROW

Separate length of yarn (shown here in a contrasting colour for clarity)

Extend loop so it won't unravel

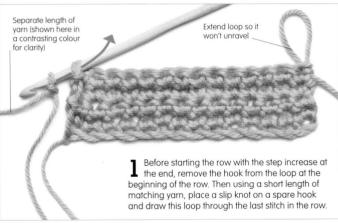

1 Before starting the row with the step increase at the end, remove the hook from the loop at the beginning of the row. Then using a short length of matching yarn, place a slip knot on a spare hook and draw this loop through the last stitch in the row.

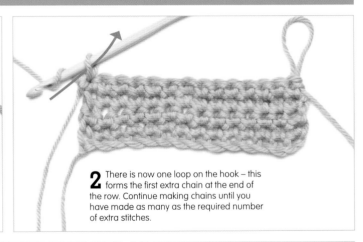

2 There is now one loop on the hook – this forms the first extra chain at the end of the row. Continue making chains until you have made as many as the required number of extra stitches.

3 So for a 3-stitch step increase, make a total of 3 chains. Then fasten off.

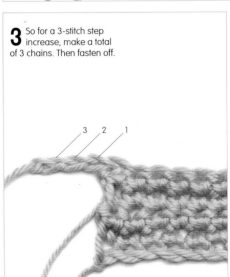

4 Return to the beginning of the row, slip the loop back onto the hook and tighten it, then work to the end of the row in the usual way until you reach the added chains.

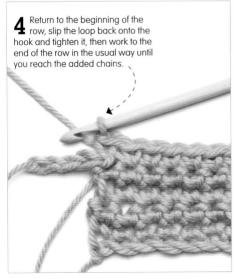

5 Work 1 dc into each of the 3 added chains. This creates a 3-dc increase. Any number of stitches can be added in this way and the same technique can be used for taller stitches.

Completed 3-dc increase

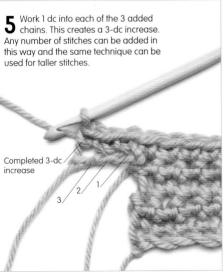

DOUBLE CROCHET DECREASES (Abbreviation = *dc2tog*)

Decreases on garment pieces, like increases, are most frequently worked as "paired decreases" – a decrease of one stitch at the beginning of the row and another at the end.

1 To decrease one stitch at the beginning of a row of double crochet, work up to the last yrh of the first dc in the usual way, but do not complete the stitch – there are now 2 loops on the hook. Insert the hook through the next stitch as shown and draw a loop through.

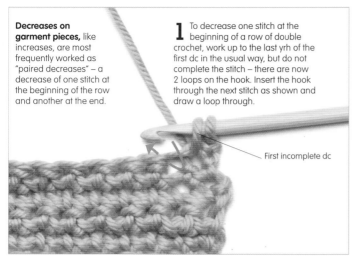

First incomplete dc

2 There are now 3 loops on the hook. Wrap the yarn around the hook and draw a loop through all 3 loops at once as shown.

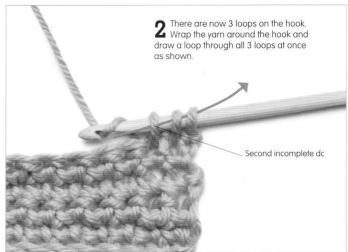

Second incomplete dc

3 This completes the decrease – where there were 2 stitches, there is now only one.

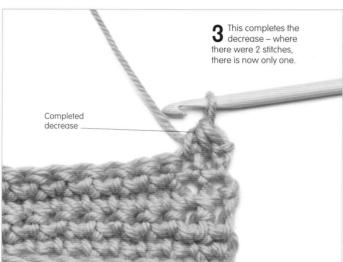

Completed decrease

4 Continue across the row, working 1 dc into each dc in the usual way up to the last 2 stitches of the row.

5 At the end of the row, insert the hook through the top of the second to last stitch and draw a loop through – there are now 2 loops on the hook.

6 Insert the hook through the last stitch in the row below as shown by the large arrow and draw a loop through.

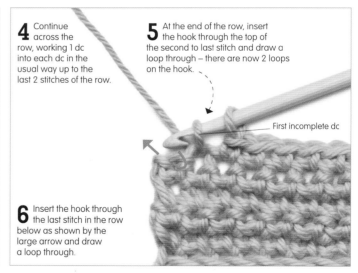

First incomplete dc

7 There are now 3 loops on the hook. Wrap the yarn around the hook and draw a loop through all 3 loops at once as shown.

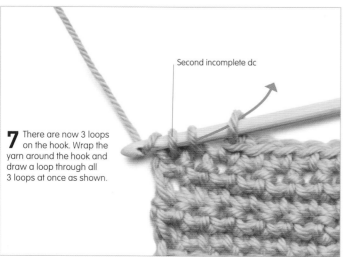

Second incomplete dc

8 This completes the decrease at the end of the row. (The same principle can be used for a "double decrease", where 2 stitches are decreased at once. For this, work 3 incomplete dc and join them together at the top with the last yrh – this is called dc3tog.)

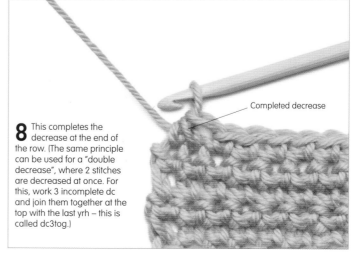

Completed decrease

TREBLE CROCHET DECREASES (Abbreviation = tr2tog)

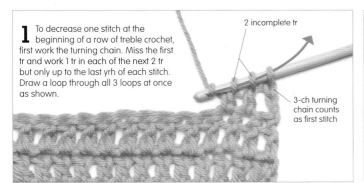

1 To decrease one stitch at the beginning of a row of treble crochet, first work the turning chain. Miss the first tr and work 1 tr in each of the next 2 tr but only up to the last yrh of each stitch. Draw a loop through all 3 loops at once as shown.

2 incomplete tr

3-ch turning chain counts as first stitch

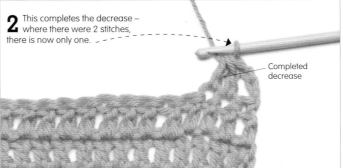

2 This completes the decrease – where there were 2 stitches, there is now only one.

Completed decrease

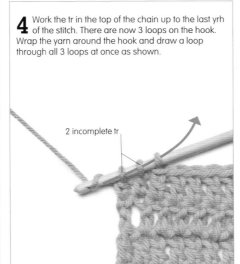

3 Continue across the row in the usual way up to the last tr in the row below. Now work a tr into the last tr but only up to the last yrh. Wrap the yarn around the hook and insert the hook into the top of the turning chain in the row below as shown.

First incomplete tr

Top of turning chain

4 Work the tr in the top of the chain up to the last yrh of the stitch. There are now 3 loops on the hook. Wrap the yarn around the hook and draw a loop through all 3 loops at once as shown.

2 incomplete tr

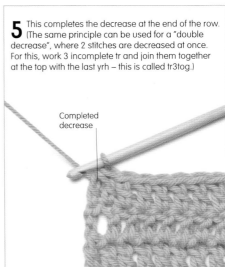

5 This completes the decrease at the end of the row. (The same principle can be used for a "double decrease", where 2 stitches are decreased at once. For this, work 3 incomplete tr and join them together at the top with the last yrh – this is called tr3tog.)

Completed decrease

STEP DECREASES

At beginning of row: Decreases, like increases, can also be worked so that they form little steps at the edge. As an example, to decrease 3 stitches at the beginning of a row of double crochet, work 1 chain and then 1 slip stitch into each of the first 4 dc. Next, work 1 chain, then work the first dc in the same place that the last slip stitch was worked. Continue along the row in the usual way.

Slip stitch to correct position

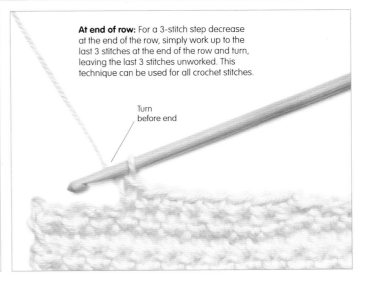

At end of row: For a 3-stitch step decrease at the end of the row, simply work up to the last 3 stitches at the end of the row and turn, leaving the last 3 stitches unworked. This technique can be used for all crochet stitches.

Turn before end

BLOCKING
AND SEAMS

Always sew the seams on a garment or accessory using a blunt-ended needle and a matching yarn (a contrasting yarn is used here just to show the seam techniques more clearly); and work them in the order given in the crochet pattern. But before sewing any seams, block your crochet pieces carefully. Press the finished seams very lightly with a cool iron on the wrong side after completion.

WET BLOCKING

If your yarn will allow it, wet blocking is the best way to even out crochet. Wet the pieces in a sink full of lukewarm water. Then squeeze out the water and roll the crochet in a towel to remove excess dampness. Smooth the crochet into shape right-side down on layers of dry towels covered with a sheet, pinning at intervals. Add as many pins as is necessary to refine the shape. Do not move the crochet until it is completely dry.

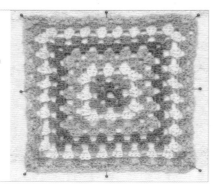

STEAM BLOCKING

For a speedier process you may prefer steam blocking (if your yarn label allows it). First, pin the crochet right-side down into the correct shape. Then steam the crochet gently using a clean damp cloth, but barely touching the cloth with the iron. Never rest the weight of an iron on your crochet or it will flatten the texture. Leave the steamed piece to dry completely before unpinning it.

BACKSTITCH SEAM

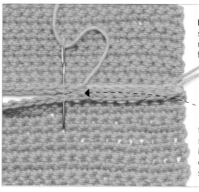

Backstitch produces durable seams and is frequently recommended in crochet patterns for garments and accessories.

1 Align the crochet pieces with right sides together and secure the yarn with two or three overcast stitches in the same place. Then inserting the needle close to the edge, work the seam taking one stitch forwards and one stitch back.

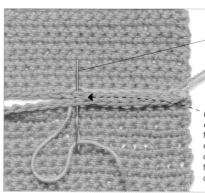

Blunt-ended yarn needle

2 On the backwards stitch, be sure to insert the needle through the same place as the end of the last stitch. At the end of the seam, secure the yarn in the same way as at the beginning of the seam.

OVERCAST STITCH SEAM

Simple overcast seam: Align the crochet pieces with right sides together and secure the yarn as for backstitch. Then inserting the needle close to the edge, make stitches through the two layers as shown.

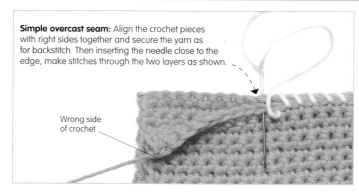

Wrong side of crochet

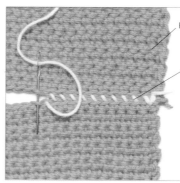

Right side of crochet

Pull seam yarn tight to make seam stitches disappear

Flat overcast seam: For a flat seam along the tops of stitches, lay the pieces right-side up and edge-to-edge. Work as for the simple overcast seam, but inserting the needle through only the back loops of the stitches.

EDGE-TO-EDGE SEAM

This method creates a neat flat seam line. It can be used, as here, on treble crochet as well as on all other types of crochet fabrics.

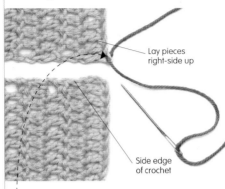

Lay pieces right-side up

Side edge of crochet

1 Align the pieces of crochet right-side up and edge-to-edge. Insert the needle through the corner of the top piece, leaving a long loose end.

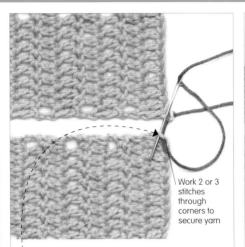

Work 2 or 3 stitches through corners to secure yarn

2 Insert the needle through the corner of the other piece, then through both pieces again in the same place at the corner to secure firmly.

3 Make the next stitch along the centre of the stitch (a treble or a turning chain) at the edge on the top piece of crochet.

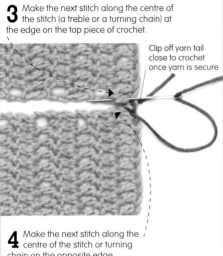

Clip off yarn tail close to crochet once yarn is secure

4 Make the next stitch along the centre of the stitch or turning chain on the opposite edge.

5 Make the next pair of stitches in the same way, working a stitch along one stitch or turning chain on the top piece then on the opposite piece.

6 Continue along the seam taking a stitch in each side alternately. Take shorter stitches on each piece if the yarn used for the pieces is bulky.

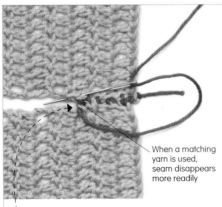

When a matching yarn is used, seam disappears more readily

7 After every few stitches, pull the yarn tight so that the seam yarn disappears and is not visible on the right side of the crochet.

SLIP STITCH SEAM

1 Instead of using a yarn needle to join your seam, you can use a crochet hook to work a quicker seam. Although seams can be worked with double crochet, slip stitch seams are less bulky. Start by placing a slip knot on the hook.

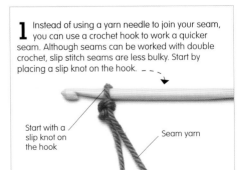

Start with a slip knot on the hook

Seam yarn

2 Align the two layers of crochet with the right sides together.

3 Then with the slip knot on the hook, insert the hook through the two layers at the starting end of the seam, wrap the yarn around the hook and draw a loop through the two layers and the loop on the hook.

4 Continue in this way and fasten off at the end. When working the seam along the tops of stitches (as here), insert the hook through only the back loops of the stitches. Along row-end edges, work through the layers one stitch in from the edge.

FINISHING
DETAILS

Finishings are often more difficult for crocheters than making the pieces. Some of the techniques most frequently used are shown here. Take your time with all finishings, and practise the methods on small swatches before adding them to your completed pieces.

DOUBLE CROCHET EDGING

Along top or bottom of a piece of crochet: Adding a simple double crochet edging is a good way to tidy up the edges of a piece of crochet. To work a double crochet edging along the top or bottom of a piece of crochet, join the yarn to the first stitch with a slip stitch, work 1 ch, 1 dc in the same place as the slip stitch, then work 1 dc in each stitch below all along the edge.

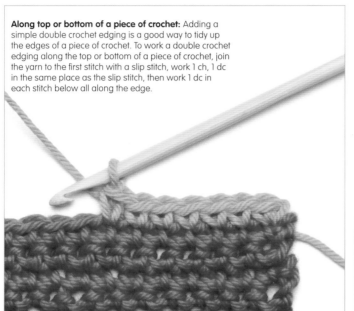

Along row-ends of a piece of crochet: A double crochet edging is worked the same way along the row-ends of a piece of crochet, but it is not as easy to achieve an even edging. To create a perfect result, experiment with how many stitches to work per row-end. If the finished edging looks flared, try working fewer stitches per row-end; and if it looks puckered, try again working more stitches per row-end.

CROCHETING EDGING DIRECTLY ONTO EDGE

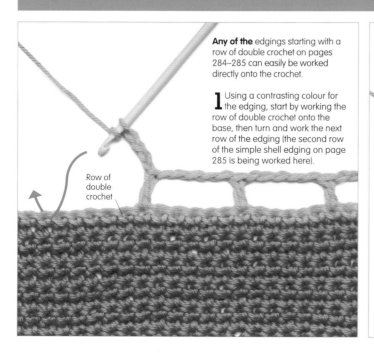

Any of the edgings starting with a row of double crochet on pages 284–285 can easily be worked directly onto the crochet.

1 Using a contrasting colour for the edging, start by working the row of double crochet onto the base, then turn and work the next row of the edging (the second row of the simple shell edging on page 285 is being worked here).

Row of double crochet

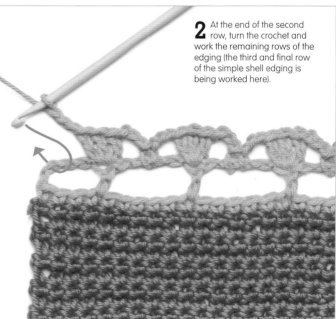

2 At the end of the second row, turn the crochet and work the remaining rows of the edging (the third and final row of the simple shell edging is being worked here).

Embellishments

There are many ways to add subtle or bold embellishments to your crochet. Adornments that will dress up your stitching include beads, ribbons, flowers, fringing, and edgings.

SIMPLE FLOWER PATTERNS

Crochet flowers are very seductive – even simple ones like these, which are all easy and very quick to stitch. They make great brooches – sew a safety pin to the back and maybe a button or an artificial pearl to the flower centre.

SHORT LOOP FLOWER

CROCHET DIAGRAM

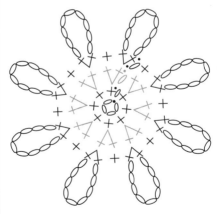

CROCHET INSTRUCTIONS

This flower is worked in 2 colours (A, B).
Using A, make 4 ch and join with a ss to first ch to form a ring.
Round 1 (RS) 1 ch (does NOT count as a st), 8 dc in ring, join with a ss to first dc of round.
Round 2 1 ch (does NOT count as a st), 2 dc in same place as ss, *2 dc in next dc; rep from * to end, join with a ss to first dc of round. 16 dc. Fasten off A.
Round 3 Using B, join with a ss to a dc, 1 ch, work (1 dc, 9 ch, 1 dc) all in same place as last ss, 1 dc in next dc, *work (1 dc, 9 ch, 1 dc) all in next dc, 1 dc in next dc; rep from * 6 times more, join with a ss to first dc of round. Fasten off.

LONG LOOP FLOWER

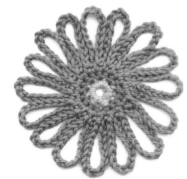

CROCHET DIAGRAM

Total of 17 ch in each loop

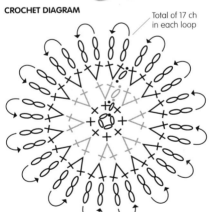

CROCHET INSTRUCTIONS

This flower is worked in 3 colours (A, B, C).
Using A, make 4 ch and join with a ss to first ch to form a ring.
Round 1 (RS) 1 ch (does NOT count as a st), 8 dc in ring, join with a ss to first dc of round. Fasten off A.
Round 2 Using B, join with a ss to a dc, 1 ch (does NOT count as a st), 2 dc in same place as last ss, *2 dc in next dc; rep from * to end, join with a ss to first dc of round. 16 dc. Fasten off B.
Round 3 Using C, join with a ss to a dc, 1 ch, work (1 dc, 17 ch, 1 dc) all in same place as last ss, *work (1 dc, 17 ch, 1 dc) all in next dc; rep from * 14 times more, join with a ss to first dc of round. Fasten off.

BUTTON FLOWER

CROCHET DIAGRAM

CROCHET INSTRUCTIONS

Note: cluster = [yrh twice and insert hook in sp, yrh and draw a loop through, (yrh and draw through first 2 loops on hook) twice] 4 times all in same sp (5 loops now on hook), yrh and draw through all 5 loops on hook.
This flower is worked in 2 colours (A, B).
Using A, make 4 ch and join with a ss to first ch to form a ring.
Round 1 (RS) 4 ch (counts as first dtr), 20 dtr in ring, join with a ss to 4th of 4-ch.
Round 2 Using B, join with a ss to same place as last ss, 1 ch (does NOT count as a st), 1 dc in same place as last ss, [5 ch, miss next 2 dtr, 1 dc in next dtr] 6 times, 5 ch, join with a ss to first dc of round.
Round 3 *Work (1 ss, 4 ch, 1 cluster, 4 ch, 1 ss) all in next 5-ch loop; rep from * 6 times more, join with a ss to last dc in round 2.
Fasten off. Sew a small button to centre of flower.

SIMPLE EDGING
PATTERNS

Adding a decorative crochet edging to an otherwise mundane-looking piece of crochet (or knitting) can transform it, giving it a touch of elegance. All the simple crochet edgings that follow are worked widthwise, so you start with a length of chain roughly equivalent to the length of edging you need. Suitable even for beginners, these edgings are perfect for dressing up towel ends, throws, baby blankets, necklines, and cuffs. When making an edging that will encircle a blanket, be sure to add extra for turning the corners; the edging can then be gathered at each corner to allow for the turning. Use a short test swatch to calculate how much extra you will need at each corner. See page 263 for abbreviations and symbols.

DIAMOND EDGING

CROCHET DIAGRAM

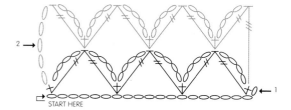

START HERE

CROCHET INSTRUCTIONS
Make a multiple of 6 ch, plus 2 extra.
Row 1 (RS) 1 dc in 2nd ch from hook, *4 ch, yrh twice and insert hook in same place as last dc, [yrh and draw first 2 loops on hook] twice, yrh twice, miss next 5 ch and insert hook in next ch, [yrh and draw first 2 loops on hook] twice, yrh and draw through all 3 loops on hook – called dtr2tog –, 4 ch, 1 dc in same place as last dtr; rep from * to end, turn.
Row 2 5 ch, 1 dtr in first dtr2tog, 4 ch, 1 dc in same place as last dtr, *4 ch, dtr2tog over last dtr worked into and next dtr, 4 ch, 1 dc in same place as last dtr; rep from *, 4 ch, yrh twice and insert hook in same place as last dc, [yrh and draw first 2 loops on hook] twice, yrh 3 times and insert hook in last dc in previous row, [yrh and draw first 2 loops on hook] 3 times, yrh and draw through all 3 loops on hook.
Fasten off.

BOLD SCALLOP EDGING

CROCHET DIAGRAM

START HERE

CROCHET INSTRUCTIONS
Make a multiple of 10 ch, plus 2 extra.
Row 1 (RS) 1 dc in 2nd ch from hook, 1 dc in each of rem ch, turn.
Row 2 1 ch, 1 dc in first dc, 2 ch, miss next 2 dc, 1 dc in next dc, 7 ch, miss next 3 dc, 1 dc in next dc, *6 ch, miss next 5 dc, 1 dc in next dc, 7 ch, miss next 3 dc, 1 dc in next dc; rep from * to last 3 dc, 2 ch, miss next 2 dc, 1 dc in last dc, turn.
Row 3 1 ch, 1 dc in first dc, 14 tr in 7-ch loop, *1 dc in next 6-ch sp, 14 tr in next 7-ch loop; rep from *, ending with 1 dc in last dc.
Fasten off.

TRIPLE PICOT EDGING

CROCHET DIAGRAM

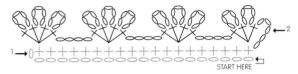

START HERE

CROCHET INSTRUCTIONS
Make a multiple of 6 ch, plus 2 extra.
Row 1 (WS) 1 dc in 2nd ch from hook, 1 dc in each of rem ch, turn.
Row 2 (RS) 5 ch, work [1 dc, (5 ch, 1 dc) twice] all in first dc, *4 ch, miss next 5 dc, [1 dc, (5 ch, 1 dc) 3 times] all in next dc; rep from * to end.
Fasten off.

PICOT SCALLOP EDGING

CROCHET DIAGRAM

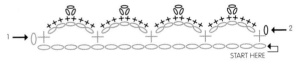

START HERE

CROCHET INSTRUCTIONS
Make a multiple of 4 ch, plus 2 extra.
Row 1 (WS) 1 dc in 2nd ch from hook, *5 ch, miss next 3 ch, 1 dc in next ch; rep from * to end, turn.
Row 2 (RS) 1 ch, *work [4 dc, 3 ch, 4 dc] all in next 5-ch loop; rep from * to end.
Fasten off.

SIMPLE SHELL EDGING

CROCHET DIAGRAM

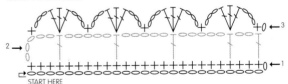

START HERE

CROCHET INSTRUCTIONS
Make a multiple of 6 ch, plus 2 extra.
Row 1 (RS) 1 dc in 2nd ch from hook, 1 dc in each of rem ch, turn.
Row 2 5 ch, miss first 3 dc, 1 tr in next dc, *5 ch, miss next 5 dc, 1 tr in next dc; rep from * to last 3 dc, 2 ch, miss next 2 dc, 1 tr in last dc, turn.
Row 3 1 ch, 1 dc in first tr, 3 ch, 3 tr in next tr, *3 ch, 1 dc in next 5-ch space, 3 ch, 3 tr in next tr; rep from *, ending with 3 ch, miss first 2 ch of last 5-ch, 1 dc in next ch.
Fasten off.

GRAND EYELET EDGING

CROCHET DIAGRAM

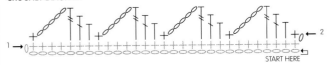

START HERE

CROCHET INSTRUCTIONS
Make a multiple of 7 ch, plus 2 extra.
Row 1 (WS) 1 dc in 2nd ch from hook, 1 dc in each of rem ch, turn.
Row 2 (RS) 1 ch, 1 dc in first dc, 1 htr in next dc, 1 tr in next dc, 1 dtr in next dc, *5 ch, miss next 3 dc, 1 dc in next dc, 1 htr in next dc, 1 tr in next dc, 1 dtr in next dc; rep from * to last 4 dc, 5 ch, miss next 3 dc, 1 dc in last dc.
Fasten off.

CIRCULAR CROCHET

Crochet can be worked not only back and forth in rows, but round and round in circles to form tubes or flat shapes started from the centre (called medallions). The basic techniques for crocheting in the round are very easy to learn, even for a beginner, so it is not surprising that many popular crochet accessories are made with circular crochet, including flowers and afghan motifs, as well as seamless toys, hats, mittens, containers, and bags.

CROCHETING TUBES

Tubular crochet is started on a long foundation chain joined into a ring, and the rounds of stitches are worked around this ring. The easiest of all crochet cylinders is double crochet worked in a spiral without turning chains.

STARTING A TUBE

1 Start the crochet cylinder, or tube, with the length of chain specified in your crochet pattern. Then, insert the hook through the first chain.

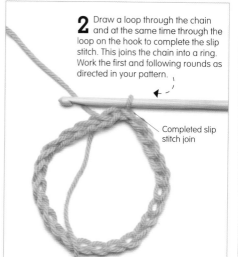

Make sure chain is not twisted

2 Draw a loop through the chain and at the same time through the loop on the hook to complete the slip stitch. This joins the chain into a ring. Work the first and following rounds as directed in your pattern.

Completed slip stitch join

DOUBLE CROCHET SPIRAL TUBE

1 Make the foundation ring and work one chain. Work the first double crochet into the same place as the slip stitch. Then work 1 dc into each of the remaining chains of the ring.

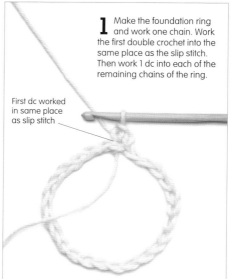

First dc worked in same place as slip stitch

2 Place a stitch marker on the last stitch of the first round to keep track of where the rounds begin and end.

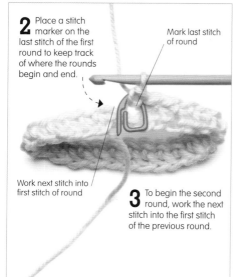

Mark last stitch of round

Work next stitch into first stitch of round

3 To begin the second round, work the next stitch into the first stitch of the previous round.

4 On the second round, work 1 dc in each dc in the round below.

Move marker up at end of each round

5 At the end of the round move the marker up onto the last stitch of this round. (As the spiral grows, the beginning of the round moves gradually to the right.)

6 Continue round and round in the same way until the crochet tube is the required length.

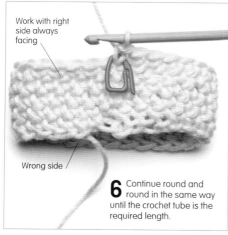

Work with right side always facing

Wrong side

FLAT
CIRCLES

The circular crochet techniques for making flat shapes are a little more difficult than those for making tubes. Making a simple circle is a good example for how other flat medallion shapes are started and then worked round and round from the centre. The circle is also used in conjunction with the crochet tube to make containers or the parts of toys, so it is well worth practising.

CROCHETING A CIRCLE

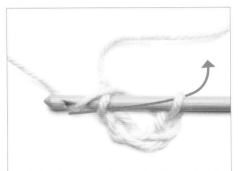

1 Follow these steps when working the simple circle below for the first time. The circle is worked from the centre outwards. Start with 4 ch. Then work a slip stitch into the first chain as shown by the large arrow.

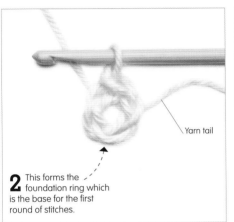

Yarn tail

2 This forms the foundation ring which is the base for the first round of stitches.

3 For a double crochet circle, start the first round with 1 chain. Then lay the yarn end around the top of the chain and start working the double crochet stitches of the first round through the centre of the ring and around the yarn tail.

Work stitches over yarn tail

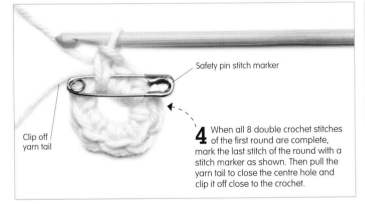

Safety pin stitch marker

Clip off yarn tail

4 When all 8 double crochet stitches of the first round are complete, mark the last stitch of the round with a stitch marker as shown. Then pull the yarn tail to close the centre hole and clip it off close to the crochet.

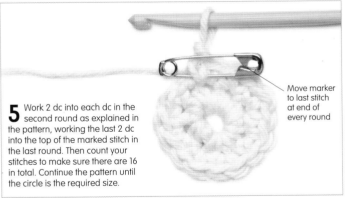

5 Work 2 dc into each dc in the second round as explained in the pattern, working the last 2 dc into the top of the marked stitch in the last round. Then count your stitches to make sure there are 16 in total. Continue the pattern until the circle is the required size.

Move marker to last stitch at end of every round

SIMPLE 11-ROUND CIRCLE MEDALLION

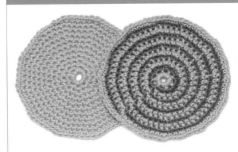

This pattern is for a classic simple crochet circle. (See page 263 for abbreviations.)

Note: Work the circle in a single colour or in two colours (A and B). For a two-colour circle, work the foundation ring and round 1 in A, then work the following rounds in B and A alternately, changing to the new colour with the last yrh of the last dc of each round and carrying the colours up the wrong side of the circle.
Make 4 ch and join with a ss in first ch to form a ring.
Round 1 (RS) 1ch, 8 dc in ring. Do not turn at end of rounds, but work with RS always facing.

Note: Mark the last stitch of round 1, and at the end of each of the following rounds, move this marker to the last stitch of the round just worked.
Round 2 2 dc in each dc. *16 dc.*
Round 3 *1 dc in next dc, 2 dc in next dc; rep from *. *24 dc.*
Round 4 1 dc in each dc.
Round 5 *1 dc in next dc, 2 dc in next dc; rep from *. *36 dc.*
Round 6 Rep round 4.
Round 7 *1 dc in each of next 2 dc, 2 dc in next dc; rep from *. *48 dc.*
Round 8 Rep round 4.

Round 9 *1 dc in each of next 3 dc, 2 dc in next dc; rep from *. *60 dc.*
Round 10 Rep round 4.
Round 11 1 dc in each of first 2 dc, 2 dc in next dc, *1 dc in each of next 4 dc, 2 dc in next dc; rep from *, ending with 1 dc in each of last 2 dc. *72 dc.*
Work 1 ss in next dc and fasten off.
To make a bigger circle, continue in this way, adding 12 extra dc in every alternate round (by working one more stitch between increases) and altering the position of the first increase on every increase round.

BABY'S HAT

This cute, quirky hat would suit a baby girl or boy. Made in one piece, crocheted in the round, the earflaps are then added to the lower edge, while the "ears" are made separately and stitched in place.

MATERIALS

Size
To fit a baby aged 9-12 months

Yarn
You can use any lightweight DK wool or wool blend yarn. We have used Debbie Bliss Baby Cashmerino 50g (125m/137yd) in 2 colours
A: 032 Sky x 1 ball
B: 064 Mink x 1 ball

032 Sky x 1   04 Mink x 1

Crochet hook
A: 3.75mm hook
B: 3mm hook

Tension
17 htr to 10cm (4in)

Notions
Stitch marker

Special Notes
Crab stitch: Work dc from left to right, instead of right to left. (Left-handed crocheters will work right to left.) After completing a round of double crochet, do not turn work. 1 ch, *insert hook into next stitch to the right (not in the stitch just completed, but the next one), draw a loop through, yrh and pull through both loops on the hook; rep from * to end.

PATTERN

HAT CROWN
With 3.75mm hook and yarn A, make 3 ch, 8 htr into 3rd ch from hook, ss in first htr to join. (8sts)
Round 1 2 ch, 1 htr in same st. 2 htr in each htr to end, ss in top of 2-ch to join. (16sts)
Round 2 2 ch, 1 htr in same st. *1 htr in next st, 2 htr in next st; rep from * to end, ss in top of 2-ch to join. (24sts)
Round 3 2 ch, 1 htr in same st, 2 htr in next st. *1 htr in each of next 2 sts, 2 htr in next st; rep from * to end, ss in top of 2-ch to join. (32sts)
Round 4 2 ch, 1 htr in each of next 2 sts, 2 htr in next st. *1 htr in each of next 3 sts, 2 htr in next st; rep from * to end, ss in top of 2-ch to join. (40sts)
Round 5 2 ch, 1 htr in each of next 3 sts, 2 htr in next st. *1 htr in each of next 4 sts, 2 htr in next st; rep from * to end, ss in top of 2-ch to join. (48sts)
Continue in this way, working an additional 1 htr between each increase per round, until there are 72sts. Work one round straight.
Next round 2 ch, 1 htr in each of next 7 sts, 2 htr in next st. *1 htr in each of next 8 sts, 2 htr in next st; rep from * to end, ss in top of 2-ch to join. (80sts)
Work straight without increasing for approximately 8cm (3in).

EARFLAPS
Rows 1-2 2 ch, 1 htr in each of next 14 sts, turn. (15sts)
Row 3 2 ch, htr2tog, 1 htr in each st to last 3 sts, htr2tog, 1 htr in last st, turn. (13sts)
Rep last row until there are 5 sts.
Fasten off yarn.
Rejoin yarn to lower edge, 20 sts to the left from first earflap.
Work second earflap to match the first.
Fasten off yarn A.

Corded edging crab stitch sometimes called "reverse double crochet" – forms a neat corded edge.

EDGING
Attach yarn B to any st along lower edge. Work 1 ch, then work evenly in dc around entire edge, including earflaps, join with ss in first dc. Do not turn, but work back around in the other direction in using crab stitch to create a corded edge. (See Special Notes.)
Fasten off yarn B and weave in ends.

EARS (make 2 in yarn A and 2 in yarn B)
Using 3mm hook, make 2 ch, 6 dc into 2nd ch from hook, ss in first dc to join. (6sts)
Round 1 1 ch, 2 dc in each dc to end, do not join. (12sts)
Round 2 *1 dc in next dc, 2 dc in next dc, rep from * to end, do not join. (18sts)
Round 3 *1 dc in each of next 2 dc, 2 dc in next dc, rep from * to end, ss in top of first dc to join. (24sts)
Round 4 1 ch, *1 dc in each of next 3 dc, 2 dc in next dc, rep from * to end, ss in top of first dc to join. (30sts)

FINISHING
Block all pieces lightly (see p.280).
Sew each yarn B ear piece to a yarn A ear piece, with wrong sides facing each other and yarn B at front. Sew one completed ear to either side of hat crown, above earflaps.

Ear Two layers of spiral rounds are joined together to form each ear. The ears are attached directly to the hat crown.

BABY'S BOOTIES

These adorable booties are made in the softest yarn for delicate skin, and in a style that is sure to stay on small feet. The booties are made in the round, starting with the sole. Be sure to use a stitch marker throughout to mark the first stitch of the round.

MATERIALS

Size
To fit a newborn baby

Yarn
Sublime Cashmere Merino Silk DK 50g

x 1 ball

Crochet hook
4mm (G-6 US) hook

Tension
Measure tension after completing the sole of each bootie. The length of the sole should be a minimum of 8.5cm (3¼in).

Notions
4 small buttons

PATTERN

BOOTIES (MAKE 2)
Work 9 ch.
Round 1 Miss 1 ch, dc in each ch to end, 4 dc in last ch. Working down other side of ch, dc in each ch to end, work 4 dc in last ch. (22sts)
Round 2 *Dc in next 7 sts, work (1 dc in next st, 2 dc in next st) twice; rep from * once more. (26sts)
Round 3 *Dc in next 7 sts, work (1 dc in each of next 2 sts, 2 dc in next st) twice; rep from * once more. (30sts)
Round 4 *Dc in next 7 sts, work (1 dc in each of next 3 sts, 2 dc in next st) twice; rep from * once more. (34sts)
Round 5 Working into back loops only, dc in each dc to end. (34sts)
Round 6 Dc in next 7 sts, work (1 dc in each of next 3 sts, dc2tog) twice, dc in next 17 sts. (32sts)
Round 7 Dc in next 7 sts, tr2tog 4 times, dc in next 7 sts, htr in next 10 sts. (28sts)
Round 8 Dc in next 7 sts, tr2tog twice, dc in next 7 sts, htr in next 10 sts, ss in first st to close. (26sts)
Do not fasten off yarn.
First strap: 9 ch, dc in 4th ch from hook and in each of next 5 chs, ss in beg st.
Fasten off.

The button loop at the end of each strap needs to fit snugly around the button. Adjust the size by adding or subtracting chains.

Second strap: Rejoin yarn on other side of bootie at corresponding st (the last dc before the htr sts) and rep instructions for first strap. Fasten off, weave in ends. Attach buttons securely, as shown in picture.

The sole of the bootie is worked in rounds without joining. Be sure to check the measurement of each sole for tension.

BABY'S CARDIGAN

A beautiful cardigan for a very special baby, this project is sure to keep your favourite little one warm and cosy. The clever, simple construction incorporates the sleeves into the body of the cardigan so no seaming is needed, making this a great introductory garment project.

MATERIALS

Size
To fit a baby aged 0–6 (6–12) months

Yarn
Jarol Heritage DK/Berroco Vintage DK 100g

A × 2   **B** × 1 ball

Crochet hook
4mm (G-6 US) hook

Notion
3 buttons, approx 1cm (½in) in diameter

Tension
17 htr per 10cm (4in)

PATTERN

FRONT (MAKE 2)
Using yarn B and 4mm hook, work 22 (25) ch.
Row 1 1 htr into 3rd ch from hook, 1 htr into each ch to end. Turn. 20 (23) sts.
Row 2 2 ch, 1 htr into each st across row. Turn. Change to yarn A and work straight in htr until piece measures 15 (16)cm/6 (6½)in.
Next row: 27(32) ch, 1 htr into 3rd ch from hook, then one htr into each ch to end of ch. 25 (30) sts increased for arm. Work across body stitches. 45 (53) htr
Work straight on these sts until piece measures approx 20 (21)cm/8 (8½) in from hem, ending at arm edge.
Next row: Work across in htr to last 6 (8) sts, 1 dc into next st, turn leaving rem sts unworked for neck opening.
Next row: Sl st across 5 sts, htr to end of row. Work straight until piece measures 24 (25)cm/ 9½ (10)in to shoulder.
Fasten off yarn.

BACK
Using yarn B and 4mm hook, work 43 (47) ch.
Row 1 1 htr into 3rd ch from hook, then 1htr into each ch to end. Turn. 41(45) htr
Row 2 2 ch, work 1htr into each st across row. Turn. Change to yarn A and work straight in htr until piece measures the same as front to one row below armhole.
Fasten off yarn.
Using yarn A, work 25 (30) ch, then work across body stitches in htr, work 27 (32) ch.
NEXT ROW: Work 1htr into 3rd ch from hook, then one htr into each ch to end of ch. 25 (30) sts increased for arm. Work in htr across body stitches, then 1 htr into each ch to end for opposite arm. 50 (60) sts in total increased for arms. 91 (105) htr
Work straight on these sts until piece measures same as front to one row below shoulder.
NEXT ROW: Work across 35 (40) sts. Fasten

off yarn, leaving rem sts unworked.
Fasten yarn to opposite arm edge, work across 35 (40) sts, fasten off yarn, leaving rem 21 (25) sts unworked for neck.

FINISHING
Block all pieces lightly to shape. Sew shoulder seams, then sew up each underarm and side seam.

NECK EDGE
Rejoin yarn A to bottom of right front edge and work evenly in dc up edge, then round neck. At top of left edge, work 5 ch for button loop, then work 4 dc down edge, 5 ch, 4 dc, 5 ch, dc to bottom of left front. Sew buttons to right front, corresponding to the button loops.

CUFFS
Using yarn B, rejoin yarn to cuff and work 2 rows of dc evenly round.
Weave in all ends.

Rows of double crochet in a contrasting colour add a neat finishing touch to the cuffs and cardigan hem.

The sleeves are made as part of the back and front pieces of the cardigan.

BABY'S BLANKET

This adorable baby blanket is made as a large Afghan (or Granny) square with a centre of mini squares and finished with a shell edging. Each new colour is joined directly to the previous square or round, so no seaming is required – just weave in the ends to finish.

MATERIALS

Size
84cm x 84cm (33in x 33in)

Yarn
Sirdar Wash 'n' Wear DK Double Crepe/Borroco Comfort DK 100g

A × 3   B × 3 balls

Crochet hook
4mm (G-6 US) hook

PATTERN

STARTING MINI SQUARE
With yarn A, work 4 ch, ss to first ch to form loop.
Round 1 3 ch, 2 tr in loop. *2 ch, 3 tr in loop; rep from * twice more, 2 ch, ss in top of beg 3-ch to join.
Fasten off.
For next mini square, use the join-as-you-go-method.
With yarn B, work 4 ch, ss to first ch to form loop.
Round 1 3 ch, 2 tr in loop. *dc in any 2-ch corner sp of starting mini square, 3 tr in loop of current square; rep from * once more. 2 ch, 3 tr in loop, 2 ch, ss in top of beg 3-ch to join.
Fasten off.
Continue making and joining the mini squares as you go, alternating colours, until centre large square is desired size. Sample blanket uses 6 x 6 mini squares.

BEGIN GRANNY SQUARE ROUNDS
Join yarn A in next ch sp after any corner.
Round 1 3 ch, 2 tr into same space. *1 ch, 3 tr into next ch sp; rep from * to corner, work (3 tr, 2 ch, 3 tr) in corner space.
Rep around piece. Fasten off yarn A.
Rounds 2–3 Attach yarn B and rep round 1. At the end of round 2, ss in top of beg 3-ch, ss in each st to next ch sp from prev round, then begin as round 1. Fasten off yarn B.
Round 4 Attach yarn A and rep round 1.
Rep rounds 1–3 to form pattern, one round of yarn A and two rounds of yarn B.

Continue with Granny rounds until blanket is desired size. Sample blanket uses 24 rounds, ending on a round 3.

EDGING
Round 1 Attach yarn B in any st. Dc in each st and ch around blanket, working 3 dc in each corner sp. Ss in first dc to join. Fasten off yarn B.
Round 2 Attach yarn A. 2 ch, *5 tr in next dc, dc into next dc. Rep from * around blanket. Fasten off.

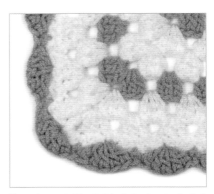

The outermost stripe in this design is actually shell edging. It finishes the blanket without breaking up the pattern of stripes.

A central block of mini squares is surrounded by rounds of traditional Afghan (or Granny) square stitch.

TEDDY BEAR

This adorable teddy is made in continuous rounds. The head is started from the top and the body from the bottom; both are decreased to the same number of stitches and then stuffed and joined. Arms, legs, and ears are added separately, as is a contrasting scarf.

MATERIALS

Size
15cm (6in)

Yarn
A (for teddy): Stylecraft Special DK/Red Heart Super Saver Solids® 100g
B (for scarf): Rowan Purelife DK 50g

A × 1   **B** × 1 ball

Crochet hook
A: 3mm (D-3 US) hook (for teddy)
B: 4mm (G-6 US) hook (for scarf)

A
B

Notions
Toy stuffing
Light brown and black embroidery thread

PATTERN

HEAD
Make 6 dc in loop (see page 287), pull tail to close.
Round 1 2 dc in each dc to end. (12sts)
Round 2 *1 dc in next dc, 2 dc in next dc; rep from * to end. (18sts)
Round 3 *1 dc in each of next 2 dc, 2 dc in next dc; rep from * to end. (24sts)
Round 4 *1 dc in each of next 3 dc, 2 dc in next dc; rep from * to end. (30sts)
Round 5 *1 dc in each of next 4 dc, 2 dc in next dc; rep from * to end. (36sts)
Round 6 *1 dc in each of next 5 dc, 2 dc in next dc; rep from * to end. (42sts)
Rounds 7–14 1 dc in each dc to end. (42sts)
Round 15 *1 dc in each of next 5 dc, dc2tog; rep from * to end. (36sts)
Round 16 *1 dc in each of next 4 dc, dc2tog; rep from * to end. (30sts)
Round 17 *1 dc in each of next 3 dc, dc2tog; rep from * to end. (24sts)
Fasten off, leaving a long tail. Embroider eyes, nose, and mouth. Stuff firmly.

EARS (Make 2)
Make 5 dc in magic loop, pull tail to close.
Round 1 2 dc in each dc to end. (10sts)
Rounds 2–3 1 dc in each dc to end. (10sts)
Fasten off, leaving a long tail. Use tail to sew open ends of ears to head.

BODY
Make 6 dc in magic loop, pull tail to close.
Round 1 2 dc in each dc to end. (12sts)
Round 2 *1 dc in next dc, 2 dc in next dc; rep from * to end. (18sts)
Round 3 *1 dc in each of next 2 dc, 2 dc in next dc; rep from * to end. (24sts)
Round 4 *1 dc in each of next 3 dc, 2 dc in next dc; rep from * to end. (30sts)
Round 5 *1 dc in each of next 4 dc, 2 dc in next dc; rep from * to end. (36sts)
Round 6 *1 dc in each of next 5 dc, 2 dc in next dc; rep from * to end. (42sts)
Rounds 7–14 1 dc in each dc to end. (42sts)
Round 15 *1 dc in each of next 5 dc, dc2tog; rep from * to end. (36sts)
Rounds 16–17 1 dc in each dc to end. (36sts)
Round 18 *1 dc in each of next 4 dc, dc2tog; rep from * to end. (30sts)
Rounds 19–20 1 dc in each dc to end. (30sts)
Round 21 *1 dc in each of next 3 dc, dc2tog; rep from * to end. (24sts)
Rounds 22–23 1 dc in each dc to end. (24sts)
Fasten off, leaving a long tail. Stuff firmly. Sew body to head.

LEGS (Make 2)
Make 6 dc in magic loop, pull tail to close.
Round 1 2 dc in each dc to end. (12sts)
Round 2 *1 dc in next dc, 2 dc in next dc; rep from * to end. (18sts)
Round 3 *1 dc in each of next 2 dc, 2 dc in next dc; rep from * to end. (24sts)
Round 4 *1 dc in each of next 3 dc, 2 dc in next dc; rep from * to end. (30sts)
Round 5 dc2tog to end. (15sts)
Rounds 6–9 1 dc in each dc to end. (15sts)
Fasten off, leaving a long tail. Stuff firmly, use tail to sew legs to body.

ARMS (Make 2)
Make 6 dc in magic loop, pull tail to close.
Round 1 2 dc in each dc to end. (12sts)
Rounds 2–8 1 dc in each dc to end. (12sts)
Fasten off, leaving a long tail. Stuff firmly, use tail to sew arms to body.

SCARF
Work 31 ch.
Row 1 Miss 1 dc, dc in rem 30 chs. (30sts)
Row 2 1 ch, dc in each dc to end.
Fasten off, weave in ends.

The head and neck are both worked to the same number of stitches, and attached to each other with matching yarn.

The teddy's eyes, nose, and mouth are embroidered on the finished head with black and light brown embroidery thread.

LACY SCARF

This lacy, openwork scarf is made using the fans stitch (see page 272) from the Techniques section. The openwork pattern is created using alternating chain loops and treble crochet stitches. It is an easy first project as it's very forgiving!

MATERIALS

Size
18cm x 180cm (7in x 71in) or desired length

Yarn
Sirdar Country Style DK/Berroco Vintage DK 100g

x 1 ball

Crochet hook
4mm (G-6 US) hook

PATTERN

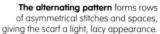

Work 33 ch
Row 1 1 tr in 5th ch from hook, *2 ch, miss 5 chs, 3 tr in next ch, 2 ch, tr in next ch; rep from * 3 times more.
Row 2 4 ch, turn. 1 tr in first 2-ch sp, *2 ch, work (4 tr, 2 ch, 1 tr) in next 2-ch sp; rep from * twice more, 2 ch, work 3 tr in last sp and 1 tr in 3rd of 4 chs of turning ch from row below.
Rep row 2 until piece is 180cm (71in) or desired length.
Fasten off, weave in ends.

The alternating pattern forms rows of asymmetrical stitches and spaces, giving the scarf a light, lacy appearance.

There is no need to add edging to either the long sides or the ends of this scarf as the stitch pattern forms its own.

BEANIE HAT

This cosy hat is made in the round starting at the top and increasing to the circumference of the head to fit the recipient. This hat has been made with two contrasting stripes near the brim, but it could easily be customized with additional stripes and colours.

MATERIALS

Size
To fit an adult male

Yarn
A Wendy Aran/Wool-Ease® Worsted 400g
B Debbie Bliss Cashmerino Aran 50g

A × 1   B × 1 ball

Crochet hook
5mm (H-8 US) hook

Tension
11sts per 10cm (4in)

Special abbreviations
fphtr: front post half treble. Yrh and insert hook from front to back to front around the post of next st. Yrh and pull up a loop. Yrh and pull through all three loops on hook.

PATTERN

With yarn A, work 4 ch, ss in first ch to form loop.
Round 1 2 ch, 11 htr in loop, ss in top of first 2-ch to join. (12sts)
Round 2 2 ch, 2 htr in next st. *1 htr in next st, 2 htr in next st; rep from * to end, ss in top of first 2-ch to join. (18sts)
Round 3 2 ch, 1 htr in next st, 2 htr in next st. *1 htr in each of next 2 sts, 2 htr in next st; rep from * to end, ss in top of first 2-ch to join. (24sts)
Round 4 2 ch, 1 htr in each of next 2 sts, 2 htr in next st. *1 htr in each of next 3 sts, 2 htr in next st; rep from * to end, ss in top of first 2-ch to join. (30sts)
Round 5 2 ch, 1 htr in each of next 3 sts, 2 htr in next st. *1 htr in each of next 4 sts, 2 htr in next st; rep from * to end, ss in top of first 2-ch to join. (36sts)
Round 6 2 ch, 1 htr in each of next 4 sts, 2 htr in next st. *1 htr in each of next 5 sts, 2 htr in next st; rep from * to end, ss in top of first 2-ch to join. (42sts)
Round 7 2 ch, 1 htr in each of next 5 sts, 2 htr in next st. *1 htr in each of next 6 sts, 2 htr in next st; rep from * to end, ss in top of first 2-ch to join. (48sts)

Round 8 2 ch, 1 htr in each of next 6 sts, 2 htr in next st. *1 htr in each of next 7 sts, 2 htr in next st; rep from * to end, ss in top of first 2-ch to join. (54sts)
Round 9 2 ch, 1 htr in each of next 7 sts, 2 htr in next st. *1 htr in each of next 8 sts, 2 htr in next st; rep from * to end, ss in top of first 2-ch to join. (60sts)
Increases can be stopped sooner or continued as set for a smaller or larger head size
Rounds 10–16 2 ch, work 1 htr in each st to end, ss in top of first 2-ch to join.
Even rounds can be added or subtracted to adjust length of hat
Round 17 With yarn B, 2 ch, work 1 htr in each st to end, ss in top of first 2-ch to join.
Rounds 18–19 With yarn A, 2 ch, work 1 htr in each st to end, ss in top of first 2-ch to join.
Round 20 With yarn B, 2 ch, work 1 htr in each st to end, ss in top of first 2-ch to join.
Round 21 With yarn B, 2 ch, *fphtr in next st, bphtr in next st; rep from * to end, ss in top of first 2-ch to join.
Fasten off, weave in ends.

Ensure that the starting hole is nearly closed after the first round. If not, pull out and start again with a shorter chain.

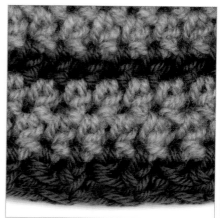

The decorative stripes are made as part of the stitch pattern. Be sure to stitch in loose ends when switching colours.

SHAWL

This lacy, feminine shawl uses a variation of the chain loop mesh (see page 267) from the Techniques section, as well as the picot and shell edgings (see page 285). The shawl is made in rows, starting from the top and decreasing naturally down to a point at the bottom.

MATERIALS

Size
135cm x 105cm (53in x 41in)

Yarn
Sublime Cashmerino Silk DK 50g

x 5 balls

Crochet hook
4.5mm (7 US) hook

PATTERN

Work 181 ch (or any multiple of 3+1).
Row 1 Miss first ch, dc in each ch to end, turn. (180sts)
Row 2 *6 ch, miss 2 sts, dc in next st; rep from * to end, turn.
Row 3 and all following rows Ss in first 3 chs, *6 ch, dc in next 6-ch loop; rep from * to end, turn.
Rep last row until left with one 6-ch loop. Fasten off, weave in ends.

TOP PICOT EDGING
Working along top of shawl, attach yarn at one end, 1 ch, dc in same st, *4 ch, ss in 4th ch from hook, dc in each of next 2 sts; rep from * across top edge, ending (4 ch, ss in 4th ch from hook, dc) all in last st. Leave yarn attached.

SIDE SHELL EDGING
Working around two remaining sides, *ss in next 6-ch loop, 5 tr in same sp, ss in same sp; rep from * around two un-edged sides, working (ss, 10 tr, ss) in loop at bottom point.
Fasten off, weave in ends.

Picot edging is used to finish the top of the shawl. The edging can be made larger by adding chains.

Shell edging finishes the long sides of the shawl. Each shell in the edging matches up with a single space in the lace pattern.

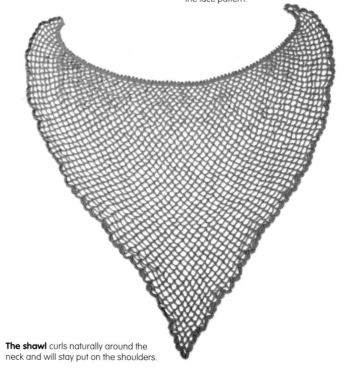

The shawl curls naturally around the neck and will stay put on the shoulders.

CLUTCH BAG

This elegant clutch is crocheted in a softly shimmering mercerized cotton and is just big enough to hold all your essentials for an evening out. It is made in rows using the cluster and shell stitch (see page 265) from the Techniques section, and forms its own edging and buttonholes. This is a quick and easy project – why not crochet one for tonight?

MATERIALS

Size
20cm x 10cm (8in x 4in)

Yarn
Rico Essentials Cotton DK/Tahki Cotton Classic 50g

× 1 ball

Crochet hook
3.5mm (E-4 US) hook

Notions
Shell button, approximately 2cm (¾in)

Special notes
Cluster: over next 5 sts, (which include 2 tr, 1 dc, 2 tr), work [yrh and insert hook in next st, yrh and draw a loop through, yrh and draw through first two loops on hook] 5 times (6 loops on hook), yrh and draw through all 6 loops on hook.

PATTERN

Work 46 ch.
Row 1 2 tr in 4th ch from hook, miss next 2 chs, 1 dc in next ch, *miss next 2 chs, 5 tr in next ch, miss next 2 chs, 1 dc in next ch; rep from * to last 3 chs, miss next 2 chs, 3 tr in last ch, turn.
Row 2 1 ch, 1 dc in first tr, *2 ch, 1 cluster over next 5 sts, 2 ch, 1 dc in centre tr of 5-tr group; rep from * to end, working last dc of last rep in top of 3-ch at end, turn.

Row 3 3 ch, 2 tr in first dc, miss next 2 chs, 1 dc in next st (top of first cluster), miss next 2 chs, *5 tr in next dc, miss next 2 chs, 1 dc in next st (top of next cluster); rep from *, ending with 3 tr in last dc, turn.
Rep rows 2 and 3 until piece measures 25cm (10in), ending on a row 3. Fold at 10cm (4in) and sew (or use slip stitch join, see page 51) 2 sides to form pocket. Fold top flap over and attach button.

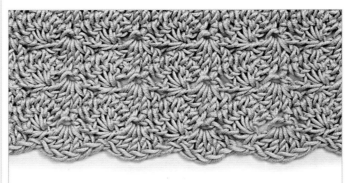

The cluster and shell stitch pattern forms its own decorative edge so there is no need to add edging.

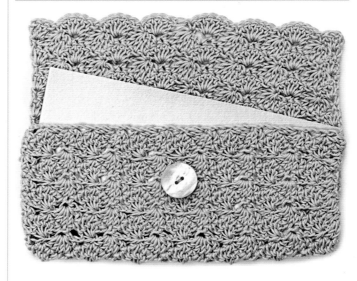

You may choose to line your clutch with fabric, or place a piece of card inside to help it keep its shape.

FRIENDSHIP BRACELETS

These bracelets are a great way to practise working into front loops, back loops, and creating chain loops using the fundamental crochet stitches: chain and slip stitch. Make an armful of bracelets, raiding your button box for suitable fastenings.

MATERIALS

Size
Patterns adapt to fit wearer

Yarn
You can use any 4-ply cotton or cotton blend yarn. Here we have used Bergère de France Coton Fifty 50g (140m/153yd) in 6 colours
A 239-56 Petrolier x 1 ball
B 244-20 Turquoise x 1 ball
C 293-11 Clementine x 1 ball
D 219-76 Perle x 1 ball
E 246-60 Bengale x 1 ball
F 253-07 Herbage x 1 ball

A x 1   B x 1   C x 1

D x 1   E x 1   F x 1

Crochet hook
2mm hook

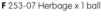

Notions
A small button for each bracelet

Special Notes
Crab stitch: Work dc from left to right, instead of right to left. (Left-handed crocheters will work right to left.) After completing a round of double crochet, do not turn work. 1 ch, *insert hook into next stitch to the right (not in the stitch just completed, but the next one), draw a loop through, yrh and pull through both loops on the hook; rep from * to end.

PATTERN

MULTI-CHAIN BRACELET
With yarn A, *make 86 ch (or any number of chains to fit wrist), ss into 1st ch, rep from * once more, then work 8 ch, ss into first of 8-ch to form button loop.
Cut yarn and fasten off. Fold both chains in half and join looped ends. Weave in yarn ends and stitch button in place where loops join.

SMALL SCALLOP BRACELET
With yarn B, make 43 ch (or an odd number of chains to fit wrist).
Row 1 *1 ch, ss in next st, rep from * to last st, 1 ch, ss in last ch; turn and work along opposite side of foundation ch.
Row 2 As row 1; do not cut yarn but work 8 ch, ss into first of 8-ch to form button loop.
Cut yarn and fasten off.
Weave in yarn ends and stitch button in place on opposite end to button loop.

MEDIUM SCALLOP BRACELET
With yarn C, make 43 ch (or an odd number of chains to fit wrist).
Row 1 *2 ch, ss in next st, rep from * to last st, 2 ch, ss in last ch; turn and work along opposite side of foundation chain.
Row 2 As row 1; do not cut yarn but work 8 ch, ss into first of 8-ch to form button loop.
Cut yarn and fasten off.
Weave in yarn ends and stitch button in place on opposite end to button loop.

LARGE SCALLOP BRACELET
With yarn D, make 43 ch (or an odd number of chains to fit wrist).

Row 1 *3 ch, ss in next st, rep from * to last st, 3 ch, ss in last ch; turn and work along opposite side of foundation chain.
Row 2 As row 1; do not cut yarn but work 8 ch, ss into first of 8-ch to form button loop.
Cut yarn and fasten off.
Weave in yarn ends and stitch button in place on opposite end to button loop.

FLAT CORD BRACELET
With yarn E, make 43 ch (or an odd number of chains to fit wrist).
Row 1 ss in 2nd ch from hook, ss in each ch to end, turn. (42sts)
Row 2 1 ch, ss into each ss of previous row, inserting hook into back loop only of every st; do not turn, work 8 ch, ss into first of 8-ch to form button loop.
Cut yarn and fasten off.
Weave in yarn ends and stitch button in place on opposite end to button loop.

SQUARE CORD BRACELET
With yarn F, make 43 ch (or an odd number of chains to fit wrist).
Row 1 Ss in 2nd ch from hook, ss in each ch to end, turn. (42sts)
Row 2 1 ch, ss into each ss of previous row, inserting hook into front loop only of every st; turn.
Row 3 As row 2; do not turn, but work 8 ch, ss into first of 8-ch to form button loop.
Cut yarn and fasten off.
Weave in yarn ends and stitch button in place on opposite end to button loop.

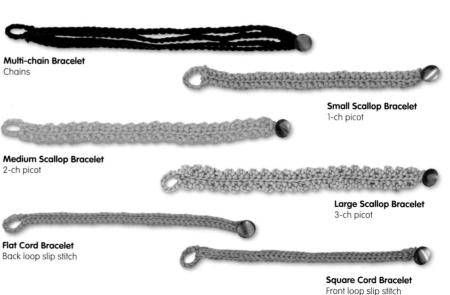

Multi-chain Bracelet
Chains

Small Scallop Bracelet
1-ch picot

Medium Scallop Bracelet
2-ch picot

Large Scallop Bracelet
3-ch picot

Flat Cord Bracelet
Back loop slip stitch

Square Cord Bracelet
Front loop slip stitch

CHEVRON CUSHION

A great introduction to colourwork, this moderately easy project uses the zigzag stitch. The entire cushion cover is made in one piece and then stitched up the sides. The buttonholes are created as part of the pattern.

MATERIALS

Size
40cm × 30cm (16in × 12in)

Yarn
A: Sirdar Click DK/Plymouth Yarn Encore 50g
B: Sirdar Country Style/Berroco Vintage DK 50g

A × 2   **B** × 1 ball

Crochet hook
4mm (G-6 US) hook

Notions
Cushion pad 40cm x 30cm/16in x 12in
(or size required for your cushion cover)
5 buttons, approx 1.5cm (½in) in diameter

PATTERN

CUSHION
With yarn B, work 81 ch.
Row 1 1 dc in 2nd ch from hook, 1 dc in each ch to end, turn. (80sts)
Rows 2–3 1 ch, 2 dc in next st, 1 dc in each of next 7 sts, miss next 2 dc, 1 dc in each of next 7 sts, *2 dc in each of next 2 sts, 1 dc in each of next 7 sts, miss next 2 dc, 1 dc in each of next 7 sts; rep from * to last st, 2 dc in last st. Turn. Change to yarn A.
Rows 4–6 2 ch, 2 htr in next st, 1 htr in each of next 7 sts, miss next 2 sts, 1 htr in each of next 7 sts, *2 htr in each of next 2 sts, 1 htr in each of next 7 sts, miss next 2 dc, 1 htr in each of next 7sts; rep from * to last st, 2 htr in last st. Turn. Change to yarn B.
Row 7 1 ch, 2 dc in next st, 1 dc in each of next 7 sts, miss next 2 dc, 1 dc in each of next 7 sts, *2 dc in each of next 2 sts, 1 dc in each of next 7 sts, miss next 2 dc, 1 dc in each of next 7 sts; rep from * to last st, 2 dc in last st. Turn. Change to yarn A.
Rep last 4 rows until work measures approximately 70cm (28in), or desired length – long enough to fit comfortably around a cushion with an overlap.
End with a row 7, then rep row 7 twice more in yarn B.
Fasten off.

Buttons are fixed to the bottom layer of the cushion cover at the bottom of each "V" in the zigzag pattern.

FINISHING
Block piece lightly to shape (see page 280). Wrap piece around cushion pad, with an overlap halfway down back of pad. Ensure top edge of piece, with 5 complete points, is on top, overlapping bottom of piece. Sew up bottom two side seams of cushion, then sew down top two side seams, overlapping bottom seam. Fasten middle flap of cushion by sewing buttons on bottom edge of piece, corresponding to first decrease hole in yarn A htr row next to end of each point. Fasten buttons and weave in all ends.

The stitch pattern forms a neat zigzag edge to the cushion cover. The buttons are simply pushed through holes in the pattern.

PROJECT BASKET

This handy, versatile basket is made in the round, starting at the centre bottom. The bottom edge and brim fold are cleverly made by crocheting only into the back loop of the stitch for one round. Size can be adjusted by adding or subtracting increase and even rounds.

MATERIALS

Size
13cm x 16cm (5in x 6in)

Yarn
Stylecraft Special DK/Takhi Cotton Classic 100g

A × 1   **B** × 1 ball

Crochet hook
4mm (G-6 US) hook

PATTERN

BASKET
With yarn A, work 2 ch, 6 dc in 2nd ch from hook.
Round 1 2 dc in each dc to end. (12sts)
Round 2 *1 dc in next dc, 2 dc in next dc; rep from * to end. (18sts)
Round 3 *1 dc in each of next 2 dc, 2 dc in next dc; rep from * to end. (24sts)
Round 4 *1 dc in each of next 3 dc, 2 dc in next dc; rep from * to end. (30sts)
Round 5 *1 dc in each of next 4 dc, 2 dc in next dc; rep from * to end. (36sts)
Round 6 *1 dc in each of next 5 dc, 2 dc in next dc; rep from * to end. (42sts)
Round 7 *1 dc in each of next 6 dc, 2 dc in next dc; rep from * to end. (48sts)
Round 8 *1 dc in each of next 7 dc, 2 dc in next dc; rep from * to end. (54sts)
Round 9 *1 dc in each of next 8 dc, 2 dc in next dc; rep from * to end. (60sts)
Round 10 *1 dc in each of next 9 dc, 2 dc in next dc; rep from * to end. (66sts)
Round 11 *1 dc in each of next 10 dc, 2 dc in next dc; rep from * to end. (72sts)
Round 12 *1 dc in each of next 11 dc, 2 dc in next dc; rep from * to end. (78sts)
Round 13 *1 dc in each of next 12 dc, 2 dc in next dc; rep from * to end. (84sts)

Round 14 *1 dc in each of next 13 dc, 2 dc in next dc; rep from * to end. (90sts)
Round 15 *1 dc in each of next 14 dc, 2 dc in next dc; rep from * to end. (96sts)
Round 16 *1 dc in each of next 15 dc, 2 dc in next dc; rep from * to end. (102sts)
Increase can be stopped earlier for a smaller basket or continued as set for a larger basket
Round 17 Working into back loops only, dc in each dc to end. (102sts)
Continue working even rounds through both loops (1 dc in each dc to end) until piece measures 13cm (5in) from Round 17, or desired height.

FOLDOVER
Round 1 Working in the front loops only, with yarn B, 1 dc in each dc to end. (102sts)
Round 2 With yarn A, 1 dc in each dc through both loops to end. (102sts)
Round 3 With yarn B, 1 dc in each dc through both loops to end. (102sts)
Rep last 2 rounds once more.
Fasten off, weave in ends.

The decorative brim with three contrasting stripes is crocheted as part of the basket and then folded down.

As rounds increase on the bottom of the basket, it begins to look more and more like a hexagon.

GRANNY-FLOWER BLANKET

This vibrant update of the vintage-inspired granny-square blanket is crocheted together, not sewn, so it looks great from either side with no obvious seams. It is perfect for draping over a chair or laying on a single bed.

MATERIALS

Size
Each flower motif measures approx 8cm (3¼in) in diameter. Final blanket measurements are approx 80cm x 120cm (90cm x 170cm, 100cm x190cm)

Yarn
For border: 4 balls of Sirdar Snuggly DK 50g in White (251)
For the flower motifs: use oddments of DK yarn
We used 1 ball of each shade.

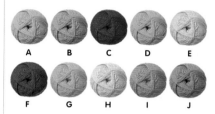

A B C D E

F G H I J

Crochet hook
4mm (G-6 US) hook
Yarn needle for darning ends

Tension
Exact tension is not essential for this project.

Special stitches
Puff – (Yrh, insert hook into st, yrh and pull through a lp, drawing it up to the height of a htr) 4 times, 9lps on hook, yrh and pull through all lps on hook.

Popcorn – Work 5tr into next st, remove hook from final stitch, insert it into first of 5tr, then back through last loop, yrh and pull through everything on hook.

PATTERN

MAKING THE FLOWER MOTIFS
Round 1 Using any contrast shade, work 3 ch to count as first tr, work 1 tr into 3rd ch from hook, then work 10 further tr into same chain. Join round with a ss.
Change colour.
Round 2 2 ch, work 1 puff into first tr, 1 ch, (1 puff, 1ch) to end of round, join round with a ss.
Change colour.
Round 3 3 ch, work popcorn into bottom of chain, 3 ch, *work popcorn into next 1-ch sp, 3 ch; rep from * to end of round, join round with ss.

Make enough flower motifs in the same way for the desired size of blanket. For a small blanket, work 96 flowers, for a medium blanket, work 153 flowers, for a large blanket work 190 flowers.

JOINING THE MOTIFS
Using the border shade, work a final row around one flower motif as follows:
Join yarn to any 3-ch sp.
3 ch, (1 tr, 3 ch, 2 tr) all into same sp, *([2 tr, 1 ch, 2 tr] into next 3-ch sp) twice, (2 tr, 3 ch, 2 tr) into next 3-ch sp; rep from * twice more, ([2 tr, 1 ch, 2 tr] into next 3-ch sp) twice, join round with a ss.
To join the next flower to first, finished motif, work border round next flower as follows:
Using the border shade, join yarn to any 3-ch sp.
3 ch, (1 tr, 3 ch, 2 tr) all into same sp, *([2 tr, 1 ch, 2 tr] into next 3-ch sp) twice, 2 tr, 1 ch into next 3 ch sp, work a ss into the central ch of any 3 ch corner sp of first motif to join the corners, 1 ch, 2 tr back into original 3-ch sp of second motif. *2 tr into next 3-ch sp, ss into next 1-ch sp of first motif, 2 tr back into original 3-ch sp of second motif; rep from * once more, 2 tr, 1 ch into next 3-ch sp, ss into central ch of next corner ch of first motif,

1 ch, 2 tr back into original 3-ch sp of second motif, ([2 tr, 1 ch, 2 tr] into next 3-ch sp) twice, (2 tr, 3 ch, 2 tr) into next 3-ch sp, ([2 tr, 1 ch, 2 tr] into next 3-ch sp) twice, join round with a ss.
Work all following motifs from first row in the same way as this, joining each subsequent flower to the previous motif along one side.
On the second row of motifs, join first flower of the row to the motif below in the same way as previously stated. For all following motifs, join along two sides to the motifs immediately adjacent and below it in the same way as before.

For a small blanket arrange 8 motifs wide by 12 motifs long.
For a medium blanket, arrange 9 motifs wide by 17 motifs long.
For a large blanket, arrange 10 motifs wide by 19 motifs long.

FINISHING THE BLANKET
Using the border shade, join yarn to any 3-ch sp. Work a border round the blanket as follows:
Using the border shade, attach yarn to any corner of blanket.
3 ch, 4 tr into same corner sp, ** *([2 tr, 1 ch, 2 tr] all into next 1-ch sp,) twice, (2 tr, 1 ch, 2 tr) into next joining sp of two motifs; rep from * to next corner of blanket, 5tr into corner sp. ** Rep between ** and ** around entire perimeter, joining round with a ss.

Weave in all ends and block very lightly to shape, being careful not to flatten the 3D nature of the flower motifs.

Crochet flowers without borders make excellent embellishments for hats and scarves, or as brooches with a safety pin sewn on the back. We've used DK weight yarn here, but you could try varying the weights of yarn to make larger and smaller blooms.

PHONE COVER

A phone cover will help to protect the screen from scratches and bumps. In addition, it's a great way to practise half treble stitches. Choose from a case with a flap or a simpler one with a button loop closure.

MATERIALS

Size
13.5cm x 8cm (5½in x 3¼in)

Yarn
You can use any Aran weight cotton or cotton blend yarn, making sure that it works to the correct tension for this pattern. Here we have used Rowan Summer Tweed 50g (120m/131yd) in 2 colours
A 00544 Jardinier x 1 ball
B 00547 Navy x 1 ball

A x 1   **B** x 1

Crochet hook
4mm hook

Notions
Design 1: 24mm (1in) buttons x 2
Design 2: 30mm (1½in) button x 1
Sewing thread to match buttons

Tension
16 htr and 12 rows to 10cm (4in)

PATTERN

PHONE COVER WITH FLAP
With yarn A, make 13 ch.
Row 1 (RS) 1 htr in 3rd ch from hook, 1 htr in each ch to end. (12 sts)
Row 2 2 ch (counts as 1 htr), 1 htr in each of next 10 htr, 1 htr in top of 2-ch.
Rep row 2 34 times.
Row 36 1 ch (does not count as a st), 1 dc in first htr, 2 ch (to form buttonhole, see tip), miss 2 htr, 1 dc in each of next 6 htr, 2 ch, miss 2 htr, 1 dc in top of 2-ch.
Row 37 1 ch, 1 dc in first dc, 2 dc in 2-ch sp, 1 dc in each of next 6 dc, 2 dc in 2-ch sp, 1 dc in last dc.
Cut yarn and fasten off.

Making up and border
Fold along top of row 14. Beg at bottom, at edge of fold, with RS facing and buttonhole edge towards the left, join in yarn B and work 1 ch (does not count as a st), then work 18 dc along side edges, inserting the hook through both thicknesses to create a decorative seam; when you reach the top edge of the front of the case, continue working along edge through single thickness up side of flap, working 8 dc, evenly spaced, then 3 dc in corner, 1 dc in each htr across top edge, 3 dc in corner, 8 dc down opposite side of flap, then through double thickness, 18 dc, evenly spaced, along side edges down to bottom corner. Cut yarn and fasten off.
Stitch buttons to front of case, to correspond with buttonholes.

PHONE COVER WITH BUTTON LOOP
With yarn A, make 13 ch.
Row 1 (RS) 1 htr in 3rd ch from hook, 1 htr in each ch to end. (12 sts)
Row 2 2 ch (counts as 1 htr), 1 htr in each of next 10 htr, 1 htr in top of 2-ch.
Rep row 2 26 times.
Cut yarn and fasten off.

Making up and border
Fold in half and join sides with a double crochet seam with yarn A. Cut yarn and fasten off.
Border Row 1: Beg at top of one of the side seams, join in yarn B and work 1 ch (does not count as a st), 1 dc in each of next 12 htr along top edge, 1 dc in side seam, continue along top edge on other side and work 1 dc in each htr, 1 dc in side seam, join with ss to 1st dc. (26 sts)
Border Row 2: 1 ch, 1 dc in each of next 13 sts along one edge, continue along top edge on other side and work 1 dc in each of next 5 sts, 18 ch to create button loop, miss next 2 sts, 1 dc in each of next 6 sts to end of row, join with a ss to 1st dc.
Cut yarn and fasten off; weave in all ends.
Stitch button to front of case, to correspond with button loop.

Index

Acknowledgements

Knitting

Project Editors Katharine Goddard, Janashree Singha, Manasvi Vohra

Senior Art Editors Glenda Fisher, Elaine Hewson, Balwant Singh

Knitting Designers Caroline Birkett, Debi Birkin, Shirley Bradford, Sian Brown, Tessa Dennison, Laura Evans, Julie Ferguson, Fiona Goble, Dr Vikki Haffenden, Zoe Halstead, Amanda Jones, Frederica Patmore, and Val Pierce

Knitters Brenda Bostock, Ruth Bridgeman, Pauline Buck, June Cole, Antonella Conti, Grace Coombs, Sally Cuthbert, Ursula Doherty, Joan Doyle, Eva Hallas, Jill Houghton, Dolly Howes, Karen Howie, Brenda Jennings, Maisie Lawrence, Patricia Liddle, Ann McFaull, Elaine Morris, Daphne Moyce, Mrs Parsons, Doreen Payne, Karen Tattersall, Jane Wales, and Brenda Willows

Pattern checkers Carol Ibbetson and Rachel Vowles

Consultant Dr Vikki Haffenden

Photography Dave King, Deepak Aggarwal

Props George & Beth and Backgrounds

Location for photography 1st Option

The following yarn manufacturers and distributors for supplying yarn for the projects Artesano Ltd, Coats Crafts UK, Designer Yarns, Kelbourne Woolens, King Cole Ltd, Rico Design, Sirdar Yarns, Sublime Yarns, Texere Yarns Ltd for providing yarn for the projects.

Gifts to Give

Project Art Editors Gemma Fletcher, Ivy Roy, Vikas Sachdeva

Project Editor Laura Palosuo

Photographer Dave King

Project makers Nicola Barter (pp182–187), Isobel de Cordova (pp121–123), Kate Davis (pp142–145), Helen Fickling (pp118–120), Glenda Fisher (pp102–105), Gemma Fletcher (pp78–83, pp136–141), Ria Holland (pp158–163), Charlotte Johnson (pp106–109, pp192–203), Kathryn Johnson (pp84–87), Paula Keogh (pp210–213), Karen Mitchell (pp164–169), Claire Montgomerie (pp94–97), Hannah Moore (pp146–151, pp176–181, pp206–209, pp214–221), Belinda Nicholson (pp98–101), Lova Rajaonarimanana (pp188–191), Victoria Read (pp152–157, pp170–175), Clara Smith (pp88–93), Caroline Stamps (pp124–127, pp132–135), The Oxford Soap Company (pp110–117, pp128–131).

Crochet

Contributors Sally Harding, Catherine Hirst, Claire Montgomerie, Erin McCarthy

Project Editors Katharine Goddard, Janashree Singha, Manasvi Vohra

Senior Art Editors Glenda Fisher, Elaine Hewson, Balwant Singh

Crochet diagrams Coral Mula

Resources Lana Pura, Willow Fabrics, House of Smocking, Usha International, and The Contented Cat